Charities Act 2011

CHAPTER 25

Explanatory Notes are available separately

GRAN*GIS* UK Publishing

Adapted and published by GRANGIS (Grand Register Library).
Online: www.grangis.com
E-mail: contact@grangis.com

In this version:
ISBN: 979-8-88559-009-9

Note: This is the original version (as it was originally enacted). Title, sub-title and the generated date is as marked on the pages.

Charities Act 2011

CHAPTER 25

CHARITIES ACT 2011

PART 1

MEANING OF "CHARITY" AND "CHARITABLE PURPOSE"

CHAPTER 1

GENERAL

CHAPTER 2

SPECIAL PROVISION FOR THIS ACT

PART 2

THE CHARITY COMMISSION AND THE OFFICIAL CUSTODIAN FOR CHARITIES

The Commission

The official custodian

PART 3

EXEMPT CHARITIES AND THE PRINCIPAL REGULATOR

Exempt charities

The principal regulator

PART 4

REGISTRATION AND NAMES OF CHARITIES

The register

Charities required to be registered

PART 6

CY-PRÈS POWERS AND ASSISTANCE AND SUPERVISION OF CHARITIES BY COURT AND COMMISSION

Cy-près powers and variation of charters

Powers of Commission to make schemes etc.

Powers of Commission to act for protection of charities etc.

Publicity relating to schemes and orders

Property vested in official custodian

Official custodian and Reverter of Sites Act 1987

CHAPTER 3

AMENDMENT OF CONSTITUTION

CHAPTER 4

CONVERSION, AMALGAMATION AND TRANSFER

Conversion of certain bodies to CIO

Amalgamation of CIOs

Transfer of CIO's undertaking to another CIO

CHAPTER 5

SUPPLEMENTARY

PART 12

INCORPORATION OF CHARITY TRUSTEES

Administrative provisions about charities

Enforcement powers of Commission etc.

Documents and evidence etc.

Offences

Regulations and orders

Interpretation

PART 19

FINAL PROVISIONS

SCHEDULES

Charities Act 2011

2011 CHAPTER 25

An Act to consolidate the Charities Act 1993 and other enactments which relate to charities. [14th December 2011]

BE IT ENACTED by the Queen's most Excellent Majesty, by and with the advice and consent of the Lords Spiritual and Temporal, and Commons, in this present Parliament assembled, and by the authority of the same, as follows:—

PART 1

MEANING OF "CHARITY" AND "CHARITABLE PURPOSE"

CHAPTER 1

GENERAL

Charity

1 Meaning of "charity"

(1) For the purposes of the law of England and Wales, "charity" means an institution which—

(a) is established for charitable purposes only, and

(b) falls to be subject to the control of the High Court in the exercise of its jurisdiction with respect to charities.

(2) The definition of "charity" in subsection (1) does not apply for the purposes of an enactment if a different definition of that term applies for those purposes by virtue of that or any other enactment.

Charitable purpose

2 Meaning of "charitable purpose"

(1) For the purposes of the law of England and Wales, a charitable purpose is a purpose which—

(a) falls within section 3(1), and

(b) is for the public benefit (see section 4).

(2) Any reference in any enactment or document (in whatever terms)—

(a) to charitable purposes, or

(b) to institutions having purposes that are charitable under the law relating to charities in England and Wales,

is to be read in accordance with subsection (1).

(3) Subsection (2) does not apply where the context otherwise requires.

(4) This section is subject to section 11 (which makes special provision for Chapter 2 of this Part onwards).

3 Descriptions of purposes

(1) A purpose falls within this subsection if it falls within any of the following descriptions of purposes—

(a) the prevention or relief of poverty;

(b) the advancement of education;

(c) the advancement of religion;

(d) the advancement of health or the saving of lives;

(e) the advancement of citizenship or community development;

(f) the advancement of the arts, culture, heritage or science;

(g) the advancement of amateur sport;

(h) the advancement of human rights, conflict resolution or reconciliation or the promotion of religious or racial harmony or equality and diversity;

(i) the advancement of environmental protection or improvement;

(j) the relief of those in need because of youth, age, ill-health, disability, financial hardship or other disadvantage;

(k) the advancement of animal welfare;

(l) the promotion of the efficiency of the armed forces of the Crown or of the efficiency of the police, fire and rescue services or ambulance services;

(m) any other purposes—

(i) that are not within paragraphs (a) to (l) but are recognised as charitable purposes by virtue of section 5 (recreational and similar trusts, etc.) or under the old law,

(ii) that may reasonably be regarded as analogous to, or within the spirit of, any purposes falling within any of paragraphs (a) to (l) or sub-paragraph (i), or

(iii) that may reasonably be regarded as analogous to, or within the spirit of, any purposes which have been recognised, under the law relating to charities in England and Wales, as falling within sub-paragraph (ii) or this sub-paragraph.

(2) In subsection (1)—

(a) in paragraph (c), "religion" includes—

(i) a religion which involves belief in more than one god, and

(ii) a religion which does not involve belief in a god,

(b) in paragraph (d), "the advancement of health" includes the prevention or relief of sickness, disease or human suffering,

(c) paragraph (e) includes—

(i) rural or urban regeneration, and

(ii) the promotion of civic responsibility, volunteering, the voluntary sector or the effectiveness or efficiency of charities,

(d) in paragraph (g), "sport" means sports or games which promote health by involving physical or mental skill or exertion,

(e) paragraph (j) includes relief given by the provision of accommodation or care to the persons mentioned in that paragraph, and

(f) in paragraph (l), "fire and rescue services" means services provided by fire and rescue authorities under Part 2 of the Fire and Rescue Services Act 2004.

(3) Where any of the terms used in any of paragraphs (a) to (l) of subsection (1), or in subsection (2), has a particular meaning under the law relating to charities in England and Wales, the term is to be taken as having the same meaning where it appears in that provision.

(4) In subsection (1)(m)(i), "the old law" means the law relating to charities in England and Wales as in force immediately before 1 April 2008.

4 The public benefit requirement

(1) In this Act "the public benefit requirement" means the requirement in section 2(1)(b) that a purpose falling within section 3(1) must be for the public benefit if it is to be a charitable purpose.

(2) In determining whether the public benefit requirement is satisfied in relation to any purpose falling within section 3(1), it is not to be presumed that a purpose of a particular description is for the public benefit.

(3) In this Chapter any reference to the public benefit is a reference to the public benefit as that term is understood for the purposes of the law relating to charities in England and Wales.

(4) Subsection (3) is subject to subsection (2).

Recreational trusts and registered sports clubs

5 Recreational and similar trusts, etc.

(1) It is charitable (and is to be treated as always having been charitable) to provide, or assist in the provision of, facilities for—

(a) recreation, or

(b) other leisure-time occupation,

if the facilities are provided in the interests of social welfare.

(2) The requirement that the facilities are provided in the interests of social welfare cannot be satisfied if the basic conditions are not met.

(3) The basic conditions are—

(a) that the facilities are provided with the object of improving the conditions of life for the persons for whom the facilities are primarily intended, and

(b) that—

(i) those persons have need of the facilities because of their youth, age, infirmity or disability, poverty, or social and economic circumstances, or

(ii) the facilities are to be available to members of the public at large or to male, or to female, members of the public at large.

(4) Subsection (1) applies in particular to—

(a) the provision of facilities at village halls, community centres and women's institutes, and

(b) the provision and maintenance of grounds and buildings to be used for purposes of recreation or leisure-time occupation,

and extends to the provision of facilities for those purposes by the organising of any activity.

But this is subject to the requirement that the facilities are provided in the interests of social welfare.

(5) Nothing in this section is to be treated as derogating from the public benefit requirement.

6 Registered sports clubs

(1) A registered sports club established for charitable purposes is to be treated as not being so established, and accordingly cannot be a charity.

(2) In subsection (1), "registered sports club" means a registered club within the meaning of Chapter 9 of Part 13 of the Corporation Tax Act 2010 (community amateur sports clubs).

Supplementary

7 Application of this Chapter in relation to Scotland

(1) This Chapter affects the law of Scotland only in so far as it affects the construction of references to—

(a) charities, or

(b) charitable purposes,

in enactments which relate to matters falling within Section A1 of Part 2 of Schedule 5 to the Scotland Act 1998 (reserved matters: fiscal policy etc.).

(2) In so far as this Chapter affects the law of Scotland—

(a) references in sections 1(1) and 2(1) to the law of England and Wales are to be read as references to the law of Scotland, and

(b) the reference in section 1(1) to the High Court is to be read as a reference to the Court of Session.

8 Application of this Chapter in relation to Northern Ireland

(1) This Chapter affects the law of Northern Ireland only in so far as it affects the construction of references to—

(a) charities, or

(b) charitable purposes,

in enactments which relate to matters falling within paragraph 9 of Schedule 2 to the Northern Ireland Act 1998 (excepted matters: taxes and duties).

(2) In so far as this Chapter affects the law of Northern Ireland—

(a) references in sections 1(1) and 2(1) to the law of England and Wales are to be read as references to the law of Northern Ireland, and

(b) the reference in section 1(1) to the High Court is to be read as a reference to the High Court in Northern Ireland.

9 Interpretation

(1) In this Chapter "enactment" includes—

(a) any provision of subordinate legislation (within the meaning of the Interpretation Act 1978), and

(b) a provision of a Measure of the Church Assembly or of the General Synod of the Church of England,

and references to enactments include enactments whenever passed or made.

(2) In section 2(2) the reference to a document includes a document whenever made.

(3) In this Act "institution" means an institution whether incorporated or not, and includes a trust or undertaking.

(4) Subsections (1) to (3) apply except where the context otherwise requires.

CHAPTER 2

SPECIAL PROVISION FOR THIS ACT

10 Ecclesiastical corporations etc. not charities in certain contexts

(1) In the rest of this Act, "charity", except in so far as the context otherwise requires, has the meaning given by section 1(1).

(2) But in the rest of this Act (apart from Chapter 3 of Part 17) "charity" is not applicable to—

(a) any ecclesiastical corporation in respect of the corporate property of the corporation, except a corporation aggregate having some purposes which are not ecclesiastical in respect of its corporate property held for those purposes,

(b) any Diocesan Board of Finance, or any subsidiary of such a Board, in respect of the diocesan glebe land of the diocese, or

(c) any trust of property for purposes for which the property has been consecrated.

(3) "Ecclesiastical corporation" means any corporation in the Church of England, whether sole or aggregate, which is established for spiritual purposes.

(4) "Diocesan Board of Finance", "subsidiary" and "diocesan glebe land" have the same meaning as in the Endowments and Glebe Measure 1976.

11 Charitable purposes

In the rest of this Act, "charitable purposes" means, except in so far as the context otherwise requires, purposes which are exclusively charitable purposes (as defined by section 2(1)).

12 Directions as to what is (or is not) a separate charity

(1) The Commission (see section 13) may direct that for all or any of the purposes of this Act an institution established for any special purposes of or in connection with a charity (being charitable purposes) is to be treated—

(a) as forming part of that charity, or

(b) as forming a distinct charity.

(2) The Commission may direct that for all or any of the purposes of this Act two or more charities having the same charity trustees are to be treated as a single charity.

PART 2

THE CHARITY COMMISSION AND THE OFFICIAL CUSTODIAN FOR CHARITIES

The Commission

13 The Charity Commission

(1) There continues to be a body corporate known as the Charity Commission for England and Wales (in this Act referred to as "the Commission").

(2) In Welsh the Commission is known as "Comisiwn Elusennau Cymru a Lloegr".

(3) The functions of the Commission are performed on behalf of the Crown.

(4) In the exercise of its functions the Commission is not subject to the direction or control of any Minister of the Crown or of another government department.

(5) But subsection (4) does not affect—

(a) any provision made by or under any enactment;

(b) any administrative controls exercised over the Commission's expenditure by the Treasury.

(6) Schedule 1 contains provisions relating to the Commission.

14 The Commission's objectives

The Commission has the following objectives—

1. *The public confidence objective*

   The public confidence objective is to increase public trust and confidence in charities.
2. *The public benefit objective*

   The public benefit objective is to promote awareness and understanding of the operation of the public benefit requirement.
3. *The compliance objective*

   The compliance objective is to promote compliance by charity trustees with their legal obligations in exercising control and management of the administration of their charities.
4. *The charitable resources objective*

   The charitable resources objective is to promote the effective use of charitable resources.
5. *The accountability objective*

   The accountability objective is to enhance the accountability of charities to donors, beneficiaries and the general public.

15 The Commission's general functions

(1) The Commission has the following general functions—

1. Determining whether institutions are or are not charities.
2. Encouraging and facilitating the better administration of charities.
3. Identifying and investigating apparent misconduct or mismanagement in the administration of charities and taking remedial or protective action in connection with misconduct or mismanagement in the administration of charities.
4. Determining whether public collections certificates should be issued, and remain in force, in respect of public charitable collections.
5. Obtaining, evaluating and disseminating information in connection with the performance of any of the Commission's functions or meeting any of its objectives.
6. Giving information or advice, or making proposals, to any Minister of the Crown on matters relating to any of the Commission's functions or meeting any of its objectives.

(2) The Commission may, in connection with its second general function, give such advice or guidance with respect to the administration of charities as it considers appropriate.

(3) Any advice or guidance so given may relate to—

(a) charities generally,

(b) any class of charities, or

(c) any particular charity,

and may take such form, and be given in such manner, as the Commission considers appropriate.

(4) The Commission's fifth general function includes (among other things) the maintenance of an accurate and up-to-date register of charities under sections 29 (the register) and 34 (removal of charities from register).

(5) The Commission's sixth general function includes (among other things) complying, so far as is reasonably practicable, with any request made by a Minister of the Crown for information or advice on any matter relating to any of its functions.

(6) In this section "public charitable collection" and "public collections certificate" have the same meaning as in Chapter 1 of Part 3 of the Charities Act 2006.

16 The Commission's general duties

The Commission has the following general duties—

1. So far as is reasonably practicable the Commission must, in performing its functions, act in a way—
   - (a) which is compatible with its objectives, and
   - (b) which it considers most appropriate for the purpose of meeting those objectives.
2. So far as is reasonably practicable the Commission must, in performing its functions, act in a way which is compatible with the encouragement of—
   - (a) all forms of charitable giving, and
   - (b) voluntary participation in charity work.
3. In performing its functions the Commission must have regard to the need to use its resources in the most efficient, effective and economic way.
4. In performing its functions the Commission must, so far as relevant, have regard to the principles of best regulatory practice (including the principles under which regulatory activities should be proportionate, accountable, consistent, transparent and targeted only at cases in which action is needed).
5. In performing its functions the Commission must, in appropriate cases, have regard to the desirability of facilitating innovation by or on behalf of charities.
6. In managing its affairs the Commission must have regard to such generally accepted principles of good corporate governance as it is reasonable to regard as applicable to it.

17 Guidance as to operation of public benefit requirement

(1) The Commission must issue guidance in pursuance of its public benefit objective (see paragraph 2 of section 14).

(2) The Commission may from time to time revise any guidance issued under this section.

(3) The Commission must carry out such public and other consultation as it considers appropriate—

- (a) before issuing any guidance under this section, or
- (b) (unless it considers that it is unnecessary to do so) before revising any guidance under this section.

(4) The Commission must publish any guidance issued or revised under this section in such manner as it considers appropriate.

(5) The charity trustees of a charity must have regard to any such guidance when exercising any powers or duties to which the guidance is relevant.

18 Supply by Commission of copies of documents

The Commission must, at the request of any person, provide that person with copies of, or extracts from, any document in the Commission's possession which is for the time being open to or available for inspection under any provision of this Act.

19 Fees and other amounts payable to Commission

(1) The Minister may by regulations require the payment to the Commission of such fees as may be prescribed by the regulations in respect of—

(a) the discharge by the Commission of such functions under the enactments relating to charities as may be so prescribed;

(b) the inspection of the register of charities or of other material kept by the Commission under those enactments, or the provision of copies of or extracts from documents so kept.

(2) Regulations under this section may—

(a) confer, or provide for the conferring of, exemptions from liability to pay a prescribed fee;

(b) provide for the remission or refunding of a prescribed fee (in whole or in part) in circumstances prescribed by the regulations.

(3) The Commission may impose charges of such amounts as it considers reasonable in respect of the supply of any publications produced by it.

(4) Any fees and other payments received by the Commission by virtue of this section are to be paid into the Consolidated Fund.

20 Incidental powers

(1) The Commission may do anything which is calculated to facilitate, or is conducive or incidental to, the performance of any of its functions or general duties.

(2) But nothing in this Act authorises the Commission—

(a) to exercise functions corresponding to those of a charity trustee in relation to a charity, or

(b) otherwise to be directly involved in the administration of a charity.

(3) Subsection (2) does not affect the operation of section 84 or 85 (power of Commission to direct specified action to be taken or to direct application of charity property).

The official custodian

21 The official custodian for charities

(1) There continues to be an officer known as the official custodian for charities (in this Act referred to as "the official custodian").

(2) The official custodian's function is to act as trustee for charities in the cases provided for by this Act.

(3) The official custodian is such individual as the Commission may from time to time designate.

(4) The official custodian's duties must be performed in accordance with such general or special directions as may be given by the Commission.

(5) Schedule 2 contains provisions relating to the official custodian.

PART 3

EXEMPT CHARITIES AND THE PRINCIPAL REGULATOR

Exempt charities

22 Meaning of "exempt charity" and Sch.3

(1) In this Act "exempt charity" means any institution, so far as it is a charity, that is within Schedule 3.

(2) Subsection (1) is subject to any other enactment by virtue of which a charity is an exempt charity.

23 Power to amend Sch.3 so as to add or remove exempt charities

(1) The Minister may by order make such amendments of Schedule 3 as the Minister considers appropriate for securing—

(a) that (so far as they are charities) institutions of a particular description become or (as the case may be) cease to be exempt charities, or

(b) that (so far as it is a charity) a particular institution becomes or (as the case may be) ceases to be an exempt charity.

(2) An order under subsection (1) may be made only if the Minister is satisfied that the order is desirable in the interests of ensuring appropriate or effective regulation of the charities or charity concerned in connection with compliance by the charity trustees of the charities or charity with their legal obligations in exercising control and management of the administration of the charities or charity.

(3) The Minister may by order make such amendments or other modifications of any enactment as the Minister considers appropriate in connection with—

(a) charities of a particular description becoming, or ceasing to be, exempt charities, or

(b) a particular charity becoming, or ceasing to be, an exempt charity,

as a result of provision made under subsection (1).

(4) In subsection (3), "enactment" includes—

(a) any provision of subordinate legislation (within the meaning of the Interpretation Act 1978), and

(b) a provision of a Measure of the Church Assembly or of the General Synod of the Church of England,

and references to enactments include enactments whenever passed or made.

24 Power to remove defunct institutions from Sch.3

The Minister may by order make such amendments of Schedule 3 as the Minister considers appropriate for removing from that Schedule an institution that has ceased to exist.

The principal regulator

25 Meaning of "the principal regulator"

In this Act "the principal regulator", in relation to an exempt charity, means such body or Minister of the Crown as is prescribed as its principal regulator by regulations made by the Minister.

26 General duty of principal regulator in relation to exempt charity

(1) This section applies to any body or Minister of the Crown who is the principal regulator in relation to an exempt charity.

(2) The body or Minister must do all that the body or Minister reasonably can to meet the compliance objective in relation to the charity.

(3) The compliance objective is to promote compliance by the charity trustees with their legal obligations in exercising control and management of the administration of the charity.

27 Power to make amendments in connection with s.26

(1) Regulations under section 25 may make such amendments or other modifications of any enactment as the Minister considers appropriate for the purpose of facilitating, or otherwise in connection with, the discharge by a principal regulator of the duty under section 26(2).

(2) In subsection (1), "enactment" includes—

(a) any provision of subordinate legislation (within the meaning of the Interpretation Act 1978), and

(b) a provision of a Measure of the Church Assembly or of the General Synod of the Church of England,

and references to enactments include enactments whenever passed or made.

28 Commission to consult principal regulator

Before exercising in relation to an exempt charity any specific power exercisable by it in relation to the charity, the Commission must consult the charity's principal regulator.

PART 4

REGISTRATION AND NAMES OF CHARITIES

The register

29 The register

(1) There continues to be a register of charities, to be kept by the Commission in such manner as it thinks fit.

(2) The register must contain—

(a) the name of every charity registered in accordance with section 30, and

(b) such other particulars of, and such other information relating to, every such charity as the Commission thinks fit.

(3) In this Act, except in so far as the context otherwise requires, "the register" means the register of charities kept under this section and "registered" is to be read accordingly.

Charities required to be registered

30 Charities required to be registered: general

(1) Every charity must be registered in the register unless subsection (2) applies to it.

(2) The following are not required to be registered—

(a) an exempt charity (see section 22 and Schedule 3),

(b) a charity which for the time being—

(i) is permanently or temporarily excepted by order of the Commission, and

(ii) complies with any conditions of the exception,

and whose gross income does not exceed £100,000,

(c) a charity which for the time being—

(i) is, or is of a description, permanently or temporarily excepted by regulations made by the Minister, and

(ii) complies with any conditions of the exception,

and whose gross income does not exceed £100,000, and

(d) a charity whose gross income does not exceed £5,000.

(3) A charity within—

(a) subsection (2)(b) or (c), or

(b) subsection (2)(d),

must, if it so requests, be registered in the register.

(4) In this section any reference to a charity's gross income is to be read, in relation to a particular time—

(a) as a reference to the charity's gross income in its financial year immediately preceding that time, or

(b) if the Commission so determines, as a reference to the amount which the Commission estimates to be the likely amount of the charity's gross income in such financial year of the charity as is specified in the determination.

31 Restrictions on extending the range of excepted charities etc.

(1) No order may be made under section 30(2)(b) so as to except any charity that was not excepted immediately before 31 January 2009.

(2) Subject to subsection (3), no regulations may be made under section 30(2)(c) so as to except any charity or description of charities that was not excepted immediately before 31 January 2009.

(3) Such regulations must be made under section 30(2)(c) as are necessary to secure that any institution ceasing to be an exempt charity by virtue of an order made under section 23 is excepted under section 30(2)(c) (subject to compliance with any conditions of the exception and the financial limit mentioned in section 30(2)(c)).

(4) Subsection (1) does not prevent an order which—

(a) was in force immediately before 31 January 2009, and

(b) has effect (by virtue of paragraph 4 of Schedule 8) as if made under section 30(2)(b),

from being varied or revoked.

(5) Subsection (2) does not prevent regulations which—

(a) were in force immediately before 31 January 2009, and

(b) have effect (by virtue of paragraph 4 of Schedule 8) as if made under section 30(2)(c),

from being varied or revoked.

32 Power to alter sums specified in s.30(2)

(1) The Minister may by order amend—

(a) section 30(2)(b) and (c), or

(b) section 30(2)(d),

by substituting a different sum for the sum for the time being specified there.

(2) The Minister may only make an order under subsection (1)—

(a) so far as it amends section 30(2)(b) and (c), if the Minister considers it expedient to do so with a view to reducing the scope of the exceptions provided by section 30(2)(b) and (c);

(b) so far as it amends section 30(2)(d), if the Minister considers it expedient to do so—

(i) in consequence of changes in the value of money, or

(ii) with a view to extending the scope of the exception provided by section 30(2)(d).

(3) No order may be made by the Minister under subsection (1)(a) unless a copy of a report under section 73 of the Charities Act 2006 has been laid before Parliament in accordance with that section.

33 Power to repeal provisions relating to excepted charities

The following provisions—

(a) section 30(2)(b) and (c) and (3)(a),

(b) section 31,

(c) section 32(1)(a), (2)(a) and (3), and

(d) this section,

cease to have effect on such day as the Minister may by order appoint for the purposes of this section.

Removal of charities from register

34 Removal of charities from register

(1) The Commission must remove from the register—

(a) any institution which it no longer considers is a charity, and

(b) any charity which has ceased to exist or does not operate.

(2) If the removal of an institution under subsection (1)(a) is due to any change in its trusts, the removal takes effect from the date of the change.

(3) A charity which is for the time being registered under section 30(3) (voluntary registration) must be removed from the register if it so requests.

Registration: duties of trustees and claims and objections

35 Duties of trustees in connection with registration

(1) If a charity required to be registered by virtue of section 30(1) is not registered, the charity trustees must—

(a) apply to the Commission for the charity to be registered, and

(b) supply the Commission with the required documents and information.

(2) The required documents and information are—

(a) copies of the charity's trusts or (if they are not set out in any extant document) particulars of them,

(b) such other documents or information as may be prescribed by regulations made by the Minister, and

(c) such other documents or information as the Commission may require for the purposes of the application.

(3) If an institution is for the time being registered, the charity trustees (or the last charity trustees) must—

(a) notify the Commission if the institution ceases to exist, or if there is any change in its trusts or in the particulars of it entered in the register, and

(b) so far as appropriate, supply the Commission with particulars of any such change and copies of any new trusts or alterations of the trusts.

(4) Nothing in subsection (3) requires a person—

(a) to supply the Commission with copies of schemes for the administration of a charity made otherwise than by the court,

(b) to notify the Commission of any change made with respect to a registered charity by such a scheme, or

(c) if the person refers the Commission to a document or copy already in the Commission's possession, to supply a further copy of the document.

36 Claims and objections to registration

(1) A person who is or may be affected by the registration of an institution as a charity may, on the ground that it is not a charity—

(a) object to its being entered by the Commission in the register, or

(b) apply to the Commission for it to be removed from the register.

(2) Provision may be made by regulations made by the Minister as to the manner in which any such objection or application is to be made, prosecuted or dealt with.

(3) Subsection (4) applies if there is an appeal to the Tribunal against any decision of the Commission—

(a) to enter an institution in the register, or

(b) not to remove an institution from the register.

(4) Until the Commission is satisfied whether the decision of the Commission is or is not to stand, the entry in the register—

(a) is to be maintained, but

(b) is in suspense and must be marked to indicate that it is in suspense.

(5) Any question affecting the registration or removal from the register of an institution—

(a) may be considered afresh by the Commission, even though it has been determined by a decision on appeal under Chapter 2 of Part 17 (appeals and applications to Tribunal), and

(b) is not concluded by that decision, if it appears to the Commission that—

(i) there has been a change of circumstances, or

(ii) the decision is inconsistent with a later judicial decision.

Effect of registration and right to inspect register

37 Effect of registration

(1) An institution is, for all purposes other than rectification of the register, conclusively presumed to be or to have been a charity at any time when it is or was on the register.

(2) For the purposes of subsection (1) an institution is to be treated as not being on the register during any period when the entry relating to it is in suspense under section 36(4).

38 Right to inspect register

(1) The register (including the entries cancelled when institutions are removed from the register) must be open to public inspection at all reasonable times.

(2) If any information contained in the register is not in documentary form, subsection (1) is to be read as requiring the information to be available for public inspection in legible form at all reasonable times.

(3) If the Commission so determines, subsection (1) does not apply to any particular information contained in the register that is specified in the determination.

(4) Copies (or particulars) of the trusts of any registered charity as supplied to the Commission under section 35 (duties of trustees in connection with registration) must, so long as the charity remains on the register—

(a) be kept by the Commission, and

(b) be open to public inspection at all reasonable times.

(5) If a copy of a document relating to a registered charity—

(a) is not required to be supplied to the Commission as the result of section 35(4), but

(b) is in the Commission's possession,

a copy of the document must be open to inspection under subsection (4) as if supplied to the Commission under section 35.

Disclosure of registered charity status

39 Statement required to be made in official publications etc.

(1) This section applies to a registered charity if its gross income in its last financial year exceeded £10,000.

(2) If this section applies to a registered charity, the fact that it is a registered charity must be stated in legible characters—

(a) in all notices, advertisements and other documents issued by or on behalf of the charity and soliciting money or other property for the benefit of the charity,

(b) in all bills of exchange, promissory notes, endorsements, cheques and orders for money or goods purporting to be signed on behalf of the charity, and

(c) in all bills rendered by it and in all its invoices, receipts and letters of credit.

(3) The statement required by subsection (2) must be in English, except that, in the case of a document which is otherwise wholly in Welsh, the statement may be in Welsh if it consists of or includes "elusen cofrestredig" (the Welsh equivalent of "registered charity").

(4) Subsection (2)(a) has effect—

(a) whether the solicitation is express or implied, and

(b) whether or not the money or other property is to be given for any consideration.

40 Power to alter sum specified in s.39(1)

The Minister may by order amend section 39(1) by substituting a different sum for the sum for the time being specified there.

41 Offences

(1) It is an offence for a person, in the case of a registered charity to which section 39 applies, to issue or authorise the issue of any document falling within section 39(2)(a) or (c) which does not contain the statement required by section 39(2).

(2) It is an offence for a person, in the case of a registered charity to which section 39 applies, to sign any document falling within section 39(2)(b) which does not contain the statement required by section 39(2).

(3) A person guilty of an offence under subsection (1) or (2) is liable on summary conviction to a fine not exceeding level 3 on the standard scale.

Power to require charity's name to be changed

42 Power to require name to be changed

(1) If this subsection applies to a charity, the Commission may give a direction requiring the name of the charity to be changed, within such period as is specified in the direction, to such other name as the charity trustees may determine with the approval of the Commission.

(2) Subsection (1) applies to a charity if—

(a) it is a registered charity and its name ("the registered name")—

(i) is the same as, or

(ii) is in the opinion of the Commission too like,

the name, at the time when the registered name was entered in the register in respect of the charity, of any other charity (whether registered or not),

(b) the name of the charity is in the opinion of the Commission likely to mislead the public as to the true nature of—

(i) the purposes of the charity as set out in its trusts, or

(ii) the activities which the charity carries on under its trusts in pursuit of those purposes,

(c) the name of the charity includes any word or expression for the time being specified in regulations made by the Minister and the inclusion in its name of that word or expression is in the opinion of the Commission likely to mislead the public in any respect as to the status of the charity,

(d) the name of the charity is in the opinion of the Commission likely to give the impression that the charity is connected in some way with Her Majesty's Government or any local authority, or with any other body of persons or any individual, when it is not so connected, or

(e) the name of the charity is in the opinion of the Commission offensive.

(3) Any direction given by virtue of subsection (2)(a) must be given within 12 months of the time when the registered name was entered in the register in respect of the charity.

(4) In subsection (2) any reference to the name of a charity is, in relation to a registered charity, a reference to the name by which it is registered.

(5) Any direction given under this section with respect to a charity must be given to the charity trustees.

43 Duty of charity trustees on receiving direction under s.42

(1) On receiving a direction under section 42 the charity trustees must give effect to it regardless of anything in the trusts of the charity.

(2) If the name of any charity is changed by virtue of section 42, the charity trustees must without delay notify the Commission of—

(a) the charity's new name, and

(b) the date on which the change occurred.

(3) Subsection (2) does not affect section 35(3) (duty of charity trustees to notify changes in registered particulars).

44 Change of name not to affect existing rights and obligations etc.

A change of name by a charity by virtue of section 42 does not affect any rights or obligations of the charity; and any legal proceedings that might have been continued or commenced by or against it in its former name may be continued or commenced by or against it in its new name.

45 Change of name where charity is a company

(1) In relation to a charitable company, any reference in section 42 or 43 to the charity trustees of a charity is to be read as a reference to the directors of the company.

(2) Subsections (3) to (5) apply if a direction is given under section 42 with respect to a charitable company.

(3) The direction is to be treated as requiring the name of the company to be changed by resolution of the directors of the company.

(4) Where a resolution of the directors is passed in accordance with subsection (3), the company must give notice of the change to the registrar of companies.

(5) Where the name of the company is changed in compliance with the direction, the registrar of companies must—

(a) if satisfied that the new name complies with the requirements of Part 5 of the Companies Act 2006, enter the new name on the register of companies in place of the former name, and

(b) issue a certificate of incorporation altered to meet the circumstances of the case;

and the change of name has effect from the date on which the altered certificate is issued.

PART 5

INFORMATION POWERS

Inquiries instituted by Commission

46 General power to institute inquiries

(1) The Commission may from time to time institute inquiries with regard to charities or a particular charity or class of charities, either generally or for particular purposes.

(2) But no such inquiry is to extend to any exempt charity except where this has been requested by its principal regulator.

(3) The Commission may—
  (a) conduct such an inquiry itself, or
  (b) appoint a person to conduct it and make a report to the Commission.

(4) This section and sections 47 to 49 (obtaining evidence and search warrants) have effect in relation to a body entered in the Scottish Charity Register which is managed or controlled wholly or mainly in or from England or Wales as they have effect in relation to a charity.

47 Obtaining evidence etc. for purposes of inquiry

(1) In this section "inquiry" means an inquiry under section 46.

(2) For the purposes of an inquiry, the Commission, or a person appointed by the Commission to conduct it, may direct any person—
  (a) if a matter in question at the inquiry is one on which the person has or can reasonably obtain information—
    (i) to provide accounts and statements in writing with respect to the matter, or to return answers in writing to any questions or inquiries addressed to the person on the matter, and
    (ii) to verify any such accounts, statements or answers by statutory declaration;
  (b) to provide copies of documents which are in the custody or under the control of the person and which relate to any matter in question at the inquiry, and to verify any such copies by statutory declaration;
  (c) to attend at a specified time and place and give evidence or produce any such documents.

But this is subject to the provisions of this section.

(3) For the purposes of an inquiry—
  (a) evidence may be taken on oath, and the person conducting the inquiry may for that purpose administer oaths, or
  (b) the person conducting the inquiry may instead of administering an oath require the person examined to make and subscribe a declaration of the truth of the matters about which that person is examined.

(4) The Commission may pay to any person attending to give evidence or produce documents for the purpose of an inquiry the necessary expenses of doing so.

(5) A direction under subsection (2)(c) may not require a person to go more than 10 miles from the person's place of residence unless those expenses are paid or tendered to the person.

48 Power to obtain search warrant for purposes of inquiry

(1) A justice of the peace may issue a warrant under this section if satisfied, on information given on oath by a member of the Commission's staff, that there are reasonable grounds for believing that each of the conditions in subsection (2) is satisfied.

(2) The conditions are—

(a) that an inquiry has been instituted under section 46,

(b) that there is on the premises to be specified in the warrant any document or information relevant to that inquiry which the Commission could require to be produced or provided under section 52(1), and

(c) that, if the Commission were to make an order requiring the document or information to be so produced or provided—

(i) the order would not be complied with, or

(ii) the document or information would be removed, tampered with, concealed or destroyed.

(3) A warrant under this section is a warrant authorising the member of the Commission's staff who is named in it ("P")—

(a) to enter and search the premises specified in it;

(b) to take such other persons with P as the Commission considers are needed to assist P in doing anything that P is authorised to do under the warrant;

(c) to take possession of any documents which appear to fall within subsection (2)(b), or to take any other steps which appear to be necessary for preserving, or preventing interference with, any such documents;

(d) to take possession of any computer disk or other electronic storage device which appears to contain information falling within subsection (2)(b), or information contained in a document so falling, or to take any other steps which appear to be necessary for preserving, or preventing interference with, any such information;

(e) to take copies of, or extracts from, any documents or information falling within paragraph (c) or (d);

(f) to require any person on the premises to provide an explanation of any such document or information or to state where any such documents or information may be found;

(g) to require any such person to give P such assistance as P may reasonably require for the taking of copies or extracts as mentioned in paragraph (e).

49 Execution of search warrant

(1) Entry and search under a warrant under section 48 must be at a reasonable hour and within one month of the date of its issue.

(2) The member of the Commission's staff who is authorised under such a warrant ("P") must, if required to do so, produce—

(a) the warrant, and

(b) documentary evidence that P is a member of the Commission's staff,

for inspection by the occupier of the premises or anyone acting on the occupier's behalf.

(3) P must make a written record of—

(a) the date and time of P's entry on the premises,

(b) the number of persons (if any) who accompanied P on to the premises and the names of any such persons,

(c) the period for which P (and any such persons) remained on the premises,

(d) what P (and any such persons) did while on the premises, and

(e) any document or device of which P took possession while there.

(4) If required to do so, P must give a copy of the record to the occupier of the premises or someone acting on the occupier's behalf.

(5) Unless it is not reasonably practicable to do so, P must before leaving the premises comply with—

(a) the requirements of subsection (3), and

(b) any requirement made under subsection (4) before P leaves the premises.

(6) Where possession of any document or device is taken under section 48—

(a) the document may be retained for so long as the Commission considers that it is necessary to retain it (rather than a copy of it) for the purposes of the relevant inquiry under section 46, or

(b) the device may be retained for so long as the Commission considers that it is necessary to retain it for the purposes of that inquiry,

as the case may be.

(7) Once it appears to the Commission that the retention of any document or device has ceased to be so necessary, it must arrange for the document or device to be returned as soon as is reasonably practicable—

(a) to the person from whose possession it was taken, or

(b) to any of the charity trustees of the charity to which it belonged or related.

For the purposes of this subsection as it has effect by virtue of section 46(4), the reference in paragraph (b) to the charity trustees of the charity is to be read as a reference to the persons having the general control and management of the administration of the body entered in the Scottish Charity Register.

(8) It is an offence for a person intentionally to obstruct the exercise of any rights conferred by a warrant under section 48.

(9) A person guilty of an offence under subsection (8) is liable on summary conviction—

(a) to imprisonment for a term not exceeding 51 weeks, or

(b) to a fine not exceeding level 5 on the standard scale,

or to both.

50 Publication of results of inquiries

(1) This section applies where an inquiry has been held under section 46.

(2) The Commission may—

(a) cause the report of the person conducting the inquiry, or such other statement of the results of the inquiry as the Commission thinks fit, to be printed and published, or

(b) publish any such report or statement in some other way which is calculated in the Commission's opinion to bring it to the attention of persons who may wish to make representations to the Commission about the action to be taken.

51 Contributions by local authorities to inquiries into local charities

(1) A council may contribute to the expenses of the Commission in connection with inquiries under section 46 into local charities in the council's area.

(2) In subsection (1) "council" means—
(a) a district council;
(b) a county council;
(c) a county borough council;
(d) a London borough council;
(e) the Common Council of the City of London.

Power to call for documents and search records

52 Power to call for documents

(1) The Commission may by order—
(a) require any person to provide the Commission with any information which is in that person's possession and which—
(i) relates to any charity, and
(ii) is relevant to the discharge of the functions of the Commission or of the official custodian;
(b) require any person who has custody or control of any document which relates to any charity and is relevant to the discharge of the functions of the Commission or of the official custodian—
(i) to provide the Commission with a copy of or extract from the document, or
(ii) to transmit the document itself to the Commission for its inspection (unless the document forms part of the records or other documents of a court or of a public or local authority).

(2) The Commission is entitled without payment to keep any copy or extract provided to it under subsection (1).

(3) If a document transmitted to the Commission under subsection (1) for it to inspect—
(a) relates only to one or more charities, and
(b) is not held by any person entitled as trustee or otherwise to the custody of it,

the Commission may keep it or may deliver it to the charity trustees or to any other person who may be so entitled.

(4) This section has effect in relation to any body entered in the Scottish Charity Register which is managed or controlled wholly or mainly in or from England or Wales as it has effect in relation to a charity.

53 Power to search records

(1) Any member of the staff of the Commission, if so authorised by it, is entitled without payment to inspect and take copies of or extracts from the records or other documents of—
(a) any court, or
(b) any public registry or office of records,

for any purpose connected with the discharge of the functions of the Commission or of the official custodian.

(2) The reference in subsection (1) to a member of the staff of the Commission includes the official custodian even if not a member of the staff of the Commission.

(3) The rights conferred by subsection (1), in relation to information recorded otherwise than in legible form, include the right to require the information to be made available in legible form—

(a) for inspection, or

(b) for a copy or extract to be made of or from it.

Disclosure of information

54 Disclosure to Commission: general

(1) A relevant public authority may disclose information to the Commission if the disclosure is made for the purpose of enabling or assisting the Commission to discharge any of its functions.

(2) Subsection (1) is subject to section 55.

(3) In this section "relevant public authority" means—

(a) any government department (including a Northern Ireland department),

(b) any local authority,

(c) any constable, and

(d) any other body or person discharging functions of a public nature (including a body or person discharging regulatory functions in relation to any description of activities).

55 Disclosure to Commission: Revenue and Customs information

(1) Revenue and Customs information may be disclosed under section 54(1) only if it relates to an institution, undertaking or body falling within one (or more) of the following paragraphs—

(a) a charity;

(b) an institution which is established for charitable, benevolent or philanthropic purposes;

(c) an institution by or in respect of which a claim for tax exemption has at any time been made;

(d) a subsidiary undertaking of a charity;

(e) a body entered in the Scottish Charity Register which is managed or controlled wholly or mainly in or from England or Wales.

(2) In subsection (1)(d) "subsidiary undertaking of a charity" means an undertaking (as defined by section 1161(1) of the Companies Act 2006) in relation to which—

(a) a charity is (or is to be treated as) a parent undertaking in accordance with the provisions of section 1162 of, and Schedule 7 to, the Companies Act 2006, or

(b) two or more charities would, if they were a single charity, be (or be treated as) a parent undertaking in accordance with those provisions.

(3) For the purposes of the references to a parent undertaking—

(a) in subsection (2), and

(b) in section 1162 of, and Schedule 7 to, the Companies Act 2006 as they apply for the purposes of subsection (2),

"undertaking" includes a charity which is not an undertaking as defined by section 1161(1) of that Act.

(4) In this section "Revenue and Customs information" means information held as mentioned in section 18(1) of the Commissioners for Revenue and Customs Act 2005.

(5) For the purposes of subsection (1)(c), "claim for tax exemption" means—

(a) a claim for exemption under section 505(1) of the Income and Corporation Taxes Act 1988,

(b) a claim for exemption under Part 10 of the Income Tax Act 2007, or

(c) a claim for exemption under Part 11 of the Corporation Tax Act 2010, if it is not—

(i) a claim for exemption under section 475, 476 or 477 (reliefs for eligible bodies and scientific research organisations), or

(ii) a claim made by virtue of section 490 or 491 (application of exemptions to eligible bodies and scientific research organisations).

56 Disclosure by Commission: general

(1) The Commission may disclose to any relevant public authority any information received by the Commission in connection with any of the Commission's functions if—

(a) the disclosure is made for the purpose of enabling or assisting the relevant public authority to discharge any of its functions, or

(b) the information so disclosed is otherwise relevant to the discharge of any of the functions of the relevant public authority.

(2) Subsection (1) is subject to subsection (3) and section 57(1) and (2).

(3) In the case of information disclosed to the Commission under section 54(1), the Commission's power to disclose the information under subsection (1) is exercisable subject to any express restriction subject to which the information was disclosed to the Commission.

(4) In this section "relevant public authority" has the same meaning as in section 54, except that it also includes any body or person within section 54(3)(d) in a country or territory outside the United Kingdom.

57 Disclosure by Commission: Revenue and Customs information

(1) Section 56(3) does not apply in relation to Revenue and Customs information disclosed to the Commission under section 54(1).

(2) But any such information may not be further disclosed (whether under section 56(1) or otherwise) except with the consent of the Commissioners for Her Majesty's Revenue and Customs.

(3) It is an offence for a responsible person to disclose information in contravention of subsection (2).

(4) A person guilty of an offence under subsection (3) is liable—

(a) on summary conviction, to imprisonment for a term not exceeding 12 months or to a fine not exceeding the statutory maximum, or both;

(b) on conviction on indictment, to imprisonment for a term not exceeding 2 years or to a fine, or both.

(5) It is a defence, where a responsible person is charged with an offence under subsection (3) of disclosing information, to prove that that person reasonably believed—

(a) that the disclosure was lawful, or

(b) that the information had already and lawfully been made available to the public.

(6) In the application of this section to Northern Ireland, the reference to 12 months in subsection (4) is to be read as a reference to 6 months.

(7) In this section "Revenue and Customs information" means information held as mentioned in section 18(1) of the Commissioners for Revenue and Customs Act 2005.

(8) In this section "responsible person" means a person who is or was—

(a) a member of the Commission,

(b) a member of the staff of the Commission,

(c) a person acting on behalf of—

(i) the Commission, or

(ii) a member of the staff of the Commission, or

(d) a member of a committee established by the Commission.

58 Disclosure to and by principal regulators of exempt charities

(1) Sections 54 to 57 apply with the modifications in subsections (2) to (4) in relation to the disclosure of information to or by the principal regulator of an exempt charity.

(2) References in those sections to the Commission or to any of its functions are to be read as references to the principal regulator of an exempt charity or to any of the functions of that body or person as principal regulator in relation to the charity.

(3) Section 55 has effect as if for subsections (1) and (2) there were substituted—

"(1) Revenue and Customs information may be disclosed under section 54(1) only if it relates to—

(a) the exempt charity in relation to which the principal regulator has functions as such, or

(b) a subsidiary undertaking of the exempt charity.

(2) In subsection (1)(b) "subsidiary undertaking of the exempt charity" means an undertaking (as defined by section 1161(1) of the Companies Act 2006) in relation to which—

(a) the exempt charity is (or is to be treated as) a parent undertaking in accordance with the provisions of section 1162 of, and Schedule 7 to, the Companies Act 2006, or

(b) the exempt charity and one or more other charities would, if they were a single charity, be (or be treated as) a parent undertaking in accordance with those provisions."

(4) Section 57 has effect as if for the definition of "responsible person" in subsection (8) there were substituted a definition specified by regulations under section 25 (meaning of "principal regulator").

(5) Regulations under section 25 may also make such amendments or other modifications of any enactment as the Minister considers appropriate for securing that any disclosure provisions that would otherwise apply in relation to the principal regulator of an exempt charity do not apply in relation to that body or person as principal regulator.

(6) In subsection (5) "disclosure provisions" means provisions having effect for authorising, or otherwise in connection with, the disclosure of information by or to the principal regulator concerned.

(7) In subsection (5) "enactment" includes—

- (a) any provision of subordinate legislation (within the meaning of the Interpretation Act 1978), and
- (b) a provision of a Measure of the Church Assembly or of the General Synod of the Church of England,

and references to enactments include enactments whenever passed or made.

59 Disclosure: supplementary

Nothing in sections 54 to 57 (or in those sections as applied by section 58(1) to (4)) authorises the making of a disclosure which—

- (a) contravenes the Data Protection Act 1998, or
- (b) is prohibited by Part 1 of the Regulation of Investigatory Powers Act 2000.

Supply of false or misleading information to Commission etc.

60 Supply of false or misleading information to Commission etc.

(1) It is an offence for a person knowingly or recklessly to provide the Commission with information which is false or misleading in a material particular if the information is provided—

- (a) in purported compliance with a requirement imposed by or under this Act, or
- (b) otherwise than as mentioned in paragraph (a) but in circumstances in which the person providing the information—
  - (i) intends, or
  - (ii) could reasonably be expected to know,

  that it would be used by the Commission for the purpose of discharging its functions under this Act.

(2) It is an offence for a person wilfully to alter, suppress, conceal or destroy any document which the person is or is liable to be required, by or under this Act, to produce to the Commission.

(3) A person guilty of an offence under this section is liable—

- (a) on summary conviction, to a fine not exceeding the statutory maximum;
- (b) on conviction on indictment, to imprisonment for a term not exceeding 2 years or to a fine, or both.

(4) In this section references to the Commission include references to any person conducting an inquiry under section 46.

PART 6

CY-PRÈS POWERS AND ASSISTANCE AND SUPERVISION OF CHARITIES BY COURT AND COMMISSION

Cy-près powers and variation of charters

61 Duty of trustees in relation to application of property cy-près

It is hereby declared that a trust for charitable purposes places a trustee under a duty, where the case permits and requires the property or some part of it to be applied cy-près, to secure its effective use for charity by taking steps to enable it to be so applied.

62 Occasions for applying property cy-près

(1) Subject to subsection (3), the circumstances in which the original purposes of a charitable gift can be altered to allow the property given or part of it to be applied cy-près are—

(a) where the original purposes, in whole or in part—

(i) have been as far as may be fulfilled, or

(ii) cannot be carried out, or not according to the directions given and to the spirit of the gift,

(b) where the original purposes provide a use for part only of the property available by virtue of the gift,

(c) where—

(i) the property available by virtue of the gift, and

(ii) other property applicable for similar purposes,

can be more effectively used in conjunction, and to that end can suitably, regard being had to the appropriate considerations, be made applicable to common purposes,

(d) where the original purposes were laid down by reference to—

(i) an area which then was but has since ceased to be a unit for some other purpose, or

(ii) a class of persons or an area which has for any reason since ceased to be suitable, regard being had to the appropriate considerations, or to be practical in administering the gift, or

(e) where the original purposes, in whole or in part, have, since they were laid down—

(i) been adequately provided for by other means,

(ii) ceased, as being useless or harmful to the community or for other reasons, to be in law charitable, or

(iii) ceased in any other way to provide a suitable and effective method of using the property available by virtue of the gift, regard being had to the appropriate considerations.

(2) In subsection (1) "the appropriate considerations" means—
- (a) (on the one hand) the spirit of the gift concerned, and
- (b) (on the other) the social and economic circumstances prevailing at the time of the proposed alteration of the original purposes.

(3) Subsection (1) does not affect the conditions which must be satisfied in order that property given for charitable purposes may be applied cy-près except in so far as those conditions require a failure of the original purposes.

(4) References in subsections (1) to (3) to the original purposes of a gift are to be read, where the application of the property given has been altered or regulated by a scheme or otherwise, as referring to the purposes for which the property is for the time being applicable.

(5) The court may by scheme made under the court's jurisdiction with respect to charities, in any case where the purposes for which the property is held are laid down by reference to any such area as is mentioned in column 1 in Schedule 4, provide for enlarging the area to any such area as is mentioned in column 2 in the same entry in that Schedule.

(6) Subsection (5) does not affect the power to make schemes in circumstances falling within subsection (1).

63 Application cy-près: donor unknown or disclaiming

(1) Property given for specific charitable purposes which fail is applicable cy-près as if given for charitable purposes generally, if it belongs—
- (a) to a donor who after—
  - (i) the prescribed advertisements and inquiries have been published and made, and
  - (ii) the prescribed period beginning with the publication of those advertisements has ended,

  cannot be identified or cannot be found, or
- (b) to a donor who has executed a disclaimer in the prescribed form of the right to have the property returned.

(2) Where the prescribed advertisements and inquiries have been published and made by or on behalf of trustees with respect to any such property, the trustees are not liable to any person in respect of the property if no claim by that person to be interested in it is received by them before the end of the period mentioned in subsection (1)(a)(ii).

(3) Where property is applied cy-près by virtue of this section, all the donor's interest in it is treated as having been relinquished when the gift was made.

(4) But where property is so applied as belonging to donors who cannot be identified or cannot be found, and is not so applied by virtue of section 64 (donors treated as unidentifiable)—
- (a) the scheme must specify the total amount of that property,
- (b) the donor of any part of that amount is entitled, on making a claim within the time limit, to recover from the charity for which the property is applied a sum equal to that part, less any expenses properly incurred by the charity trustees after the scheme's date in connection with claims relating to the donor's gift, and

(c) the scheme may include directions as to the provision to be made for meeting any claims made in accordance with paragraph (b).

(5) For the purposes of subsection (4)(b)—

(a) a claim is made within the time limit only if it is made no later than 6 months after the date on which the scheme is made, and

(b) "the scheme's date" means the date on which the scheme is made.

(6) Subsection (7) applies if—

(a) any sum is, in accordance with any directions included in the scheme under subsection (4)(c), set aside for meeting claims made in accordance with subsection (4)(b), but

(b) the aggregate amount of any such claims actually made exceeds the relevant amount;

and for this purpose "the relevant amount" means the amount of the sum so set aside after deduction of any expenses properly incurred by the charity trustees in connection with claims relating to the donors' gifts.

(7) If the Commission so directs, each of the donors in question is entitled only to such proportion of the relevant amount as the amount of the donor's claim bears to the aggregate amount referred to in subsection (6)(b).

64 Donors treated as unidentifiable

(1) For the purposes of section 63 property is conclusively presumed (without any advertisement or inquiry) to belong to donors who cannot be identified, in so far as it consists of—

(a) the proceeds of cash collections made—

(i) by means of collecting boxes, or

(ii) by other means not adapted for distinguishing one gift from another, or

(b) the proceeds of any lottery, competition, entertainment, sale or similar money-raising activity, after allowing for property given to provide prizes or articles for sale or otherwise to enable the activity to be undertaken.

(2) The court or the Commission may by order direct that property not falling within subsection (1) is for the purposes of section 63 to be treated (without any advertisement or inquiry) as belonging to donors who cannot be identified if it appears to the court or the Commission—

(a) that it would be unreasonable, having regard to the amounts likely to be returned to the donors, to incur expense with a view to returning the property, or

(b) that it would be unreasonable, having regard to the nature, circumstances and amounts of the gifts, and to the lapse of time since the gifts were made, for the donors to expect the property to be returned.

65 Donors treated as disclaiming

(1) This section applies to property given—

(a) for specific charitable purposes, and

(b) in response to a solicitation within subsection (2).

(2) A solicitation is within this subsection if—

(a) it is made for specific charitable purposes, and

(b) it is accompanied by a statement to the effect that property given in response to it will, in the event of those purposes failing, be applicable cy-près as if given for charitable purposes generally, unless the donor makes a relevant declaration at the time of making the gift.

(3) A relevant declaration is a declaration in writing by the donor to the effect that, in the event of the specific charitable purposes failing, the donor wishes to be given the opportunity by the trustees holding the property to request the return of the property in question (or a sum equal to its value at the time of the making of the gift).

(4) Subsections (5) and (6) apply if—

(a) a person has given property as mentioned in subsection (1),

(b) the specific charitable purposes fail, and

(c) the donor has made a relevant declaration.

(5) The trustees holding the property must take the prescribed steps for the purpose of—

(a) informing the donor of the failure of the purposes,

(b) enquiring whether the donor wishes to request the return of the property (or a sum equal to its value), and

(c) if within the prescribed period the donor makes such a request, returning the property (or such a sum) to the donor.

(6) If those trustees have taken all appropriate prescribed steps but—

(a) they have failed to find the donor, or

(b) the donor does not within the prescribed period request the return of the property (or a sum equal to its value),

section 63(1) applies to the property as if it belonged to a donor within section 63(1)(b) (application of property where donor has disclaimed right to return of property).

(7) If—

(a) a person has given property as mentioned in subsection (1),

(b) the specific charitable purposes fail, and

(c) the donor has not made a relevant declaration,

section 63(1) similarly applies to the property as if it belonged to a donor within section 63(1)(b).

(8) For the purposes of this section—

(a) "solicitation" means a solicitation made in any manner and however communicated to the persons to whom it is addressed,

(b) it is irrelevant whether any consideration is or is to be given in return for the property in question, and

(c) where any appeal consists of—

(i) solicitations that are accompanied by statements within subsection (2)(b), and

(ii) solicitations that are not so accompanied,

a person giving property as a result of the appeal is to be presumed, unless the contrary is proved, to have responded to the former solicitations and not the latter.

66 Unknown and disclaiming donors: supplementary

(1) For the purposes of sections 63 and 65, charitable purposes are to be treated as failing if any difficulty in applying property to those purposes makes that property or the part not applicable cy-près available to be returned to the donors.

(2) In sections 63 to 65 and this section—
- (a) references to a donor include persons claiming through or under the original donor, and
- (b) references to property given include the property for the time being representing the property originally given or property derived from it.

(3) Subsection (2) applies except in so far as the context otherwise requires.

(4) In sections 63 and 65 "prescribed" means prescribed by regulations made by the Commission.

(5) Any such regulations are to be published by the Commission in such manner as it thinks fit.

(6) Any such regulations may, as respects the advertisements which are to be published for the purposes of section 63(1)(a), make provision as to the form and content of such advertisements as well as the manner in which they are to be published.

67 Cy-près schemes

(1) The power of the court or the Commission to make schemes for the application of property cy-près must be exercised in accordance with this section.

(2) Where any property given for charitable purposes is applicable cy-près, the court or the Commission may make a scheme providing for the property to be applied—
- (a) for such charitable purposes, and
- (b) (if the scheme provides for the property to be transferred to another charity) by or on trust for such other charity,

as it considers appropriate, having regard to the matters set out in subsection (3).

(3) The matters are—
- (a) the spirit of the original gift,
- (b) the desirability of securing that the property is applied for charitable purposes which are close to the original purposes, and
- (c) the need for the relevant charity to have purposes which are suitable and effective in the light of current social and economic circumstances.

The "relevant charity" means the charity by or on behalf of which the property is to be applied under the scheme.

(4) If a scheme provides for the property to be transferred to another charity, the scheme may impose on the charity trustees of that charity a duty to secure that the property is applied for purposes which are, so far as is reasonably practicable, similar in character to the original purposes.

(5) In this section references to property given include the property for the time being representing the property originally given or property derived from it.

(6) In this section references to the transfer of property to a charity are references to its transfer—

(a) to the charity,
(b) to the charity trustees,
(c) to any trustee for the charity, or
(d) to a person nominated by the charity trustees to hold it in trust for the charity,

as the scheme may provide.

(7) In this section references to the original purposes of a gift are to be read, where the application of the property given has been altered or regulated by a scheme or otherwise, as referring to the purposes for which the property is for the time being applicable.

68 Charities governed by charter, or by or under statute

(1) Subsection (2) applies where a Royal charter establishing or regulating a body corporate is amendable by the grant and acceptance of a further charter.

(2) A scheme relating to the body corporate or to the administration of property held by the body (including a scheme for the cy-près application of any such property)—

(a) may be made by the court under the court's jurisdiction with respect to charities even though the scheme cannot take effect without the alteration of the charter, but
(b) must be so framed that the scheme, or such part of it as cannot take effect without the alteration of the charter, does not purport to come into operation unless or until Her Majesty thinks fit to amend the charter in such manner as will permit the scheme or that part of it to have effect.

(3) Subsection (4) applies where, under—

(a) the court's jurisdiction with respect to charities or the corresponding jurisdiction of a court in Northern Ireland, or
(b) powers conferred by this Act or by any Northern Ireland legislation relating to charities,

a scheme is made with respect to a body corporate and it appears to Her Majesty expedient, having regard to the scheme, to amend any Royal charter relating to that body.

(4) Her Majesty may, on the application of the body corporate, amend the charter accordingly by Order in Council in any way in which the charter could be amended by the grant and acceptance of a further charter; and any such Order in Council may be revoked or varied in the same manner as the charter it amends.

(5) The jurisdiction of the court with respect to charities is not excluded or restricted in the case of a charity of a description mentioned in Schedule 5 by the operation of the enactments or instruments there mentioned in relation to that description.

(6) A scheme established for a charity of a description mentioned in Schedule 5—

(a) may modify or supersede in relation to it the provision made by any such enactment or instrument as if made by a scheme of the court, and
(b) may also make any such provision as is authorised by that Schedule.

Powers of Commission to make schemes etc.

69 Commission's concurrent jurisdiction with High Court for certain purposes

(1) The Commission may by order exercise the same jurisdiction and powers as are exercisable by the High Court in charity proceedings for the following purposes—

(a) establishing a scheme for the administration of a charity;

(b) appointing, discharging or removing a charity trustee or trustee for a charity, or removing an officer or employee;

(c) vesting or transferring property, or requiring or entitling any person to call for or make any transfer of property or any payment.

(2) Subsection (1) is subject to the provisions of this Act.

(3) If the court directs a scheme for the administration of a charity to be established—

(a) the court may by order refer the matter to the Commission for it to prepare or settle a scheme in accordance with such directions (if any) as the court sees fit to give, and

(b) any such order may provide for the scheme to be put into effect by order of the Commission as if prepared under subsection (1) and without any further order of the court.

70 Restrictions on Commission's concurrent jurisdiction

(1) The Commission does not have jurisdiction under section 69 to try or determine—

(a) the title at law or in equity to any property as between—

(i) a charity or trustee for a charity, and

(ii) a person holding or claiming the property or an interest in it adversely to the charity, or

(b) any question as to the existence or extent of any charge or trust.

(2) Subject to the following subsections, the Commission must not exercise its jurisdiction under section 69 as respects any charity except—

(a) on the application of the charity,

(b) on an order of the court under section 69(3), or

(c) on the application of the Attorney General.

(3) In the case of a charity whose gross income does not exceed £500 a year, the Commission may exercise its jurisdiction under section 69 on the application of—

(a) any one or more of the charity trustees,

(b) any person interested in the charity, or

(c) any two or more inhabitants of the area of the charity if it is a local charity.

(4) Subsection (5) applies where in the case of a charity, other than an exempt charity, the Commission—

(a) is satisfied that the charity trustees—

(i) ought in the interests of the charity to apply for a scheme, but

(ii) have unreasonably refused or neglected to do so, and

(b) has given the charity trustees an opportunity to make representations to it.

(5) The Commission—

(a) may proceed as if an application for a scheme had been made by the charity, but

(b) may not, where it acts by virtue of this subsection, alter the purposes of a charity unless 40 years have elapsed from the date of the charity's foundation.

(6) Where—

(a) a charity cannot apply to the Commission for a scheme because of any vacancy among the charity trustees or the absence or incapacity of any of them, but

(b) such an application is made by such number of the charity trustees as the Commission considers appropriate in the circumstances of the case,

the Commission may nevertheless proceed as if the application were an application made by the charity.

(7) The Commission may on the application of any charity trustee or trustee for a charity exercise its jurisdiction under section 69 for the purpose of discharging the applicant from trusteeship.

(8) The Commission must not exercise its jurisdiction under section 69 in any case (not referred to it by order of the court) which—

(a) because of its contentious character, or any special question of law or of fact which it may involve, or

(b) for other reasons,

the Commission may consider more fit to be adjudicated on by the court.

71 Exercise of Commission's concurrent jurisdiction: notice

(1) Before exercising any jurisdiction under section 69 otherwise than on an order of the court, the Commission must give notice of its intention to do so to each of the charity trustees except any—

(a) that cannot be found or has no known address in the United Kingdom, or

(b) who is party or privy to an application for the exercise of the jurisdiction.

(2) Any such notice—

(a) may be given by post, and

(b) if given by post, may be addressed to the recipient's last known address in the United Kingdom.

72 Power to alter sum specified in s.70(3)

If the Minister thinks it expedient to do so—

(a) in consequence of changes in the value of money, or

(b) with a view to increasing the number of charities in respect of which the Commission may exercise its jurisdiction under section 69 in accordance with section 70(3),

the Minister may by order amend section 70(3) by substituting a different sum for the sum for the time being specified there.

73 Powers to make schemes altering provision made by Acts, etc.

(1) If it appears to the Commission that a scheme should be established for the administration of a charity, but also—

(a) that it is necessary or desirable for the scheme—
 (i) to alter the provision made by an Act establishing or regulating the charity, or
 (ii) to make any other provision which goes or might go beyond the powers exercisable by the Commission apart from this section, or
(b) that it is for any reason proper for the scheme to be subject to parliamentary review,

the Commission may (subject to subsection (7)) settle a scheme accordingly with a view to its being given effect under this section.

(2) A scheme settled by the Commission under this section may be given effect by order of the Minister.

(3) Subject to subsections (4) and (6), an order under subsection (2) is subject to annulment in pursuance of a resolution of either House of Parliament.

(4) In the case of a scheme which goes beyond the powers exercisable apart from this section in altering a statutory provision contained in or having effect under any public general Act, no order may be made unless a draft of the order has been laid before and approved by a resolution of each House of Parliament.

(5) Subject to subsection (6), any provision of a scheme brought into effect under this section may be modified or superseded by the court or the Commission as if it were a scheme brought into effect by order of the Commission under section 69.

(6) Where subsection (4) applies to a scheme, the order giving effect to it—
(a) may direct that the scheme must not be modified or superseded by a scheme brought into effect otherwise than under this section, and
(b) may also direct that subsection (4) is to apply to any scheme modifying or superseding the scheme to which the order gives effect.

(7) The Commission must not proceed under this section without the same application, and the same notice to the charity trustees, as would be required if the Commission was proceeding (without an order of the court) under section 69.

(8) But on any application for a scheme, or in a case where it acts by virtue of section 70(5) or (6), the Commission may proceed under this section or section 69 as appears to it appropriate.

74 Restriction on expenditure on promoting Bills

(1) No expenditure incurred in preparing or promoting a Bill in Parliament is to be defrayed without the consent of the court or the Commission out of any money applicable for the purposes of a charity.

(2) Subsection (1) applies regardless of anything in the trusts of a charity.

75 Further powers to alter application of charitable property

(1) Subsection (2) applies where the Commission is satisfied that—
(a) the whole of the income of a charity cannot in existing circumstances be effectively applied for the purposes of the charity,
(b) if those circumstances continue, a scheme might be made for applying the surplus cy-près, and

(c) it is for any reason not yet desirable to make such a scheme.

(2) The Commission may by order authorise the charity trustees at their discretion (but subject to any conditions imposed by the order) to apply any accrued or accruing income for any purposes for which it might be made applicable by such a scheme.

(3) Any application of accrued or accruing income authorised by an order under subsection (2) is to be treated as being within the purposes of the charity.

(4) An order under subsection (2) must not extend—

(a) to more than £300 out of income accrued before the date of the order,

(b) to income accruing more than 3 years after that date, or

(c) to more than £100 out of the income accruing in any of those 3 years.

Powers of Commission to act for protection of charities etc.

76 Suspension of trustees etc. and appointment of interim managers

(1) Subsection (3) applies where, at any time after it has instituted an inquiry under section 46 with respect to any charity, the Commission is satisfied—

(a) that there is or has been any misconduct or mismanagement in the administration of the charity, or

(b) that it is necessary or desirable to act for the purpose of—

(i) protecting the property of the charity, or

(ii) securing a proper application for the purposes of the charity of that property or of property coming to the charity.

(2) The reference in subsection (1) to misconduct or mismanagement extends (regardless of anything in the trusts of the charity) to the employment—

(a) for the remuneration or reward of persons acting in the affairs of the charity, or

(b) for other administrative purposes,

of sums which are excessive in relation to the property which is or is likely to be applied or applicable for the purposes of the charity.

(3) The Commission may of its own motion do one or more of the following—

(a) by order suspend any person who is a trustee, charity trustee, officer, agent or employee of the charity from office or employment pending consideration being given to the person's removal (whether under section 79 or 80 or otherwise);

(b) by order appoint such number of additional charity trustees as it considers necessary for the proper administration of the charity;

(c) by order—

(i) vest any property held by or in trust for the charity in the official custodian,

(ii) require the persons in whom any such property is vested to transfer it to the official custodian, or

(iii) appoint any person to transfer any such property to the official custodian;

(d) order any person who holds any property on behalf of the charity, or of any trustee for it, not to part with the property without the approval of the Commission;

(e) order any debtor of the charity not to make any payment in or towards the discharge of the debtor's liability to the charity without the approval of the Commission;

(f) by order restrict (regardless of anything in the trusts of the charity) the transactions which may be entered into, or the nature or amount of the payments which may be made, in the administration of the charity without the approval of the Commission;

(g) by order appoint (in accordance with section 78) an interim manager, to act as receiver and manager in respect of the property and affairs of the charity.

(4) The Commission may not make an order under subsection (3)(a) so as to suspend a person from office or employment for a period of more than 12 months.

(5) But any order under subsection (3)(a) made in the case of any person ("P") may make provision, as respects the period of P's suspension for matters arising out of it, and in particular—

(a) for enabling any person to execute any instrument in P's name or otherwise act for P, and

(b) in the case of a charity trustee, for adjusting any rules governing the proceedings of the charity trustees to take account of the reduction in the number capable of acting.

This does not affect the generality of section 337(1) and (2).

(6) The Commission—

(a) must, at such intervals as it thinks fit, review any order made by it under paragraph (a), or any of paragraphs (c) to (g), of subsection (3), and

(b) if on any such review it appears to the Commission that it would be appropriate to discharge the order in whole or in part, must so discharge it (whether subject to any savings or other transitional provisions or not).

77 Offence of contravening certain orders under s.76

(1) It is an offence for a person to contravene an order under—

(a) section 76(3)(d) (order prohibiting person from parting with property),

(b) section 76(3)(e) (order prohibiting debtor of charity from discharging liability), or

(c) section 76(3)(f) (order restricting transactions or payments).

(2) A person guilty of an offence under subsection (1) is liable on summary conviction to a fine not exceeding level 5 on the standard scale.

(3) This section is not to be treated as precluding the bringing of proceedings for breach of trust against any charity trustee or trustee for a charity in respect of a contravention of an order under section 76(3)(d) or (f) (whether or not proceedings in respect of the contravention are brought against the trustee under this section).

78 Interim managers: supplementary

(1) The Commission may under section 76(3)(g) appoint to be interim manager in respect of a charity such person (other than a member of its staff) as it thinks fit.

(2) An order made by the Commission under section 76(3)(g) may make provision with respect to the functions to be discharged by the interim manager appointed by the order.

This does not affect the generality of section 337(1) and (2).

(3) Those functions are to be discharged by the interim manager under the supervision of the Commission.

(4) In connection with the discharge of those functions, an order under section 76(3)(g) may provide—

(a) for the interim manager appointed by the order to have such powers and duties of the charity trustees of the charity concerned (whether arising under this Act or otherwise) as are specified in the order;

(b) for any powers or duties specified by virtue of paragraph (a) to be exercisable or performed by the interim manager to the exclusion of those trustees.

(5) Where a person has been appointed interim manager by any such order—

(a) section 110 (power to give advice and guidance) applies to the interim manager and the interim manager's functions as it applies to a charity trustee of the charity concerned and to the charity trustee's duties as such, and

(b) the Commission may apply to the High Court for directions in relation to any particular matter arising in connection with the discharge of those functions.

(6) The High Court may on an application under subsection (5)(b)—

(a) give such directions, or

(b) make such orders declaring the rights of any persons (whether before the court or not),

as it thinks just.

(7) The costs of an application under subsection (5)(b) must be paid by the charity concerned.

(8) Regulations made by the Minister may make provision with respect to—

(a) the appointment and removal of persons appointed in accordance with this section;

(b) the remuneration of such persons out of the income of the charities concerned;

(c) the making of reports to the Commission by such persons.

(9) Regulations under subsection (8) may, in particular, authorise the Commission—

(a) to require security for the due discharge of the functions of a person so appointed to be given by that person;

(b) to determine the amount of such a person's remuneration;

(c) to disallow any amount of remuneration in such circumstances as are prescribed by the regulations.

79 Removal of trustee or officer etc. for protective etc. purposes

(1) Subsection (2) applies where, at any time after it has instituted an inquiry under section 46 with respect to any charity, the Commission is satisfied both as mentioned in section 76(1)(a) (misconduct or mismanagement etc.) and as mentioned in section 76(1)(b) (need to protect property etc.).

(2) The Commission may of its own motion do either or both of the following—

(a) by order remove any trustee, charity trustee, officer, agent or employee of the charity—

(i) who has been responsible for or privy to the misconduct or mismanagement, or

(ii) whose conduct contributed to it or facilitated it;

(b) by order establish a scheme for the administration of the charity.

80 Other powers to remove or appoint charity trustees

(1) The Commission may remove a charity trustee by order made of its own motion if—

(a) within the last 5 years, the trustee—

(i) having previously been adjudged bankrupt, has been discharged, or

(ii) having previously made a composition or arrangement with, or granted a trust deed for, creditors, has been discharged in respect of it;

(b) the trustee is a corporation in liquidation;

(c) the trustee is incapable of acting because of mental disorder within the meaning of the Mental Health Act 1983;

(d) the trustee has not acted, and will not make a declaration of willingness or unwillingness to act;

(e) the trustee—

(i) is outside England and Wales or cannot be found, or

(ii) does not act,

and the trustee's absence or failure to act impedes the proper administration of the charity.

(2) The Commission may by order made of its own motion appoint a person to be a charity trustee—

(a) in place of a charity trustee removed by the Commission under section 79 or subsection (1) or otherwise;

(b) if there are no charity trustees, or if because of vacancies in their number or the absence or incapacity of any of their number the charity cannot apply for the appointment;

(c) if there is a single charity trustee who is not a corporation aggregate and the Commission is of opinion that it is necessary to increase the number for the proper administration of the charity;

(d) if the Commission is of opinion that it is necessary for the proper administration of the charity to have an additional charity trustee because one of the existing charity trustees who ought nevertheless to remain a charity trustee—

(i) is outside England and Wales or cannot be found, or

(ii) does not act.

(3) In subsection (1)(a)(i), the reference to the trustee having been adjudged bankrupt includes a reference to the trustee's estate having been sequestrated.

(4) This section does not apply in relation to an exempt charity except at a time after the Commission has instituted an inquiry under section 46 with respect to it.

81 Removal or appointment of charity trustees etc.: supplementary

(1) The powers of the Commission under sections 76, 79 and 80 to remove or appoint charity trustees of its own motion include power to make any such order with respect

to the vesting in or transfer to the charity trustees of any property as the Commission could make on the removal or appointment of a charity trustee by it under section 69 (Commission's concurrent jurisdiction with High Court for certain purposes).

(2) Any order under any of those sections or this section—

(a) for the removal or appointment of a charity trustee or trustee for a charity, or

(b) for the vesting or transfer of any property,

has the same effect as an order made under section 69.

(3) Subsection (1) does not apply in relation to an exempt charity except at a time after the Commission has instituted an inquiry under section 46 with respect to it.

82 Removal of trustees etc.: notice

(1) Before exercising any jurisdiction by virtue of section 79 or 80, the Commission must give notice of its intention to do so to each of the charity trustees, except any that cannot be found or has no known address in the United Kingdom.

(2) Any such notice—

(a) may be given by post, and

(b) if given by post, may be addressed to the recipient's last known address in the United Kingdom.

83 Power to suspend or remove trustees etc. from membership of charity

(1) Subsection (2) applies where—

(a) the Commission makes an order under section 76(3) suspending from office or employment a person who is a trustee, charity trustee, officer, agent or employee of a charity, and

(b) the person is a member of the charity.

(2) The Commission may also make an order suspending the person's membership of the charity for the period for which the person is suspended from office or employment.

(3) Subsection (4) applies where—

(a) the Commission makes an order under section 79(2) removing from office or employment a person who is an officer, agent or employee of a charity, and

(b) the person is a member of the charity.

(4) The Commission may also make an order—

(a) terminating the person's membership of the charity, and

(b) prohibiting the person from resuming membership of the charity without the Commission's consent.

(5) If an application for the Commission's consent under subsection (4)(b) is made 5 years or more after the order was made, the Commission must grant the application unless satisfied that, because of any special circumstances, it should be refused.

84 Power to direct specified action to be taken

(1) This section applies where, at any time after the Commission has instituted an inquiry under section 46 with respect to any charity, it is satisfied either as mentioned in

section 76(1)(a) (misconduct or mismanagement etc.) or as mentioned in section 76(1)(b) (need to protect property etc.).

(2) The Commission may by order direct—

(a) the charity trustees,

(b) any trustee for the charity,

(c) any officer or employee of the charity, or

(d) (if a body corporate) the charity itself,

to take any action specified in the order which the Commission considers to be expedient in the interests of the charity.

(3) An order under this section—

(a) may require action to be taken whether or not it would otherwise be within the powers exercisable by the person or persons concerned, or by the charity, in relation to the administration of the charity or to its property, but

(b) may not require any action to be taken which is prohibited by any Act or expressly prohibited by the trusts of the charity or is inconsistent with its purposes.

(4) Anything done by a person or body under the authority of an order under this section is to be treated as properly done in the exercise of the powers mentioned in subsection (3)(a).

(5) Subsection (4) does not affect any contractual or other rights arising in connection with anything which has been done under the authority of such an order.

85 Power to direct application of charity property

(1) This section applies where the Commission is satisfied—

(a) that a person or persons in possession or control of any property held by or on trust for a charity is or are unwilling to apply it properly for the purposes of the charity, and

(b) that it is necessary or desirable to make an order under this section for the purpose of securing a proper application of that property for the purposes of the charity.

(2) The Commission may by order direct the person or persons concerned to apply the property in such manner as is specified in the order.

(3) An order under this section—

(a) may require action to be taken whether or not it would otherwise be within the powers exercisable by the person or persons concerned in relation to the property, but

(b) may not require any action to be taken which is prohibited by any Act or expressly prohibited by the trusts of the charity.

(4) Anything done by a person under the authority of an order under this section is to be treated as properly done in the exercise of the powers mentioned in subsection (3)(a).

(5) Subsection (4) does not affect any contractual or other rights arising in connection with anything which has been done under the authority of such an order.

86 Copy of certain orders, and reasons, to be sent to charity

(1) Where the Commission makes an order under a provision mentioned in subsection (2) it must send the documents mentioned in subsection (3)—

(a) to the charity concerned (if a body corporate), or

(b) (if not) to each of the charity trustees.

(2) The provisions are—

section 76 (suspension of trustees etc. and appointment of interim managers);

section 79 (removal of trustee or officer etc. for protective etc. purposes);

section 80 (other powers to remove or appoint charity trustees);

section 81 (removal or appointment of charity trustees etc.: supplementary);

section 83 (power to suspend or remove trustees etc. from membership of charity);

section 84 (power to direct specified action to be taken);

section 85 (power to direct application of charity property).

(3) The documents are—

(a) a copy of the order, and

(b) a statement of the Commission's reasons for making it.

(4) The documents must be sent to the charity or charity trustees as soon as practicable after the making of the order.

(5) The Commission need not comply with subsection (4) in relation to the documents, or (as the case may be) the statement of its reasons, if it considers that to do so—

(a) would prejudice any inquiry or investigation, or

(b) would not be in the interests of the charity;

but, once the Commission considers that this is no longer the case, it must send the documents, or (as the case may be) the statement, to the charity or charity trustees as soon as practicable.

(6) Nothing in this section requires any document to be sent to a person who—

(a) cannot be found, or

(b) has no known address in the United Kingdom.

(7) Any documents required to be sent to a person under this section may be sent to, or otherwise served on, the person in the same way as an order made by the Commission under this Act could be served on the person in accordance with section 339.

87 Supervision by Commission of certain Scottish charities

(1) Sections 76 to 82 (except section 79(2)(b)) and sections 84 to 86 have effect in relation to any body which—

(a) is entered in the Scottish Charity Register, and

(b) is managed or controlled wholly or mainly in or from England or Wales,

as they have effect in relation to a charity.

(2) Subsection (3) applies where—

(a) a body entered in the Scottish Charity Register is managed or controlled wholly or mainly in or from Scotland, but

(b) any person in England and Wales holds any property on behalf of the body or of any person concerned in its management or control.

(3) If the Commission is satisfied, on the basis of such information as may be supplied to it by the Scottish Charity Regulator, as to the matters mentioned in subsection (4), it may make an order requiring the person holding the property not to part with it without the Commission's approval.

(4) The matters are—

(a) that there has been any misconduct or mismanagement in the administration of the body, and

(b) that it is necessary or desirable to make an order under subsection (3) for the purpose of protecting the property of the body or securing a proper application of such property for the purposes of the body.

(5) Subsection (6) applies where—

(a) any person in England and Wales holds any property on behalf of a body entered in the Scottish Charity Register or of any person concerned in the management or control of such a body, and

(b) the Commission is satisfied (whether on the basis of such information as may be supplied to it by the Scottish Charity Regulator or otherwise)—

(i) that there has been any misconduct or mismanagement in the administration of the body, and

(ii) that it is necessary or desirable to make an order under subsection (6) for the purpose of protecting the property of the body or securing a proper application of such property for the purposes of the body.

(6) The Commission may by order—

(a) vest the property in such body or charity as is specified in the order in accordance with subsections (7) and (8),

(b) require any persons in whom the property is vested to transfer it to any such body or charity, or

(c) appoint any person to transfer the property to any such body or charity.

(7) The Commission may specify in an order under subsection (6)—

(a) such other body entered in the Scottish Charity Register, or

(b) such charity,

as it considers appropriate, if the purposes of the body or charity are, in the opinion of the Commission, as similar in character to those of the body referred to in subsection (5)(a) as is reasonably practicable.

(8) But the Commission must not so specify any body or charity unless it has received from—

(a) the persons concerned in the management or control of the body, or

(b) (as the case may be) the charity trustees of the charity,

written confirmation that they are willing to accept the property.

Publicity relating to schemes and orders

88 Publicity relating to schemes

(1) The Commission may not—

(a) make any order under this Act to establish a scheme for the administration of a charity, or

(b) submit such a scheme to the court or the Minister for an order giving it effect,

unless, before doing so, the Commission has complied with the publicity requirements in subsection (2).

This is subject to any disapplication of those requirements under subsection (4).

(2) The publicity requirements are—

(a) that the Commission must give public notice of its proposals, inviting representations to be made to it within a period specified in the notice, and

(b) that, in the case of a scheme relating to a local charity (other than an ecclesiastical charity) in a parish, or in a community in Wales, the Commission must communicate a draft of the scheme to—

(i) the parish council or, if the parish has no council, the chairman of the parish meeting, or

(ii) the community council or, if the community has no council, the county council or county borough council.

(3) The time when any such notice is given or any such communication takes place is to be decided by the Commission.

(4) The Commission may determine that either or both of the publicity requirements is or are not to apply in relation to a particular scheme if it is satisfied that—

(a) because of the nature of the scheme, or

(b) for any other reason,

compliance with the requirement or requirements is unnecessary.

(5) Where the Commission gives public notice of any proposals under this section—

(a) it must take into account any representations made to it within the period specified in the notice, and

(b) it may (without further notice) proceed with the proposals either without modifications or with such modifications as it thinks desirable.

(6) Where the Commission makes an order under this Act to establish a scheme for the administration of a charity, a copy of the order must be available, for at least a month after the order is published, for public inspection at all reasonable times—

(a) at the Commission's office, and

(b) if the charity is a local charity, at some convenient place in the area of the charity.

(7) Subsection (6)(b) does not apply if the Commission is satisfied that for any reason it is unnecessary for a copy of the scheme to be available locally.

(8) Any public notice of any proposals which is to be given under this section—

(a) is to contain such particulars of the proposals, or such directions for obtaining information about them, as the Commission thinks sufficient and appropriate, and

(b) is to be given in such manner as the Commission thinks sufficient and appropriate.

89 Publicity for orders relating to trustees or other individuals

(1) The Commission may not make any order under this Act to appoint, discharge or remove a charity trustee or trustee for a charity, other than—

(a) an order relating to the official custodian, or

(b) an order under section 76(3)(b) (appointment of additional charity trustees),

unless, before doing so, the Commission has complied with the publicity requirement in subsection (2).

This is subject to any disapplication of that requirement under subsection (4).

(2) The publicity requirement is that the Commission must give public notice of its proposals, inviting representations to be made to it within a period specified in the notice.

(3) The time when any such notice is given is to be decided by the Commission.

(4) The Commission may determine that the publicity requirement is not to apply in relation to a particular order if it is satisfied that for any reason compliance with the requirement is unnecessary.

(5) Before the Commission makes an order under this Act to remove a person who is—

(a) a charity trustee or trustee for a charity, or

(b) an officer, agent or employee of a charity,

without the person's consent, the Commission must give the person not less than one month's notice of its proposals, inviting representations to be made to it within a period specified in the notice.

This does not apply if the person cannot be found or has no known address in the United Kingdom.

(6) Where the Commission gives notice of any proposals under this section—

(a) it must take into account any representations made to it within the period specified in the notice, and

(b) it may (without further notice) proceed with the proposals either without modifications or with such modifications as it thinks desirable.

(7) Any notice of any proposals which is to be given under this section—

(a) is to contain such particulars of the proposals, or such directions for obtaining information about them, as the Commission thinks sufficient and appropriate, and

(b) (in the case of a public notice) is to be given in such manner as the Commission thinks sufficient and appropriate.

(8) Any notice to be given under subsection (5)—

(a) may be given by post, and

(b) if given by post, may be addressed to the recipient's last known address in the United Kingdom.

Property vested in official custodian

90 Entrusting charity property to official custodian, and termination of trust

(1) The court may by order—

(a) vest in the official custodian any land held by or in trust for a charity,

(b) authorise or require the persons in whom any such land is vested to transfer it to the official custodian, or

(c) appoint any person to transfer any such land to the official custodian.

(2) But subsection (1) does not apply to any interest in land by way of mortgage or other security.

(3) Where property is vested in the official custodian in trust for a charity, the court may make an order discharging the official custodian from the trusteeship as respects all or any of that property.

(4) Where—

(a) the official custodian is discharged from the trusteeship of any property, or

(b) the trusts on which the official custodian holds any property come to an end,

the court may make such vesting orders and give such directions as may seem to the court to be necessary or expedient in consequence.

(5) No person is liable for any loss occasioned by—

(a) acting in conformity with an order under this section, or

(b) giving effect to anything done in pursuance of such an order.

(6) No person is excused from—

(a) acting in conformity with an order under this section, or

(b) giving effect to anything done in pursuance of such an order,

because the order has been in any respect improperly obtained.

91 Supplementary provisions as to property vested in official custodian

(1) Subject to the provisions of this Act, where property is vested in the official custodian in trust for a charity, the official custodian—

(a) must not exercise any powers of management, but

(b) as trustee of any property—

(i) has all the same powers, duties and liabilities,

(ii) is entitled to the same rights and immunities, and

(iii) is subject to the control and orders of the court in the same way,

as a corporation appointed custodian trustee under section 4 of the Public Trustee Act 1906.

(2) Subsection (1) does not confer on the official custodian a power to charge fees.

(3) Subject to subsection (4), where any land is vested in the official custodian in trust for a charity, the charity trustees may, in the name and on behalf of the official custodian, execute and do all assurances and things which they could properly execute or do in their own name and on their own behalf if the land were vested in them.

(4) If any land is so vested in the official custodian by virtue of an order under section 76(3)(c), the power conferred on the charity trustees by subsection (3) is not exercisable by them in relation to any transaction affecting the land, unless the transaction is authorised by order of the court or of the Commission.

(5) Where any land is vested in the official custodian in trust for a charity—

(a) the charity trustees have the same power to make obligations entered into by them binding on the land as if it were vested in them, and

(b) any covenant, agreement or condition which is enforceable by or against the official custodian because the land is vested in the official custodian is enforceable by or against the charity trustees as if the land were vested in them.

(6) In relation to a corporate charity, subsections (3) to (5) apply with the substitution of references to the charity for references to the charity trustees.

(7) Subsections (3) to (5) do not authorise any charity trustees or charity to impose any personal liability on the official custodian.

(8) Where the official custodian is entitled as trustee for a charity to the custody of securities or documents of title relating to the trust property, the official custodian may permit them to be in the possession or under the control of the charity trustees without incurring any liability by doing so.

Official custodian and Reverter of Sites Act 1987

92 Divestment of official custodian where 1987 Act due to operate

(1) Subsection (2) applies where—

(a) any land is vested in the official custodian in trust for a charity, and

(b) it appears to the Commission that section 1 of the 1987 Act (right of reverter replaced by trust) will, or is likely to, operate in relation to the land at a particular time or in particular circumstances.

(2) The jurisdiction which, under section 69, is exercisable by the Commission for the purpose of discharging a trustee for a charity may, at any time before section 1 of the 1987 Act operates in relation to the land, be exercised by the Commission of its own motion for the purpose of—

(a) making an order discharging the official custodian from the trusteeship of the land, and

(b) making such vesting orders and giving such directions as appear to the Commission to be necessary or expedient in consequence.

(3) In this section and sections 93 to 95—

(a) "the 1987 Act" means the Reverter of Sites Act 1987, and

(b) any reference to section 1 of the 1987 Act operating in relation to any land is a reference to a trust arising in relation to the land under that section.

93 Divestment of official custodian where 1987 Act has operated

(1) Subsection (2) applies where—

(a) section 1 of the 1987 Act has operated in relation to any land which, immediately before the time when that section so operated, was vested in the official custodian in trust for a charity, and

(b) the land remains vested in the official custodian but on the trust arising under that section.

(2) The court or the Commission (of its own motion) may—

(a) make an order discharging the official custodian from the trusteeship of the land, and

(b) (subject to sections 94 and 95) make such vesting orders and give such directions as appear to it to be necessary or expedient in consequence.

94 Vesting of land in relevant charity trustees following divestment

(1) Subsection (2) applies where an order discharging the official custodian from the trusteeship of any land—

(a) is made by—

(i) the court under section 90(3), or

(ii) the Commission under section 69,

on the ground that section 1 of the 1987 Act will, or is likely to, operate in relation to the land, or

(b) is made by the court or the Commission under section 93.

(2) The persons in whom the land is to be vested on the discharge of the official custodian are the relevant charity trustees, unless the court or (as the case may be) the Commission is satisfied that it would be appropriate for it to be vested in some other persons.

(3) In subsection (2) "the relevant charity trustees" means—

(a) in relation to an order made as mentioned in subsection (1)(a), the charity trustees of the charity in trust for which the land is vested in the official custodian immediately before the time when the order takes effect, or

(b) in relation to an order made under section 93, the charity trustees of the charity in trust for which the land was vested in the official custodian immediately before the time when section 1 of the 1987 Act operated in relation to the land.

95 Supplementary provisions in connection with 1987 Act

(1) Subsection (2) applies where—

(a) section 1 of the 1987 Act has operated in relation to any such land as is mentioned in section 93(1)(a), and

(b) the land remains vested in the official custodian as mentioned in section 93(1)(b).

(2) Subject to subsection (3)—

(a) all the powers, duties and liabilities that would, apart from this section, be those of the official custodian as trustee of the land are instead to be those of the charity trustees of the charity concerned, and

(b) those trustees may, in the name and on behalf of the official custodian, execute and do all assurances and things which they could properly execute or do in their own name and on their own behalf if the land were vested in them.

(3) Subsection (2) is not to be treated as requiring or authorising those trustees to sell the land at a time when it remains vested in the official custodian.

(4) Where—

(a) the official custodian has been discharged from the trusteeship of any land by an order under section 93, and

(b) the land has, in accordance with section 94, been vested in the charity trustees concerned or (as the case may be) in any persons other than those trustees,

the land is to be held by those trustees, or (as the case may be) by those persons, as trustees on the terms of the trust arising under section 1 of the 1987 Act.

(5) The official custodian is not liable to any person in respect of any loss or misapplication of any land vested in the official custodian in accordance with section 1 of the 1987 Act unless it is occasioned by or through any wilful neglect or default of—

(a) the official custodian, or

(b) any person acting for the official custodian.

(6) But the Consolidated Fund is liable to make good to any person any sums for which the official custodian may be liable because of any such neglect or default.

Establishment of common investment or deposit funds

96 Power to make common investment schemes

(1) The court or the Commission may by order make and bring into effect schemes for the establishment of common investment funds under trusts which provide—

(a) for property transferred to the fund by or on behalf of a charity participating in the scheme to be invested under the control of trustees appointed to manage the fund, and

(b) for the participating charities to be entitled (subject to the provisions of the scheme) to the capital and income of the fund in shares determined by reference to the amount or value of the property transferred to it by or on behalf of each of them and to the value of the fund at the time of the transfers.

(2) In this section and sections 97 to 99 "common investment scheme" means a scheme under subsection (1).

(3) The court or the Commission may make a common investment scheme on the application of any two or more charities.

97 Bodies which may participate in common investment schemes

(1) A common investment scheme—

(a) may be made in terms admitting any charity to participate, or

(b) may restrict the right to participate in any manner.

(2) A common investment scheme may provide for appropriate bodies to be admitted to participate in the scheme (in addition to the participating charities) to such extent as the trustees appointed to manage the fund may determine.

(3) In this section "appropriate body" means—

(a) a Scottish recognised body, or

(b) a Northern Ireland charity,

and, in the application of the relevant provisions in relation to a scheme which contains provisions authorised by subsection (2), "charity" includes an appropriate body.

(4) The relevant provisions are—

(a) section 96(1) (power to make common investment schemes),

(b) section 98 (provisions which may be included in common investment schemes),

(c) section 99(1) (provisions relating to rights of participating charity etc.), and

(d) (in relation only to a Northern Ireland charity) section 99(2) (power to participate in common investment schemes).

98 Provisions which may be included in common investment schemes

(1) A common investment scheme may make provision for, and for all matters connected with, the establishment, investment, management and winding up of the common investment fund, and may in particular include provision—

(a) for remunerating persons appointed trustees to hold or manage the fund or any part of it, with or without provision authorising a person to receive the remuneration even though the person is also a charity trustee of or trustee for a participating charity;

(b) for restricting the size of the fund, and for regulating as to time, amount or otherwise the right to transfer property to or withdraw it from the fund, and for enabling sums to be advanced out of the fund by way of loan to a participating charity pending the withdrawal of property from the fund by the charity;

(c) for enabling income to be withheld from distribution with a view to avoiding fluctuations in the amounts distributed, and generally for regulating distributions of income;

(d) for enabling money to be borrowed temporarily for the purpose of meeting payments to be made out of the funds;

(e) for enabling questions arising under the scheme as to the right of a charity to participate, or as to the rights of participating charities, or as to any other matter, to be conclusively determined by the decision of the trustees managing the fund or in any other manner;

(f) for regulating the accounts and information to be supplied to participating charities.

(2) A common investment scheme, in addition to the provision for property to be transferred to the fund on the basis that the charity is to be entitled to a share in the capital and income of the fund, may include provision for enabling sums to be deposited by or on behalf of a charity on the basis that (subject to the provisions of the scheme) the charity is to be entitled—

(a) to repayment of the sums deposited, and

(b) to interest on them at a rate determined by or under the scheme.

(3) Where a scheme makes any such provision it must also provide for excluding from the amount of capital and income to be shared between charities participating otherwise than by way of deposit such amounts (not exceeding the amounts properly attributable to the making of deposits) as are from time to time reasonably required in respect of the liabilities of the fund—

(a) for the repayment of deposits, and

(b) for the interest on deposits,

including amounts required by way of reserve.

99 Further provisions relating to common investment schemes and funds

(1) Except in so far as a common investment scheme provides to the contrary—

(a) the rights under it of a participating charity are not capable of being assigned or charged;

(b) a trustee or other person concerned in the management of the common investment fund is not required or entitled to take account of any trust or other equity affecting a participating charity or its property or rights.

(2) The powers of investment of every charity include power to participate in common investment schemes unless the power is excluded by a provision specifically referring to common investment schemes in the trusts of the charity.

(3) A common investment fund is to be treated for all purposes as being a charity.

(4) Subsection (3) applies not only to common investment funds established under section 96, but also to any similar fund established for the exclusive benefit of charities by or under any enactment relating to any particular charities or class of charities.

100 Power to make common deposit schemes

(1) The court or the Commission may by order make and bring into effect schemes for the establishment of common deposit funds under trusts which provide—

(a) for sums to be deposited by or on behalf of a charity participating in the scheme and invested under the control of trustees appointed to manage the fund, and

(b) for any such charity to be entitled (subject to the provisions of the scheme) to repayment of any sums so deposited and to interest on them at a rate determined under the scheme.

(2) In this section and sections 101 to 103 "common deposit scheme" means a scheme under subsection (1).

(3) The court or the Commission may make a common deposit scheme on the application of any two or more charities.

101 Bodies which may participate in common deposit schemes

(1) A common deposit scheme—

(a) may be made in terms admitting any charity to participate, or

(b) may restrict the right to participate in any manner.

(2) A common deposit scheme may provide for appropriate bodies to be admitted to participate in the scheme (in addition to the participating charities) to such extent as the trustees appointed to manage the fund may determine.

(3) In this section "appropriate body" means—

(a) a Scottish recognised body, or

(b) a Northern Ireland charity,

and, in the application of the relevant provisions in relation to a scheme which contains provisions authorised by subsection (2), "charity" includes an appropriate body.

(4) The relevant provisions are—

(a) section 100(1) (power to make common deposit schemes),

(b) section 102 (provisions which may be included in common deposit schemes),

(c) section 103(1) (provisions relating to rights of participating charity etc.), and

(d) (in relation only to a Northern Ireland charity) section 103(2) (power to participate in common deposit schemes).

102 Provisions which may be included in common deposit schemes

A common deposit scheme may make provision for, and for all matters connected with, the establishment, investment, management and winding up of the common deposit fund, and may in particular include provision—

(a) for remunerating persons appointed trustees to hold or manage the fund or any part of it, with or without provision authorising a person to receive the remuneration even though the person is also a charity trustee of or trustee for a participating charity;

(b) for regulating as to time, amount or otherwise the right to repayment of sums deposited in the fund;

(c) for authorising a part of the income for any year to be credited to a reserve account maintained for the purpose of counteracting any losses accruing to the fund, and generally for regulating the manner in which the rate of interest on deposits is to be determined from time to time;

(d) for enabling money to be borrowed temporarily for the purpose of meeting payments to be made out of the funds;

(e) for enabling questions arising under the scheme as to the right of a charity to participate, or as to the rights of participating charities, or as to any other matter, to be conclusively determined by the decision of the trustees managing the fund or in any other manner;

(f) for regulating the accounts and information to be supplied to participating charities.

103 Further provisions relating to common deposit schemes and funds

(1) Except in so far as a common deposit scheme provides to the contrary—

(a) the rights under it of a participating charity are not capable of being assigned or charged;

(b) a trustee or other person concerned in the management of the common deposit fund is not required or entitled to take account of any trust or other equity affecting a participating charity or its property or rights.

(2) The powers of investment of every charity include power to participate in common deposit schemes unless the power is excluded by a provision specifically referring to common deposit schemes in the trusts of the charity.

(3) A common deposit fund is to be treated for all purposes as being a charity.

(4) Subsection (3) applies not only to common deposit funds established under section 100, but also to any similar fund established for the exclusive benefit of

charities by or under any enactment relating to any particular charities or class of charities.

104 Meaning of "Scottish recognised body" and "Northern Ireland charity"

(1) In sections 97 and 101 "Scottish recognised body" means a body–

(a) established under the law of Scotland, or

(b) managed or controlled wholly or mainly in or from Scotland,

to which HMRC have given intimation, which has not subsequently been withdrawn, that tax relief is due in respect of income of the body which is applicable and applied to charitable purposes only.

(2) In sections 97 and 101 "Northern Ireland charity" means an institution—

(a) which is a charity under the law of Northern Ireland, and

(b) to which HMRC have given intimation, which has not subsequently been withdrawn, that tax relief is due in respect of income of the institution which is applicable and applied to charitable purposes only.

(3) For the purposes of this section—

"HMRC" means the Commissioners for Her Majesty's Revenue and Customs;

"tax relief" means relief under—

(a) Part 10 of the Income Tax Act 2007, or

(b) any provision of Part 11 of the Corporation Tax Act 2010 other than sections 480 (exemption for profits of small-scale trades) and 481 (exemption from charges under provisions to which section 1173 applies).

Power to authorise dealings with charity property, ex gratia payments etc.

105 Power to authorise dealings with charity property etc.

(1) Subject to the provisions of this section, where it appears to the Commission that any action proposed or contemplated in the administration of a charity is expedient in the interests of the charity, the Commission may by order sanction that action, whether or not it would otherwise be within the powers exercisable by the charity trustees in the administration of the charity.

(2) Anything done under the authority of an order under this section is to be treated as properly done in the exercise of those powers.

(3) An order under this section—

(a) may be made so as to authorise a particular transaction, compromise or the like, or a particular application of property, or so as to give a more general authority, and

(b) may authorise a charity to use common premises, or employ a common staff, or otherwise combine for any purpose of administration, with any other charity.

Paragraph (b) does not affect the generality of subsection (1).

(4) An order under this section may give directions—

(a) as to the manner in which any expenditure is to be borne, and

(b) as to other matters connected with or arising out of the action authorised by the order.

(5) Where anything is done in pursuance of an authority given by an order under this section, any directions given in connection with that authority—

(a) are binding on the charity trustees for the time being as if contained in the trusts of the charity, but

(b) may on the application of the charity be modified or superseded by a further order.

(6) The directions which may be given by an order under this section in particular include directions—

(a) for meeting any expenditure out of a specified fund,

(b) for charging any expenditure to capital or to income,

(c) for requiring expenditure charged to capital to be recouped out of income within a specified period,

(d) for restricting the costs to be incurred at the expense of the charity, or

(e) for the investment of money arising from any transaction.

This does not affect the generality of subsection (4).

(7) An order under this section may authorise any act even though—

(a) it is prohibited by the Ecclesiastical Leases Act 1836, or

(b) the trusts of the charity provide for the act to be done by or under the authority of the court.

(8) But an order under this section may not—

(a) authorise the doing of any act expressly prohibited by any Act other than the Ecclesiastical Leases Act 1836, or by the trusts of the charity, or

(b) extend or alter the purposes of the charity.

(9) In the case of a charitable company, an order under this section may authorise an act even though it involves the breach of a duty imposed on a director of the company under Chapter 2 of Part 10 of the Companies Act 2006 (general duties of directors).

(10) An order under this section does not confer any authority in relation to a building which has been consecrated and of which the use or disposal is regulated, and can be further regulated, by a scheme having effect or treated as having effect under or by virtue of the Mission and Pastoral Measure 2011.

(11) The reference in subsection (10) to a building is to be treated as including—

(a) part of a building, and

(b) any land which under such a scheme is to be used or disposed of with a building to which the scheme applies.

106 Power to authorise ex gratia payments etc.

(1) Subject to subsection (5), the Commission may by order exercise the same power as is exercisable by the Attorney General to authorise the charity trustees of a charity to take any action falling within subsection (2)(a) or (b) in a case where the charity trustees—

(a) (apart from this section) have no power to take the action, but

(b) in all the circumstances regard themselves as being under a moral obligation to take it.

(2) The actions are—

(a) making any application of property of the charity, or

(b) waiving to any extent, on behalf of the charity, its entitlement to receive any property.

(3) The power conferred on the Commission by subsection (1) is exercisable by the Commission under the supervision of, and in accordance with such directions as may be given by, the Attorney General.

(4) Any such directions may in particular require the Commission, in such circumstances as are specified in the directions—

(a) to refrain from exercising the power conferred by subsection (1), or

(b) to consult the Attorney General before exercising it.

(5) Where—

(a) an application is made to the Commission for it to exercise the power conferred by subsection (1) in a case where it is not precluded from doing so by any such directions, but

(b) the Commission considers that it would nevertheless be desirable for the application to be entertained by the Attorney General rather than by the Commission,

the Commission must refer the application to the Attorney General.

(6) It is hereby declared that where—

(a) an application is made to the Commission as mentioned in subsection (5)(a), and

(b) the Commission determines the application by refusing to authorise charity trustees to take any action falling within subsection (2)(a) or (b),

that refusal does not preclude the Attorney General, on an application subsequently made to the Attorney General by the charity trustees, from authorising them to take that action.

Power to give directions about dormant bank accounts of charities

107 Power to direct transfer of credits in dormant bank accounts

(1) The Commission may give a direction under subsection (2) where—

(a) it is informed by a relevant institution—

(i) that it holds one or more accounts in the name of or on behalf of a particular charity ("the relevant charity"), and

(ii) that the account, or (if it so holds two or more accounts) each of the accounts, is dormant, and

(b) it is unable, after making reasonable inquiries, to locate that charity or any of its trustees.

(2) A direction under this subsection is a direction which—

(a) requires the institution concerned to transfer the amount, or (as the case may be) the aggregate amount, standing to the credit of the relevant charity in the account or accounts in question to such other charity as is specified in the direction in accordance with subsection (3), or

(b) requires the institution concerned to transfer to each of two or more other charities so specified in the direction such part of that amount or aggregate amount as is there specified in relation to that charity.

(3) The Commission—

(a) may specify in a direction under subsection (2) such other charity or charities as it considers appropriate, having regard, in a case where the purposes of the relevant charity are known to the Commission, to those purposes and to the purposes of the other charity or charities, but

(b) must not so specify any charity unless it has received from the charity trustees written confirmation that those trustees are willing to accept the amount proposed to be transferred to the charity.

(4) Any amount received by a charity by virtue of this section is to be received by the charity on terms that—

(a) it is to be held and applied by the charity for the purposes of the charity, but

(b) as property of the charity, it is nevertheless subject to any restrictions on expenditure to which it was subject as property of the relevant charity.

(5) The receipt of any charity trustees or trustee for a charity in respect of any amount received from a relevant institution by virtue of this section is a complete discharge of the institution in respect of that amount.

108 Accounts which cease to be dormant before transfer

(1) This section applies where—

(a) the Commission has been informed as mentioned in section 107(1)(a) by any relevant institution, and

(b) before any transfer is made by the institution in pursuance of a direction under section 107(2), the institution has, by reason of any circumstances, cause to believe that the account, or (as the case may be) any of the accounts, held by it in the name of or on behalf of the relevant charity is no longer dormant.

(2) The institution must without delay notify those circumstances in writing to the Commission.

(3) If it appears to the Commission that the account or accounts in question is or are no longer dormant, it must revoke any direction under section 107(2) which has previously been given by it to the institution with respect to the relevant charity.

109 Dormant bank accounts: supplementary

(1) No obligation as to secrecy or other restriction on disclosure (however imposed) precludes a relevant institution from disclosing any information to the Commission for the purpose of enabling the Commission to discharge its functions under sections 107 and 108.

(2) For the purposes of sections 107 and 108 and this section, an account is dormant if no transaction, other than—

(a) a transaction consisting in a payment into the account, or

(b) a transaction which the institution holding the account has itself caused to be effected,

has been effected in relation to the account within the period of 5 years immediately preceding the date when the Commission is informed as mentioned in section 107(1)(a).

(3) For the purposes of sections 107 and 108 and this section, a "relevant institution" means—

(a) the Bank of England,

(b) a person who has permission under Part 4 of the Financial Services and Markets Act 2000 to accept deposits,

(c) an EEA firm of the kind mentioned in paragraph 5(b) of Schedule 3 to that Act which has permission under paragraph 15 of that Schedule (as a result of qualifying for authorisation under paragraph 12(1) of that Schedule) to accept deposits, or

(d) such other person who may lawfully accept deposits in the United Kingdom as may be prescribed by the Minister.

(4) In subsection (3), paragraphs (b) to (d) are to be read with—

(a) section 22 of the Financial Services and Markets Act 2000,

(b) any relevant order under that section, and

(c) Schedule 2 to that Act.

(5) For the purposes of sections 107 and 108, references to the transfer of any amount to a charity are references to its transfer—

(a) to the charity trustees, or

(b) to any trustee for the charity,

as the charity trustees may determine (and any reference to any amount received by a charity is to be read accordingly).

(6) For the purpose of determining the matters in respect of which any of the powers conferred by sections 46 to 53 (inquiries and searches) may be exercised it is to be assumed that the Commission has no functions under section 107 or 108 in relation to accounts to which this subsection applies.

(This has the result that, for example, a relevant institution is not, in connection with the Commission's functions under sections 107 and 108, required under section 47(2)(a) to provide any statements, or answer any questions or inquiries, with respect to any such accounts held by the institution.)

(7) Subsection (6) applies to accounts which—

(a) are dormant accounts by virtue of subsection (2), but

(b) would not be dormant accounts if subsection (2)(a) were omitted.

Additional powers of Commission

110 Power to give advice

(1) The Commission may, on the written application of any charity trustee or trustee for a charity, give the applicant its opinion or advice in relation to any matter—

(a) relating to the performance of any duties of the applicant, as such a trustee, in relation to the charity concerned, or

(b) otherwise relating to the proper administration of the charity.

(2) A person ("P") who—

(a) is a charity trustee or trustee for a charity, and

(b) acts in accordance with any opinion or advice given by the Commission under subsection (1) (whether to P or another trustee),

is to be treated, as regards P's responsibility for so acting, as having acted in accordance with P's trust.

(3) But subsection (2) does not apply to P if, when so acting—

(a) P knows or has reasonable cause to suspect that the opinion or advice was given in ignorance of material facts, or

(b) a decision of the court or the Tribunal has been obtained on the matter or proceedings are pending to obtain one.

111 Power to determine membership of charity

(1) The Commission may—

(a) on the application of a charity, or

(b) at any time after the institution of an inquiry under section 46 with respect to a charity,

determine who are the members of the charity.

(2) The Commission's power under subsection (1) may also be exercised by a person appointed by the Commission for the purpose.

(3) In a case within subsection (1)(b) the Commission may, if it thinks fit, so appoint the person appointed to conduct the inquiry.

112 Power to order assessment of solicitor's bill

(1) The Commission may order that a solicitor's bill of costs for business done for a charity, or for charity trustees or trustees for a charity, is to be assessed, together with the costs of the assessment—

(a) by a costs officer in such division of the High Court as may be specified in the order, or

(b) by the costs officer of any other court having jurisdiction to order the assessment of the bill.

(2) On any order under this section for the assessment of a solicitor's bill—

(a) the assessment is to proceed,

(b) the costs officer has the same powers and duties, and

(c) the costs of the assessment are to be borne,

as if the order had been made, on the application of the person chargeable with the bill, by the court in which the costs are assessed.

(3) No order under this section for the assessment of a solicitor's bill is to be made after payment of the bill, unless the Commission is of opinion that it contains exorbitant charges.

(4) No order under this section is to be made in any case where the solicitor's costs are not subject to assessment on an order of the High Court because of—

(a) an agreement as to the solicitor's remuneration, or

(b) the lapse of time since payment of the bill.

Legal proceedings relating to charities

113 Petitions for winding up charities under Insolvency Act

(1) This section applies where a charity may be wound up by the High Court under the Insolvency Act 1986.

(2) A petition for the charity to be wound up under the 1986 Act by any court in England or Wales having jurisdiction may be presented by the Attorney General, as well as by any person authorised by that Act.

(3) Such a petition may also be presented by the Commission if, at any time after it has instituted an inquiry under section 46 with respect to the charity, it is satisfied either as mentioned in section 76(1)(a) (misconduct or mismanagement etc.) or as mentioned in section 76(1)(b) (need to protect property etc.).

(4) The power exercisable by the Commission by virtue of this section is exercisable—

(a) by the Commission of its own motion, but

(b) only with the agreement of the Attorney General on each occasion.

114 Proceedings by the Commission

(1) Subject to subsection (2), the Commission may exercise the same powers with respect to—

(a) the taking of legal proceedings with reference to charities or the property or affairs of charities, or

(b) the compromise of claims with a view to avoiding or ending such proceedings,

as are exercisable by the Attorney General acting ex officio.

(2) Subsection (1) does not apply to the power of the Attorney General under section 113(2) to present a petition for the winding up of a charity.

(3) The practice and procedure to be followed in relation to any proceedings taken by the Commission under subsection (1) are the same in all respects (and in particular as regards costs) as if they were proceedings taken by the Attorney General acting ex officio.

(4) No rule of law or practice is to be treated as requiring the Attorney General to be a party to any such proceedings.

(5) The powers exercisable by the Commission by virtue of this section are exercisable—

(a) by the Commission of its own motion, but

(b) only with the agreement of the Attorney General on each occasion.

115 Proceedings by other persons

(1) Charity proceedings may be taken with reference to a charity by—

(a) the charity,

(b) any of the charity trustees,

(c) any person interested in the charity, or

(d) if it is a local charity, any two or more inhabitants of the area of the charity,

but not by any other person.

(2) Subject to the following provisions of this section, no charity proceedings relating to a charity are to be entertained or proceeded with in any court unless the taking of the proceedings is authorised by order of the Commission.

(3) The Commission must not, without special reasons, authorise the taking of charity proceedings where in its opinion the case can be dealt with by the Commission under the powers of this Act other than those conferred by section 114.

(4) This section does not require an order for the taking of proceedings—

(a) in a pending cause or matter, or

(b) for the bringing of any appeal.

(5) Where subsections (1) to (4) require the taking of charity proceedings to be authorised by an order of the Commission, the proceedings may nevertheless be entertained or proceeded with if, after the order had been applied for and refused, leave to take the proceedings was obtained from one of the judges of the High Court attached to the Chancery Division.

(6) Nothing in subsections (1) to (5) applies—

(a) to the taking of proceedings by the Attorney General, with or without a relator, or

(b) to the taking of proceedings by the Commission in accordance with section 114.

(7) If it appears to the Commission, on an application for an order under this section or otherwise, that it is desirable—

(a) for legal proceedings to be taken with reference to any charity or its property or affairs, and

(b) for the proceedings to be taken by the Attorney General,

the Commission must so inform the Attorney General and send the Attorney General such statements and particulars as the Commission thinks necessary to explain the matter.

(8) In this section "charity proceedings" means proceedings in any court in England or Wales brought under—

(a) the court's jurisdiction with respect to charities, or

(b) the court's jurisdiction with respect to trusts in relation to the administration of a trust for charitable purposes.

Supplementary

116 Effect of provisions relating to vesting or transfer of property

No vesting or transfer of any property in pursuance of any provision of this Part operates as a breach of a covenant or condition against alienation or gives rise to a forfeiture.

PART 7

CHARITY LAND

Restrictions on dispositions of land in England and Wales

117 Restrictions on dispositions of land: general

(1) No land held by or in trust for a charity is to be conveyed, transferred, leased or otherwise disposed of without an order of—

(a) the court, or

(b) the Commission.

But this is subject to the following provisions of this section, sections 119 to 121 (further provisions about restrictions on dispositions) and section 127 (release of charity rentcharges).

(2) Subsection (1) does not apply to a disposition of such land if—

(a) the disposition is made to a person who is not—

(i) a connected person (as defined in section 118), or

(ii) a trustee for, or nominee of, a connected person, and

(b) the requirements of—

(i) section 119(1) (dispositions other than certain leases), or

(ii) section 120(2) (leases which are for 7 years or less etc.),

have been complied with in relation to it.

(3) The restrictions on disposition imposed by this section and sections 119 to 121 apply regardless of anything in the trusts of a charity; but nothing in this section or sections 119 to 121 applies to—

(a) any disposition for which general or special authority is expressly given (without the authority being made subject to the sanction of an order of the court) by—

(i) any statutory provision contained in or having effect under an Act, or

(ii) any scheme legally established,

(b) any disposition for which the authorisation or consent of the Secretary of State is required under the Universities and College Estates Act 1925,

(c) any disposition of land held by or in trust for a charity which—

(i) is made to another charity otherwise than for the best price that can reasonably be obtained, and

(ii) is authorised to be so made by the trusts of the first-mentioned charity, or

(d) the granting, by or on behalf of a charity and in accordance with its trusts, of a lease to any beneficiary under those trusts where the lease—

(i) is granted otherwise than for the best rent that can reasonably be obtained, and

(ii) is intended to enable the demised premises to be occupied for the purposes, or any particular purposes, of the charity.

(4) Nothing in this section or sections 119 to 121 applies to—

(a) any disposition of land held by or in trust for an exempt charity,

(b) any disposition of land by way of mortgage or other security, or
(c) any disposition of an advowson.

118 Meaning of "connected person" in s.117(2)

(1) In section 117(2) "connected person", in relation to a charity, means any person who falls within subsection (2)—
(a) at the time of the disposition in question, or
(b) at the time of any contract for the disposition in question.

(2) The persons are—
(a) a charity trustee or trustee for the charity,
(b) a person who is the donor of any land to the charity (whether the gift was made on or after the establishment of the charity),
(c) a child, parent, grandchild, grandparent, brother or sister of any such trustee or donor,
(d) an officer, agent or employee of the charity,
(e) the spouse or civil partner of any person falling within any of paragraphs (a) to (d),
(f) a person carrying on business in partnership with any person falling within any of paragraphs (a) to (e),
(g) an institution which is controlled—
(i) by any person falling within any of paragraphs (a) to (f), or
(ii) by two or more such persons taken together, or
(h) a body corporate in which—
(i) any connected person falling within any of paragraphs (a) to (g) has a substantial interest, or
(ii) two or more such persons, taken together, have a substantial interest.

(3) Sections 350 to 352 (meaning of child, spouse and civil partner, controlled institution and substantial interest) apply for the purposes of subsection (2).

119 Requirements for dispositions other than certain leases

(1) The requirements mentioned in section 117(2)(b) are that the charity trustees must, before entering into an agreement for the sale, or (as the case may be) for a lease or other disposition, of the land—
(a) obtain and consider a written report on the proposed disposition from a qualified surveyor instructed by the trustees and acting exclusively for the charity,
(b) advertise the proposed disposition for such period and in such manner as is advised in the surveyor's report (unless it advises that it would not be in the best interests of the charity to advertise the proposed disposition), and
(c) decide that they are satisfied, having considered the surveyor's report, that the terms on which the disposition is proposed to be made are the best that can reasonably be obtained for the charity.

(2) Subsection (1) does not apply where the proposed disposition is the granting of such a lease as is mentioned in section 120(1).

(3) For the purposes of subsection (1) a qualified surveyor is a person who—

(a) is a fellow or professional associate of the Royal Institution of Chartered Surveyors or satisfies such other requirement or requirements as may be prescribed by regulations made by the Minister, and

(b) is reasonably believed by the charity trustees to have ability in, and experience of, the valuation of land of the particular kind, and in the particular area, in question.

(4) Any report prepared for the purposes of subsection (1) must contain such information, and deal with such matters, as may be prescribed by regulations made by the Minister.

120 Requirements for leases which are for 7 years or less etc.

(1) Subsection (2) applies where the proposed disposition is the granting of a lease for a term ending not more than 7 years after it is granted (other than one granted wholly or partly in consideration of a fine).

(2) The requirements mentioned in section 117(2)(b) are that the charity trustees must, before entering into an agreement for the lease—

(a) obtain and consider the advice on the proposed disposition of a person who is reasonably believed by the trustees to have the requisite ability and practical experience to provide them with competent advice on the proposed disposition, and

(b) decide that they are satisfied, having considered that person's advice, that the terms on which the disposition is proposed to be made are the best that can reasonably be obtained for the charity.

121 Additional restrictions where land held for stipulated purposes

(1) Subsection (2) applies where—

(a) any land is held by or in trust for a charity, and

(b) the trusts on which it is so held stipulate that it is to be used for the purposes, or any particular purposes, of the charity.

(2) The land must not be conveyed, transferred, leased or otherwise disposed of unless the charity trustees have before the relevant time—

(a) given public notice of the proposed disposition, inviting representations to be made to them within a time specified in the notice, which must be not less than one month from the date of the notice, and

(b) taken into consideration any representations made to them within that time about the proposed disposition.

(3) Subsection (2)—

(a) is subject to subsections (5) and (6), and

(b) does not affect the operation of sections 117 to 120.

(4) In subsection (2) "the relevant time" means—

(a) where the charity trustees enter into an agreement for the sale, or (as the case may be) for the lease or other disposition, the time when they enter into that agreement, and

(b) in any other case, the time of the disposition.

(5) Subsection (2) does not apply to any such disposition of land as is there mentioned if—

(a) the disposition is to be effected with a view to acquiring by way of replacement other property which is to be held on the trusts referred to in subsection (1)(b), or

(b) the disposition is the granting of a lease for a term ending not more than 2 years after it is granted (other than one granted wholly or partly in consideration of a fine).

(6) The Commission may, if the condition in subsection (7) is met, direct—

(a) that subsection (2) is not to apply to dispositions of land held by or in trust for a charity or class of charities (whether generally or only in the case of a specified class of dispositions or land, or otherwise as may be provided in the direction), or

(b) that subsection (2) is not to apply to a particular disposition of land held by or in trust for a charity.

(7) The condition is that the Commission, on an application made to it in writing by or behalf of the charity or charities in question, is satisfied that it would be in the interests of the charity or charities for the Commission to give the direction.

122 Instruments concerning dispositions of land: required statements, etc.

(1) Subsection (2) applies to any of the following instruments—

(a) a contract for the sale, or for a lease or other disposition, of land which is held by or in trust for a charity, and

(b) a conveyance, transfer, lease or other instrument effecting a disposition of such land.

(2) An instrument to which this subsection applies must state—

(a) that the land is held by or in trust for a charity,

(b) whether the charity is an exempt charity and whether the disposition is one falling within section 117(3)(a), (b), (c) or (d), and

(c) if it is not an exempt charity and the disposition is not one falling within section 117(3)(a), (b), (c) or (d), that the land is land to which the restrictions on disposition imposed by sections 117 to 121 apply.

(3) Where any land held by or in trust for a charity is conveyed, transferred, leased or otherwise disposed of by a disposition to which section 117(1) or (2) applies, the charity trustees must certify in the instrument by which the disposition is effected—

(a) (where section 117(1) applies) that the disposition has been sanctioned by an order of the court or of the Commission (as the case may be), or

(b) (where section 117(2) applies) that the charity trustees have power under the trusts of the charity to effect the disposition and have complied with sections 117 to 121 so far as applicable to it.

(4) Where subsection (3) has been complied with in relation to any disposition of land, then in favour of a person who (whether under the disposition or afterwards) acquires an interest in the land for money or money's worth, it is conclusively presumed that the facts were as stated in the certificate.

(5) Subsection (6) applies where—

(a) any land held by or in trust for a charity is conveyed, transferred, leased or otherwise disposed of by a disposition to which section 117(1) or (2) applies, but

(b) subsection (3) has not been complied with in relation to the disposition.

(6) In favour of a person who (whether under the disposition or afterwards) in good faith acquires an interest in the land for money or money's worth, the disposition is valid whether or not—

(a) the disposition has been sanctioned by an order of the court or of the Commission, or

(b) the charity trustees have power under the trusts of the charity to effect the disposition and have complied with sections 117 to 121 so far as applicable to it.

(7) Subsection (8) applies to any of the following instruments—

(a) a contract for the sale, or for a lease or other disposition, of land which will, as a result of the disposition, be held by or in trust for a charity, and

(b) a conveyance, transfer, lease or other instrument effecting a disposition of such land.

(8) An instrument to which this subsection applies must state—

(a) that the land will, as a result of the disposition, be held by or in trust for a charity,

(b) whether the charity is an exempt charity, and

(c) if it is not an exempt charity, that the restrictions on disposition imposed by sections 117 to 121 will apply to the land (subject to section 117(3)).

(9) In this section and section 123 references to a disposition of land do not include references to—

(a) a disposition of land by way of mortgage or other security,

(b) any disposition of an advowson, or

(c) any release of a rentcharge falling within section 127(1).

123 Charity land and land registration

(1) Where the disposition to be effected by any such instrument as is mentioned in section 122(1)(b) or (7)(b) will be—

(a) a registrable disposition, or

(b) a disposition which triggers the requirement of registration,

the statement which, by virtue of section 122(2) or (8), is to be contained in the instrument must be in such form as may be prescribed by land registration rules.

(2) Where the registrar approves an application for registration of—

(a) a disposition of registered land, or

(b) a person's title under a disposition of unregistered land,

and the instrument effecting the disposition contains a statement complying with section 122(8) and subsection (1), the registrar must enter in the register a restriction reflecting the limitation under sections 117 to 121 on subsequent disposal.

(3) Where—

(a) any such restriction is entered in the register in respect of any land, and

(b) the charity by or in trust for which the land is held becomes an exempt charity,

the charity trustees must apply to the registrar for the removal of the entry.

(4) On receiving any application duly made under subsection (3) the registrar must remove the entry.

(5) Where—

(a) any registered land is held by or in trust for an exempt charity and the charity ceases to be an exempt charity, or

(b) any registered land becomes, as a result of a declaration of trust by the registered proprietor, land held in trust for a charity (other than an exempt charity),

the charity trustees must apply to the registrar for such a restriction as is mentioned in subsection (2) to be entered in the register in respect of the land.

(6) On receiving any application duly made under subsection (5) the registrar must enter such a restriction in the register in respect of the land.

Restrictions on mortgages of land in England and Wales

124 Restrictions on mortgages

(1) Subject to subsection (2), no mortgage of land held by or in trust for a charity is to be granted without an order of—

(a) the court, or

(b) the Commission.

(2) Subsection (1) does not apply to a mortgage of any such land if the charity trustees have, before executing the mortgage, obtained and considered proper advice, given to them in writing, on the relevant matters or matter mentioned in subsection (3) or (4) (as the case may be).

(3) In the case of a mortgage to secure the repayment of a proposed loan or grant, the relevant matters are—

(a) whether the loan or grant is necessary in order for the charity trustees to be able to pursue the particular course of action in connection with which they are seeking the loan or grant,

(b) whether the terms of the loan or grant are reasonable having regard to the status of the charity as the prospective recipient of the loan or grant, and

(c) the ability of the charity to repay on those terms the sum proposed to be paid by way of loan or grant.

(4) In the case of a mortgage to secure the discharge of any other proposed obligation, the relevant matter is whether it is reasonable for the charity trustees to undertake to discharge the obligation, having regard to the charity's purposes.

(5) Subsection (3) or (as the case may be) subsection (4) applies in relation to such a mortgage as is mentioned in that subsection whether the mortgage—

(a) would only have effect to secure the repayment of the proposed loan or grant or the discharge of the proposed obligation, or

(b) would also have effect to secure the repayment of sums paid by way of loan or grant, or the discharge of other obligations undertaken, after the date of its execution.

(6) Subsection (7) applies where—

(a) the charity trustees of a charity have executed a mortgage of land held by or in trust for a charity in accordance with subsection (2), and

(b) the mortgage has effect to secure the repayment of sums paid by way of loan or grant, or the discharge of other obligations undertaken, after the date of its execution.

(7) In such a case, the charity trustees must not after that date enter into any transaction involving—

(a) the payment of any such sums, or

(b) the undertaking of any such obligations,

unless they have, before entering into the transaction, obtained and considered proper advice, given to them in writing, on the matters or matter mentioned in subsection (3)(a) to (c) or (4) (as the case may be).

(8) For the purposes of this section proper advice is the advice of a person—

(a) who is reasonably believed by the charity trustees to be qualified by ability in and practical experience of financial matters, and

(b) who has no financial interest in relation to the loan, grant or other transaction in connection with which the advice is given;

and such advice may constitute proper advice for those purposes even though the person giving it does so in the course of employment as an officer or employee of the charity or of the charity trustees.

(9) This section applies regardless of anything in the trusts of a charity; but nothing in this section applies to any mortgage—

(a) for which general or special authority is given as mentioned in section 117(3)(a), or

(b) for which the authorisation or consent of the Secretary of State is required as mentioned in section 117(3)(b).

(10) Nothing in this section applies to an exempt charity.

125 Mortgages: required statements, etc.

(1) Any mortgage of land held by or in trust for a charity must state—

(a) that the land is held by or in trust for a charity,

(b) whether the charity is an exempt charity and whether the mortgage is one falling within section 124(9), and

(c) if it is not an exempt charity and the mortgage is not one falling within section 124(9), that the mortgage is one to which the restrictions imposed by section 124 apply.

(2) Where section 124(1) or (2) applies to any mortgage of land held by or in trust for a charity, the charity trustees must certify in the mortgage—

(a) (where section 124(1) applies) that the mortgage has been sanctioned by an order of the court or of the Commission (as the case may be), or

(b) (where section 124(2) applies) that the charity trustees have power under the trusts of the charity to grant the mortgage, and have obtained and considered such advice as is mentioned in section 124(2).

(3) Where subsection (2) has been complied with in relation to any mortgage, then in favour of a person who (whether under the mortgage or afterwards) acquires an interest

in the land in question for money or money's worth, it is conclusively presumed that the facts were as stated in the certificate.

(4) Subsection (5) applies where—

(a) section 124(1) or (2) applies to any mortgage of land held by or in trust for a charity, but

(b) subsection (2) has not been complied with in relation to the mortgage.

(5) In favour of a person who (whether under the mortgage or afterwards) in good faith acquires an interest in the land for money or money's worth, the mortgage is valid whether or not—

(a) the mortgage has been sanctioned by an order of the court or of the Commission, or

(b) the charity trustees have power under the trusts of the charity to grant the mortgage and have obtained and considered such advice as is mentioned in section 124(2).

(6) Where section 124(7) applies to any mortgage of land held by or in trust for a charity, the charity trustees must certify in relation to any transaction falling within section 124(7) that they have obtained and considered such advice as is mentioned in section 124(7).

(7) Where subsection (6) has been complied with in relation to any transaction, then, in favour of a person who (whether under the mortgage or afterwards) has acquired or acquires an interest in the land for money or money's worth, it is conclusively presumed that the facts were as stated in the certificate.

126 Mortgages of charity land and land registration

(1) Where the mortgage referred to in section 125(1) will be a registrable disposition, the statement required by section 125(1) must be in such form as may be prescribed by land registration rules.

(2) Where any such mortgage will be one to which section 4(1)(g) of the Land Registration Act 2002 applies—

(a) the statement required by section 125(1) must be in such form as may be prescribed by land registration rules, and

(b) if the charity is not an exempt charity, the mortgage must also contain a statement, in such form as may be prescribed by land registration rules, that the restrictions on disposition imposed by sections 117 to 121 apply to the land (subject to section 117(3)).

(3) Where—

(a) the registrar approves an application for registration of a person's title to land in connection with such a mortgage as is mentioned in subsection (2),

(b) the mortgage contains statements complying with section 125(1) and subsection (2), and

(c) the charity is not an exempt charity,

the registrar must enter in the register a restriction reflecting the limitation under sections 117 to 121 on subsequent disposal.

(4) Subsections (3) and (4) of section 123 (removal of entry) apply in relation to any restriction entered under subsection (3) as they apply in relation to any restriction entered under section 123(2).

Release of charity rentcharges

127 Release of charity rentcharges

(1) Section 117(1) does not apply to the release by a charity of a rentcharge which it is entitled to receive if the release is given in consideration of the payment of an amount which is not less than 10 times the annual amount of the rentcharge.

(2) Where a charity which is entitled to receive a rentcharge releases it in consideration of the payment of an amount not exceeding £1,000, any costs incurred by the charity in connection with proving its title to the rentcharge are recoverable by the charity from the person or persons in whose favour the rentcharge is being released.

(3) Neither section 117(1) nor subsection (2) of this section applies where a rentcharge which a charity is entitled to receive is redeemed under sections 8 to 10 of the Rentcharges Act 1977.

128 Power to alter sum specified in s.127(2)

The Minister may by order amend section 127(2) by substituting a different sum for the sum for the time being specified there.

Interpretation

129 Interpretation

(1) In sections 117 to 126 "land" means land in England and Wales.

(2) In sections 124 to 126 "mortgage" includes a charge.

(3) Sections 123 and 126 are to be construed as one with the Land Registration Act 2002.

PART 8

CHARITY ACCOUNTS, REPORTS AND RETURNS

CHAPTER 1

INDIVIDUAL ACCOUNTS

130 Accounting records

(1) The charity trustees of a charity must ensure that accounting records are kept in respect of the charity which are sufficient to show and explain all the charity's transactions, and which are such as to—

(a) disclose at any time, with reasonable accuracy, the financial position of the charity at that time, and

(b) enable the trustees to ensure that, where any statements of accounts are prepared by them under section 132(1), those statements of accounts comply with the requirements of regulations under section 132(1).

(2) The accounting records must in particular contain—

(a) entries showing from day to day all sums of money received and expended by the charity, and the matters in respect of which the receipt and expenditure takes place, and

(b) a record of the assets and liabilities of the charity.

131 Preservation of accounting records

(1) The charity trustees of a charity must preserve any accounting records made for the purposes of section 130 in respect of the charity for at least 6 years from the end of the financial year of the charity in which they are made.

(2) Subsection (3) applies if a charity ceases to exist within the period of 6 years mentioned in subsection (1) as it applies to any accounting records.

(3) The obligation to preserve the accounting records in accordance with subsection (1) must continue to be discharged by the last charity trustees of the charity, unless the Commission consents in writing to the records being destroyed or otherwise disposed of.

132 Preparation of statement of accounts

(1) The charity trustees of a charity must (subject to section 133) prepare in respect of each financial year of the charity a statement of accounts complying with such requirements as to its form and contents as may be prescribed by regulations made by the Minister.

(2) Regulations under subsection (1) may in particular make provision—

(a) for any such statement to be prepared in accordance with such methods and principles as are specified or referred to in the regulations;

(b) as to any information to be provided by way of notes to the accounts.

(3) Regulations under subsection (1) may also make provision for determining the financial years of a charity for the purposes of this Act and any regulations made under it.

(4) But regulations under subsection (1) may not impose on the charity trustees of a charity that is a charitable trust created by any person ("the settlor") any requirement to disclose, in any statement of accounts prepared by them under subsection (1)—

(a) the identities of recipients of grants made out of the funds of the charity, or

(b) the amounts of any individual grants so made,

if the disclosure would fall to be made at a time when the settlor or any spouse or civil partner of the settlor was still alive.

133 Account and statement an option for lower-income charities

If a charity's gross income in any financial year does not exceed £250,000, the charity trustees may, in respect of that year, elect to prepare—

(a) a receipts and payments account, and
(b) a statement of assets and liabilities,

instead of a statement of accounts under section 132(1).

134 Preservation of statement of accounts or account and statement

(1) The charity trustees of a charity must preserve—
(a) any statement of accounts prepared by them under section 132(1), or
(b) any account and statement prepared by them under section 133,

for at least 6 years from the end of the financial year to which any such statement relates or (as the case may be) to which any such account and statement relate.

(2) Subsection (3) applies if a charity ceases to exist within the period of 6 years mentioned in subsection (1) as it applies to any statement of accounts or account and statement.

(3) The obligation to preserve the statement or account and statement in accordance with subsection (1) must continue to be discharged by the last charity trustees of the charity, unless the Commission consents in writing to the statement or account and statement being destroyed or otherwise disposed of.

135 Charitable companies

Nothing in sections 130 to 134 (preparation and preservation of individual accounts) applies to a charitable company.

136 Exempt charities

(1) Nothing in sections 130 to 134 (preparation and preservation of individual accounts) applies to an exempt charity.

(2) But the charity trustees of an exempt charity—
(a) must keep proper books of account with respect to the affairs of the charity, and
(b) if not required by or under the authority of any other Act to prepare periodical statements of account must prepare consecutive statements of account consisting on each occasion of—
(i) an income and expenditure account relating to a period of not more than 15 months, and
(ii) a balance sheet relating to the end of that period.

(3) The books of accounts and statements of account relating to an exempt charity must be preserved for a period of at least 6 years unless—
(a) the charity ceases to exist, and
(b) the Commission consents in writing to their being destroyed or otherwise disposed of.

CHAPTER 2

GROUP ACCOUNTS

137 Accounting records

(1) The charity trustees of a parent charity or of any charity which is a subsidiary undertaking must ensure that the accounting records kept in respect of the charity under—

(a) section 130(1) (individual accounts: accounting records), or

(b) (as the case may be) section 386 of the Companies Act 2006 (duty to keep accounting records),

are such as to enable the charity trustees of the parent charity to ensure that, where any group accounts are prepared by them under section 138(2), those accounts comply with the requirements of regulations under section 142.

(2) The duty in subsection (1) is in addition to the duty to ensure that the accounting records comply with the requirements of—

(a) section 130(1), or

(b) section 386 of the Companies Act 2006.

(3) Subsection (4) applies if a parent charity has a subsidiary undertaking in relation to which the requirements of—

(a) section 130(1), or

(b) section 386 of the Companies Act 2006,

do not apply.

(4) The charity trustees of the parent charity must take reasonable steps to secure that the undertaking keeps such accounting records as to enable the trustees to ensure that, where any group accounts are prepared by them under section 138(2), those accounts comply with the requirements of regulations under section 142.

138 Preparation of group accounts

(1) This section applies in relation to a financial year of a charity if—

(a) the charity is a parent charity at the end of that year, and

(b) (where it is a company) it is not required to prepare consolidated accounts for that year under section 399 of the Companies Act 2006 (duty to prepare group accounts), whether or not such accounts are in fact prepared.

(2) The charity trustees of the parent charity must prepare group accounts in respect of that year.

(3) If the requirement in subsection (2) applies to the charity trustees of a parent charity (other than a parent charity which is a company) in relation to a financial year—

(a) that requirement so applies in addition to the requirement in section 132(1) (statement of accounts), and

(b) the option of preparing the documents mentioned in section 133 (account and statement) is not available in relation to that year (whatever the amount of the charity's gross income for that year).

(4) If—

(a) the requirement in subsection (2) applies to the charity trustees of a parent charity in relation to a financial year, and

(b) the charity is a company,

that requirement so applies in addition to the requirement in section 394 of the Companies Act 2006 (duty to prepare individual accounts).

(5) Subsection (2) is subject to section 139.

139 Exceptions to requirement to prepare group accounts

(1) The requirement in section 138(2) does not apply to the charity trustees of a parent charity in relation to a financial year if at the end of that year it is itself a subsidiary undertaking in relation to another charity.

(2) The requirement in section 138(2) does not apply to the charity trustees of a parent charity in relation to a financial year if the aggregate gross income of the group for that year does not exceed such sum as is specified in regulations made by the Minister.

(3) Regulations made by the Minister may prescribe circumstances in which a subsidiary undertaking may or (as the case may be) must be excluded from group accounts required to be prepared under section 138(2) for a financial year.

(4) Where, by virtue of such regulations, each of the subsidiary undertakings which are members of a group is—

(a) permitted to be excluded from any such group accounts for a financial year, or

(b) required to be so excluded,

the requirement in section 138(2) does not apply to the charity trustees of the parent charity in relation to that year.

140 Preservation of group accounts

(1) The charity trustees of a charity must preserve any group accounts prepared by them under section 138(2) for at least 6 years from the end of the financial year to which the accounts relate.

(2) Subsection (3) applies if a charity ceases to exist within the period of 6 years mentioned in subsection (1) as it applies to any group accounts.

(3) The obligation to preserve the accounts in accordance with subsection (1) must continue to be discharged by the last charity trustees of the charity, unless the Commission consents in writing to the accounts being destroyed or otherwise disposed of.

141 "Parent charity", "subsidiary undertaking" and "group"

(1) This section applies for the purposes of this Part.

(2) A charity is a parent charity if it is (or is to be treated as) a parent undertaking in relation to one or more other undertakings in accordance with the provisions of section 1162 of, and Schedule 7 to, the Companies Act 2006.

(3) Each undertaking in relation to which a parent charity is (or is to be treated as) a parent undertaking in accordance with those provisions is a subsidiary undertaking in relation to the parent charity.

(4) But subsection (3) does not have the result that any of the following is a subsidiary undertaking—

(a) any special trusts of a charity,

(b) any institution which, by virtue of a direction under section 12(1), is to be treated as forming part of a charity for the purposes of this Part, or

(c) any charity to which a direction under section 12(2) applies for the purposes of this Part.

(5) "The group", in relation to a parent charity, means that charity and its subsidiary undertaking or undertakings, and any reference to the members of the group is to be read accordingly.

(6) For the purposes of this section and the operation for those purposes of section 1162 of, and Schedule 7 to, the Companies Act 2006 "undertaking" means—

(a) an undertaking as defined by section 1161(1) of the 2006 Act, or

(b) a charity which is not an undertaking as so defined.

142 "Group accounts"

(1) For the purposes of this Part, "group accounts" means consolidated accounts—

(a) relating to the group, and

(b) complying with such requirements as to their form and contents as may be prescribed by regulations made by the Minister.

(2) Regulations under subsection (1) may in particular make provision—

(a) for any such accounts to be prepared in accordance with such methods and principles as are specified or referred to in the regulations;

(b) for dealing with cases where the financial years of the members of the group do not all coincide;

(c) as to any information to be provided by way of notes to the accounts.

(3) Regulations under subsection (1) may also make provision—

(a) for determining the financial years of subsidiary undertakings for the purposes of this Part;

(b) for imposing on the charity trustees of a parent charity requirements with respect to securing that such financial years coincide with that of the charity.

143 Exempt charities

Nothing in sections 137 to 142 (preparation and preservation of group accounts) applies to an exempt charity.

CHAPTER 3

AUDIT OR EXAMINATION OF ACCOUNTS

Audit or examination of individual accounts

144 Audit of accounts of larger charities

(1) Subsection (2) applies to a financial year of a charity if—

(a) the charity's gross income in that year exceeds £500,000, or

(b) the charity's gross income in that year exceeds the accounts threshold and at the end of the year the aggregate value of its assets (before deduction of liabilities) exceeds £3.26 million.

"The accounts threshold" means the sum for the time being specified in section 133 (account and statement an option for lower-income charities).

(2) If this subsection applies to a financial year of a charity, the accounts of the charity for that year must be audited by a person who—

(a) is eligible for appointment as a statutory auditor under Part 42 of the Companies Act 2006, or

(b) is a member of a body for the time being specified in regulations under section 154 and is under the rules of that body eligible for appointment as auditor of the charity.

145 Examination of accounts an option for lower-income charities

(1) If section 144(2) does not apply to a financial year of a charity but its gross income in that year exceeds £25,000, the accounts of the charity for that year must, at the election of the charity trustees, be—

(a) examined by an independent examiner, that is, an independent person who is reasonably believed by the trustees to have the requisite ability and practical experience to carry out a competent examination of the accounts, or

(b) audited by a person within section 144(2)(a) or (b).

(2) Subsection (1) is subject to—

(a) subsection (3), and

(b) any order under section 146(1).

(3) If subsection (1) applies to the accounts of a charity for a year and the charity's gross income in that year exceeds £250,000, a person qualifies as an independent examiner for the purposes of subsection (1)(a) if (and only if) the person is independent and—

(a) a member of one of the bodies listed in subsection (4), or

(b) a Fellow of the Association of Charity Independent Examiners.

(4) The bodies referred to in subsection (3)(a) are—

(a) the Institute of Chartered Accountants in England and Wales;

(b) the Institute of Chartered Accountants of Scotland;

(c) the Institute of Chartered Accountants in Ireland;

(d) the Association of Chartered Certified Accountants;

(e) the Association of Authorised Public Accountants;

(f) the Association of Accounting Technicians;
(g) the Association of International Accountants;
(h) the Chartered Institute of Management Accountants;
(i) the Institute of Chartered Secretaries and Administrators;
(j) the Chartered Institute of Public Finance and Accountancy.

(5) The Commission may—
(a) give guidance to charity trustees in connection with the selection of a person for appointment as an independent examiner;
(b) give such directions as it thinks appropriate with respect to the carrying out of an examination in pursuance of subsection (1)(a);

and any such guidance or directions may either be of general application or apply to a particular charity only.

(6) The Minister may by order—
(a) amend subsection (3) by adding or removing a description of person to or from the list in that subsection or by varying any entry for the time being included in that list;
(b) amend subsection (4) by adding or removing a body to or from the list in that subsection or by varying any entry for the time being included in that list.

146 Commission's powers to order audit

(1) The Commission may by order require the accounts of a charity for a financial year to be audited by a person within section 144(2)(a) or (b) if it appears to the Commission that—
(a) section 144(2), or (as the case may be) section 145(1), has not been complied with in relation to that year within 10 months from the end of that year, or
(b) although section 144(2) does not apply to that year, it would nevertheless be desirable for the accounts of the charity for that year to be audited by a person within section 144(2)(a) or (b).

(2) If the Commission makes an order under subsection (1) with respect to a charity, the auditor must be a person appointed by the Commission unless—
(a) the order is made by virtue of subsection (1)(b), and
(b) the charity trustees themselves appoint an auditor in accordance with the order.

(3) The expenses of any audit carried out by an auditor appointed by the Commission under subsection (2), including the auditor's remuneration, are recoverable by the Commission—
(a) from the charity trustees of the charity concerned, who are personally liable, jointly and severally, for those expenses, or
(b) to the extent that it appears to the Commission not to be practical to seek recovery of those expenses in accordance with paragraph (a), from the funds of the charity.

147 Accounts required to be audited under Companies Act

(1) Nothing in sections 144 to 146 applies in relation to the accounts of a charitable company for a financial year if those accounts are required to be audited in accordance with Part 16 of the Companies Act 2006 ("Part 16 accounts").

(2) In the case of a charitable company, the Commission may by order require that the condition and Part 16 accounts of the company for such period as the Commission thinks fit are to be investigated and audited by an auditor who—

(a) is eligible for appointment as a statutory auditor under Part 42 of the Companies Act 2006, and

(b) is appointed by the Commission.

(3) An auditor acting under subsection (2)—

(a) has a right of access to all books, accounts and documents relating to the company which are in the possession or control of the charity trustees or to which the charity trustees have access;

(b) is entitled to require from any charity trustee, past or present, and from any past or present officer or employee of the company such information and explanation as the auditor thinks necessary for the performance of the auditor's duties;

(c) must at the conclusion or during the progress of the audit make such reports to the Commission about the audit or about the accounts or affairs of the company as the auditor thinks the case requires, and must send a copy of any such report to the charity trustees.

(4) The expenses of any audit under subsection (2) including the remuneration of the auditor, are to be paid by the Commission.

(5) If any person fails to afford an auditor any facility to which the auditor is entitled under subsection (3), the Commission may by order give to that person or to the charity trustees for the time being such directions as the Commission thinks appropriate for securing that the default is made good.

148 NHS charities: general

Nothing in sections 144 to 146 applies in relation to a financial year of a charity where, at any time in the year, it is—

(a) an English NHS charity (as defined in section 149), or

(b) a Welsh NHS charity (as defined in section 150).

149 Audit or examination of English NHS charity accounts

(1) This section applies in relation to a financial year of a charity where, at any time in the year, it is an English NHS charity.

(2) If section 144(1)(a) or (b) is satisfied in relation to that financial year of the charity, the accounts of the charity for that year must be audited by a person appointed by the Audit Commission.

(3) In any other case, the accounts of the charity for that financial year must, at the election of the Audit Commission, be—

(a) audited by a person appointed by the Audit Commission, or

(b) examined by a person so appointed.

(4) Section 3 of the Audit Commission Act 1998 applies in relation to any appointment under subsection (2) or (3)(a).

(5) The Charity Commission may give such directions as it thinks appropriate with respect to the carrying out of an examination in pursuance of subsection (3)(b); and any such directions may either be of general application or apply to a particular charity only.

(6) The Comptroller and Auditor General may at any time examine and inspect—

- (a) the accounts of the charity for the financial year,
- (b) any records relating to those accounts, and
- (c) any report of a person appointed under subsection (2) or (3) to audit or examine those accounts.

(7) In this section, "English NHS charity" means a charitable trust, the trustees of which are—

- (a) a Strategic Health Authority,
- (b) a Primary Care Trust,
- (c) a National Health Service trust all or most of whose hospitals, establishments and facilities are situated in England,
- (d) trustees appointed in pursuance of paragraph 10 of Schedule 4 to the National Health Service Act 2006 for a National Health Service trust falling within paragraph (c),
- (e) special trustees appointed in pursuance of section 29(1) of the National Health Service Reorganisation Act 1973, section 95(1) of the National Health Service Act 1977 and section 212(1) of the National Health Service Act 2006 for such a National Health Service trust, or
- (f) trustees for a Primary Care Trust appointed in pursuance of paragraph 12 of Schedule 3 to the National Health Service Act 2006.

(8) In this Chapter "the Audit Commission" means the Audit Commission for Local Authorities and the National Health Service in England.

150 Audit or examination of Welsh NHS charity accounts

(1) This section applies in relation to a financial year of a charity where, at any time in the year, it is a Welsh NHS charity.

(2) If section 144(1)(a) or (b) is satisfied in relation to that financial year of the charity, the accounts of the charity for that year must be audited by the Auditor General for Wales.

(3) In any other case, the accounts of the charity for that financial year must, at the election of the Auditor General for Wales, be audited or examined by the Auditor General for Wales.

(4) In this section "Welsh NHS charity" means a charitable trust, the trustees of which are—

- (a) a Local Health Board,
- (b) a National Health Service trust all or most of whose hospitals, establishments and facilities are situated in Wales,
- (c) trustees appointed in pursuance of paragraph 10 of Schedule 3 to the National Health Service (Wales) Act 2006 for a National Health Service trust falling within paragraph (b), or
- (d) special trustees appointed in pursuance of section 29(1) of the National Health Service Reorganisation Act 1973, section 95(1) of the National Health Service

Act 1977 and section 160(1) of the National Health Service (Wales) Act 2006 for such a National Health Service trust.

(5) References in this Act to an auditor or an examiner have effect in relation to this section as references to the Auditor General for Wales acting under this section as an auditor or examiner.

Audit or examination of group accounts

151 Audit of accounts of larger groups

(1) This section applies where group accounts are prepared for a financial year of a parent charity under section 138(2) and—

(a) the aggregate gross income of the group in that year exceeds the relevant income threshold (see section 176(1)), or

(b) the aggregate gross income of the group in that year exceeds the relevant income threshold and at the end of the year the aggregate value of the assets of the group (before deduction of liabilities) exceeds the relevant assets threshold (see section 176(2)).

(2) This section also applies where—

(a) group accounts are prepared for a financial year of a parent charity under section 138(2), and

(b) the appropriate audit provision applies in relation to the parent charity's own accounts for that year.

(3) In this section "the appropriate audit provision", in relation to a financial year of a parent charity, means—

(a) (subject to paragraph (b), (c) or (d)) section 144(2) (audit of accounts of larger charities);

(b) if section 149 (audit or examination of English NHS charity accounts) applies in relation to that year, section 149(2);

(c) if section 150 (audit or examination of Welsh NHS charity accounts) applies in relation to that year, section 150(2);

(d) if the parent charity is a company—

(i) section 144(2), or

(ii) (as the case may be) Part 16 of the Companies Act 2006.

(4) If this section applies in relation to a financial year of a parent charity by virtue of subsection (1) or (2), the group accounts for that year must be audited—

(a) (subject to paragraph (b) or (c)) by a person within section 144(2)(a) or (b);

(b) if section 149 applies in relation to that year, by a person appointed by the Audit Commission;

(c) if section 150 applies in relation to that year, by the Auditor General for Wales.

(5) If this section applies in relation to a financial year of a parent charity by virtue of subsection (1)—

(a) (subject to paragraph (b)) the appropriate audit provision applies in relation to the parent charity's own accounts for that year (whether or not it would otherwise so apply);

(b) if the parent charity is a company and its own accounts for that year are not required to be audited in accordance with Part 16 of the Companies Act 2006, section 144(2) applies in relation to those accounts (whether or not it would otherwise so apply).

(6) Subsections (4) and (6) of section 149 apply in relation to any appointment under subsection (4)(b) as they apply in relation to an appointment under section 149(2).

(7) References in this Act to an auditor have effect in relation to subsection (4)(c) as references to the Auditor General for Wales acting under subsection (4)(c) as an auditor.

152 Examination of accounts an option for smaller groups

(1) This section applies if—

(a) group accounts are prepared for a financial year of a parent charity under section 138(2), and

(b) section 151 (audit of accounts of larger groups) does not apply in relation to that year.

(2) If—

(a) this section applies in relation to a financial year of a parent charity,

(b) the aggregate gross income of the group in that year exceeds the sum specified in section 145(1), and

(c) subsection (6) or (7) (NHS charity: group accounts) does not apply in relation to it,

the group accounts for that year must, at the election of the charity trustees of the parent charity, be examined by an independent examiner (as defined in section 145(1)(a)) or audited by a person within section 144(2)(a) or (b).

(3) Subsection (2) is subject to—

(a) subsection (4), and

(b) any order under section 153(1).

(4) If subsection (2) applies to the group accounts for a year and the aggregate gross income of the group in that year exceeds the sum specified in section 145(3), a person qualifies as an independent examiner for the purposes of subsection (2) if (and only if) the person is independent and meets the requirements of section 145(3)(a) or (b).

(5) The Commission may—

(a) give guidance to charity trustees of a parent charity in connection with the selection of a person for appointment as an independent examiner;

(b) give such directions as it thinks appropriate with respect to the carrying out of an examination in pursuance of subsection (2);

and any such guidance or directions may either be of general application or apply to a particular charity only.

(6) If—

(a) this section applies in relation to a financial year of a parent charity, and

(b) section 149 (audit or examination of English NHS charity accounts) also applies in relation to that year, the group accounts for that year must at the election of the Audit Commission be audited by a person appointed by the Audit Commission or examined by a person so appointed.

Subsections (4) to (6) of section 149 apply for the purposes of this subsection as they apply for the purposes of section 149(3).

(7) If—

(a) this section applies in relation to a financial year of a parent charity, and

(b) section 150 (audit or examination of Welsh NHS charity accounts) also applies in relation to that year,

the group accounts for that year must, at the election of the Auditor General for Wales, be audited or examined by the Auditor General for Wales.

References in this Act to an auditor or an examiner have effect in relation to this subsection as references to the Auditor General for Wales acting under this subsection as an auditor or examiner.

(8) If the group accounts for a financial year of a parent charity are to be examined or audited in accordance with subsection (2), section 145(1) applies in relation to the parent charity's own accounts for that year (whether or not it would otherwise so apply).

(9) Nothing in subsection (6) or (7) affects the operation of section 149(3) to (6) or (as the case may be) section 150(3) in relation to the parent charity's own accounts for the financial year in question.

153 Commission's powers to order audit of group accounts

(1) The Commission may by order require the group accounts of a parent charity for a financial year to be audited by a person within section 144(2)(a) or (b) if it appears to the Commission that—

(a) section 151(4)(a), or (as the case may be) section 152(2), has not been complied with in relation to that year within 10 months from the end of that year, or

(b) although section 151(4)(a) does not apply to that year, it would nevertheless be desirable for the group accounts for that year to be audited by a person within section 144(2)(a) or (b).

But this subsection does not apply if section 149 or 150 (audit or examination of NHS charity accounts) applies in relation to the parent charity for that year.

(2) If the Commission makes an order under subsection (1) with respect to group accounts, the auditor must be a person appointed by the Commission unless—

(a) the order is made by virtue of subsection (1)(b), and

(b) the charity trustees of the parent charity themselves appoint an auditor in accordance with the order.

(3) The expenses of any audit carried out by an auditor appointed by the Commission under subsection (2), including the auditor's remuneration, are recoverable by the Commission—

(a) from the charity trustees of the parent charity, who are personally liable, jointly and severally, for those expenses, or

(b) to the extent that it appears to the Commission not to be practical to seek recovery of those expenses in accordance with paragraph (a), from the funds of the parent charity.

Regulations relating to audits and examinations

154 Regulations relating to audits and examinations

(1) The Minister may by regulations make provision—

(a) specifying one or more bodies for the purposes of section 144(2)(b);

(b) with respect to the duties of an auditor carrying out an audit of individual or group accounts, including provision with respect to the making by the auditor of a report on—

(i) the statement of accounts prepared for the financial year in question under section 132(1),

(ii) the account and statement so prepared under section 133,

(iii) the accounts so prepared under section 394 of the Companies Act 2006 (duty to prepare individual accounts), or

(iv) group accounts so prepared under section 138(2),

as the case may be;

(c) with respect to the making of a report in respect of an examination of individual or group accounts by the independent examiner or examiner who has carried out the examination;

(d) conferring on an auditor or on an independent examiner or examiner a right of access with respect to books, documents and other records (however kept) which relate to—

(i) the charity (if the audit or examination is of individual accounts), or

(ii) any member of the group (if the audit or examination is of group accounts);

(e) entitling an auditor or an independent examiner or examiner to require information and explanations from—

(i) past or present charity trustees or trustees for, or past or present officers or employees of, the charity (if the audit or examination is of individual accounts), or

(ii) past or present charity trustees or trustees for, or past or present officers or employees of, any member of the group (if the audit or examination is of group accounts);

(f) enabling the Commission, in circumstances specified in the regulations, to dispense with the requirements of section 144(2), 145(1), 151(4)(a) or 152(2) —

(i) in the case of a particular charity, or

(ii) in the case of any particular financial year of a charity.

(2) Regulations under subsection (1)(e) may in particular make, in relation to audits or examinations of group accounts, provision corresponding or similar to any provision made by section 499 or 500 of the Companies Act 2006 in connection with the rights exercisable by an auditor of a company in relation to a subsidiary undertaking of the company.

(3) In this section—

"audit of individual or group accounts" means an audit under—

(a) section 144, 145, 146, 149 or 150 (individual accounts), or

(b) section 151, 152 or 153 (group accounts);

"examination of individual or group accounts" means an examination under—

(a) section 145, 149 or 150 (individual accounts), or

(b) section 152 (group accounts);

and the references in this section and section 155 to an audit or examination of individual accounts and to an audit or examination of group accounts are to be read accordingly.

155 Power of Commission to direct compliance with certain regulations

If any person fails to afford an auditor or an independent examiner or examiner any facility to which the auditor, independent examiner or examiner is entitled by virtue of section 154(1)(d) or (e), the Commission, for securing that the default is made good, may by order give such directions as it thinks appropriate—

(a) to that person,

(b) if the audit or examination is of individual accounts, to the charity trustees for the time being of the charity concerned, or

(c) if the audit or examination is of group accounts, to the charity trustees for the time being of such member of the group as the Commission thinks appropriate.

Duty of auditors etc. to report matters to Commission

156 Duty of auditors etc. to report matters to Commission

(1) This section applies to a person ("P") who—

(a) is acting as an auditor or independent examiner appointed by or in relation to a charity under sections 144 to 146 (audit or examination of individual accounts),

(b) is acting as an auditor or examiner appointed under section 149(2) or (3) (audit or examination of English NHS charity accounts), or

(c) is the Auditor General for Wales acting under section 150(2) or (3) (audit or examination of Welsh NHS charity accounts).

(2) If, in the course of acting in the capacity mentioned in subsection (1), P becomes aware of a matter—

(a) which relates to the activities or affairs of the charity or of any connected institution or body, and

(b) which P has reasonable cause to believe is likely to be of material significance for the purposes of the exercise by the Commission of its functions under the provisions mentioned in subsection (3),

P must immediately make a written report on the matter to the Commission.

(3) The provisions are—

(a) sections 46, 47 and 50 (inquiries by Commission);

(b) sections 76 and 79 to 82 (Commission's powers to act for protection of charities).

(4) If, in the course of acting in the capacity mentioned in subsection (1), P becomes aware of any matter—

(a) which does not appear to P to be one that P is required to report under subsection (2), but

(b) which P has reasonable cause to believe is likely to be relevant for the purposes of the exercise by the Commission of any of its functions,

P may make a report on the matter to the Commission.

(5) Where the duty or power under subsection (2) or (4) has arisen in relation to P when acting in the capacity mentioned in subsection (1), the duty or power is not affected by P's subsequently ceasing to act in that capacity.

(6) Where P makes a report as required or authorised by subsection (2) or (4), no duty to which P is subject is to be regarded as contravened merely because of any information or opinion contained in the report.

157 Meaning of "connected institution or body" in s.156(2)

(1) In section 156(2) "connected institution or body", in relation to a charity, means—

(a) an institution which is controlled by, or

(b) a body corporate in which a substantial interest is held by,

the charity or any one or more of the charity trustees acting as such.

(2) Sections 351 and 352 (meaning of controlled institution and substantial interest) apply for the purposes of subsection (1).

158 Application of duty in relation to auditors etc. of group accounts

(1) Subsections (2) to (6) of section 156 (duty of auditors etc. of individual accounts to report matters to Commission) apply in relation to a person appointed to audit, or report on, any group accounts under sections 151 to 153 as they apply in relation to the person referred to in section 156 as "P".

(2) In section 156(2)(a), as it applies in accordance with subsection (1), the reference to the charity or any connected institution or body is to be read as a reference to the parent charity or any of its subsidiary undertakings.

159 Application of duty in relation to Companies Act auditors

(1) Sections 156(2) to (6) and 157 (duty of auditors etc. of individual accounts to report matters to Commission) apply in relation to a person acting as a Companies Act auditor of a charitable company as they apply in relation to the person referred to in section 156 as "P", but reading any reference to P's acting in the capacity mentioned in section 156(1) as a reference to the person acting as a Companies Act auditor.

(2) In subsection (1), "Companies Act auditor" means an auditor appointed under Chapter 2 of Part 16 of the Companies Act 2006 (appointment of auditors).

Exempt and excepted charities

160 Exempt charities

(1) Nothing in sections 144 to 155 (audit or examination of accounts) applies to an exempt charity.

(2) Sections 156(2) to (6) and 157 (duty of auditors etc. of individual accounts to report matters to Commission) apply in relation to a person appointed to audit, or report on, the accounts of an exempt charity which is not a company as they apply in relation to the person referred to in section 156 as "P", but reading—

(a) any reference to P's acting in the capacity mentioned in section 156(1) as a reference to the person acting as a person so appointed, and

(b) any reference to the Commission or to any of its functions as a reference to the charity's principal regulator or to any of the latter's functions as principal regulator in relation to the charity.

(3) Nothing in section 158 (duty of auditors etc. in relation to group accounts) applies to an exempt charity.

161 Excepted charities

(1) Nothing in sections 144 to 146 (audit or examination of individual accounts) applies to any charity which—

(a) falls within section 30(2)(d) (whether or not it also falls within section 30(2)(b) or (c)), and

(b) is not registered.

(2) Except in accordance with subsections (3) and (4), nothing in—

(a) section 154 or 155 (regulations relating to audits and examinations), or

(b) section 156 or 157 (duty of auditors etc. to report matters to Commission),

applies to a charity mentioned in subsection (1).

(3) Sections 154 to 157 apply to a charity mentioned in subsection (1) which is also—

(a) an English NHS charity (as defined in section 149), or

(b) a Welsh NHS charity (as defined in section 150).

(4) Sections 156 and 157 apply in accordance with section 160(2) to a charity mentioned in subsection (1) which is also an exempt charity.

CHAPTER 4

ANNUAL REPORTS AND RETURNS AND PUBLIC ACCESS TO ACCOUNTS ETC.

Annual reports etc.

162 Charity trustees to prepare annual reports

(1) The charity trustees of a charity must prepare in respect of each financial year of the charity an annual report containing—

(a) such a report by the trustees on the activities of the charity during that year, and

(b) such other information relating to the charity or to its trustees or officers,

as may be prescribed by regulations made by the Minister.

(2) Regulations under subsection (1) may in particular make provision—

(a) for any such report as is mentioned in subsection (1)(a) to be prepared in accordance with such principles as are specified or referred to in the regulations;

(b) enabling the Commission to dispense with any requirement prescribed by virtue of subsection (1)(b)—

(i) in the case of a particular charity or a particular class of charities, or

(ii) in the case of a particular financial year of a charity or of any class of charities.

163 Transmission of annual reports to Commission in certain cases

(1) Where a charity's gross income in any financial year exceeds £25,000, a copy of the annual report required to be prepared under section 162 in respect of that year must be transmitted to the Commission by the charity trustees within—

(a) 10 months from the end of that year, or

(b) such longer period as the Commission may for any special reason allow in the case of that report.

(2) Where a charity's gross income in any financial year does not exceed £25,000, a copy of the annual report required to be prepared under section 162 in respect of that year must, if the Commission so requests, be transmitted to it by the charity trustees—

(a) in the case of a request made before the end of 7 months from the end of the financial year to which the report relates, within 10 months from the end of that year, and

(b) in the case of a request not so made, within 3 months from the date of the request,

or, in either case, within such longer period as the Commission may for any special reason allow in the case of that report.

(3) In the case of a charity which is constituted as a CIO—

(a) the requirement imposed by subsection (1) applies whatever the charity's gross income is, and

(b) subsection (2) does not apply.

164 Documents to be transmitted with annual report

(1) Subject to subsection (3), any copy of an annual report transmitted to the Commission under section 163 must have attached to it—

(a) a copy of the statement of accounts prepared for the financial year in question under section 132(1), or

(b) (as the case may be) a copy of the account and statement so prepared under section 133,

and a copy of the relevant auditor's or examiner's report.

(2) In subsection (1), "the relevant auditor's or examiner's report" means—

(a) if the accounts of the charity for that year have been audited under section 144, 145, 146, 149 or 150, the report made by the auditor on that statement of accounts or (as the case may be) on that account and statement;

(b) if the accounts of the charity for that year have been examined under section 145, 149 or 150, the report made by the person carrying out the examination.

(3) Subsections (1) and (2) do not apply to a charitable company, and any copy of an annual report transmitted by the charity trustees of a charitable company under section 163 must have attached to it—

(a) a copy of the company's annual accounts prepared for the financial year in question under Part 15 of the Companies Act 2006, and

(b) a copy of the relevant auditor's or examiner's report.

(4) In subsection (3), "the relevant auditor's or examiner's report" means—

(a) if the accounts of the company for that year have been audited under Part 16 of the Companies Act 2006, the report made by the auditor on those accounts;

(b) if the accounts of the company for that year have been audited under section 144, 145 or 146, the report made by the auditor on those accounts;

(c) if the accounts of the company for that year have been examined under section 145, the report made by the person carrying out the examination.

165 Preservation of annual reports etc.

(1) Any copy of an annual report transmitted to the Commission under section 163, together with the documents attached to it, is to be kept by the Commission for such period as it thinks fit.

(2) The charity trustees of a charity must preserve for at least 6 years from the end of the financial year to which it relates an annual report prepared by them under section 162(1) if they have not been required to transmit a copy of it to the Commission.

(3) Subsection (4) applies if a charity ceases to exist within the period of 6 years mentioned in subsection (2) as it applies to any annual report.

(4) The obligation to preserve the annual report in accordance with subsection (2) must continue to be discharged by the last charity trustees of the charity, unless the Commission consents in writing to the annual report being destroyed or otherwise disposed of.

166 Annual reports and group accounts

(1) This section applies where group accounts are prepared for a financial year of a parent charity under section 138(2).

(2) The annual report prepared by the charity trustees of the parent charity in respect of that year under section 162 must include—

(a) such a report by the trustees on the activities of the charity's subsidiary undertakings during that year, and

(b) such other information relating to any of those undertakings,

as may be prescribed by regulations made by the Minister.

(3) Regulations under subsection (2) may in particular make provision—

(a) for any such report as is mentioned in subsection (2)(a) to be prepared in accordance with such principles as are specified or referred to in the regulations;

(b) enabling the Commission to dispense with any requirement prescribed by virtue of subsection (2)(b) in the case of—

(i) a particular subsidiary undertaking, or

(ii) a particular class of subsidiary undertakings.

(4) Section 163 (transmission of annual report to Commission in certain cases) applies in relation to the annual report referred to in subsection (2) as if any reference to the charity's gross income in the financial year in question were a reference to the aggregate gross income of the group in that year.

(5) When transmitted to the Commission in accordance with subsection (4), the copy of the annual report must have attached to it both a copy of the group accounts prepared for that year under section 138(2) and—

(a) a copy of the report made by the auditor on those accounts, or

(b) if those accounts have been examined under section 152, a copy of the report made by the person carrying out the examination.

(6) The requirements in this section are in addition to those in sections 162 to 165.

167 Exempt charities

Nothing in sections 162 to 166 (annual reports etc.) applies to any exempt charity.

168 Excepted charities

(1) Nothing in sections 162 to 165 (annual reports etc.) applies to any charity which—

(a) falls within section 30(2)(d) (whether or not it also falls within section 30(2)(b) or (c)), and

(b) is not registered.

(2) Except in accordance with subsection (5), nothing in sections 162 to 165 applies to any charity which—

(a) falls within section 30(2)(b) or (c) but does not fall within section 30(2)(d), and

(b) is not registered.

(3) If requested to do so by the Commission, the charity trustees of any such charity as is mentioned in subsection (2) must prepare an annual report in respect of such financial year of the charity as is specified in the Commission's request.

(4) Any report prepared under subsection (3) must contain—

(a) such a report by the charity trustees on the activities of the charity during the year in question, and

(b) such other information relating to the charity or to its trustees or officers,

as may be prescribed by regulations made under section 162(1) in relation to annual reports prepared under section 162(1).

(5) The following provisions apply in relation to any report required to be prepared under subsection (3) as if it were an annual report required to be prepared under section 162(1)—

(a) section 163(1) (transmission of annual report in certain cases), with the omission of the words preceding "a copy of the annual report", and

(b) sections 164 (documents to be transmitted with annual report) and 165(1) (preservation of annual reports etc.).

(6) Subsections (7) and (8) apply where—

(a) a charity is required to prepare an annual report in respect of a financial year by virtue of subsection (3),

(b) the charity is a parent charity at the end of the year, and

(c) group accounts are prepared for that year under section 138(2) by the charity trustees of the charity.

(7) When transmitted to the Commission in accordance with subsection (5), the copy of the annual report must have attached to it both a copy of the group accounts and—

(a) a copy of the report made by the auditor on those accounts, or

(b) if those accounts have been examined under section 152, a copy of the report made by the person carrying out the examination.

(8) The requirement in subsection (7) is in addition to that in subsection (4).

Annual returns

169 Annual returns by registered charities

(1) Subject to subsection (2), every registered charity must prepare in respect of each of its financial years an annual return in such form, and containing such information, as may be prescribed by regulations made by the Commission.

(2) Subsection (1) does not apply in relation to any financial year of a charity in which the charity's gross income does not exceed £10,000 (but this subsection does not apply if the charity is constituted as a CIO).

(3) Any such return must be transmitted to the Commission by the date by which the charity trustees are, by virtue of section 163(1), required to transmit to the Commission the annual report required to be prepared in respect of the financial year in question.

(4) The Commission may dispense with the requirements of subsection (1)—

(a) in the case of a particular charity or a particular class of charities, or

(b) in the case of a particular financial year of a charity or of any class of charities.

Availability of documents to public

170 Public inspection of annual reports etc. kept by Commission

Any document kept by the Commission in pursuance of section 165(1) (preservation of annual reports etc.) must be open to public inspection at all reasonable times—

(a) during the period for which it is so kept, or

(b) if the Commission so determines, during such lesser period as it may specify.

171 Supply by charity trustees of copy of most recent annual report

(1) This section applies if an annual report has been prepared in respect of any financial year of a charity in pursuance of section 162(1) or 168(3).

(2) If the charity trustees of a charity—

(a) are requested in writing by any person to provide that person with a copy of its most recent annual report, and

(b) are paid by that person such reasonable fee (if any) as they may require in respect of the costs of complying with the request,

they must comply with the request within the period of 2 months beginning with the date on which it is made.

(3) The reference in subsection (2) to a charity's most recent annual report is a reference to the annual report prepared in pursuance of section 162(1) or 168(3) in respect of the last financial year of the charity in respect of which an annual report has been so prepared.

172 Supply by charity trustees of copy of most recent accounts

(1) If the charity trustees of a charity—

(a) are requested in writing by any person to provide that person with a copy of the charity's most recent accounts, and

(b) are paid by that person such reasonable fee (if any) as they may require in respect of the costs of complying with the request,

they must comply with the request within the period of 2 months beginning with the date on which it is made.

(2) The reference in subsection (1) to a charity's most recent accounts is—

(a) in the case of a charity other than one falling within paragraph (b) or (c), a reference to—

(i) the statement of accounts prepared in pursuance of section 132(1), or

(ii) the account and statement prepared in pursuance of section 133,

in respect of the last financial year of the charity in respect of which a statement of accounts or account and statement has or have been so prepared;

(b) in the case of a charitable company, a reference to the most recent annual accounts of the company prepared under Part 16 of the Companies Act 2006 in relation to which any of the following conditions is satisfied—

(i) they have been audited,

(ii) they have been examined by an independent examiner under section 145(1)(a), or

(iii) they relate to a year in respect of which the company is exempt from audit under Part 16 of the Companies Act 2006 and neither section 144(2) nor section 145(1) applied to them, and

(c) in the case of an exempt charity, a reference to the accounts of the charity most recently audited in pursuance of any statutory or other requirement or, if its accounts are not required to be audited, the accounts most recently prepared in respect of the charity.

(3) In subsection (1), the reference to a charity's most recent accounts includes, in relation to a charity whose charity trustees have prepared any group accounts under section 138(2), the group accounts most recently prepared by them.

Offences

173 Offences of failing to supply certain documents

(1) If any requirement within subsection (2) is not complied with, each person who immediately before the specified date for compliance was a charity trustee of the charity is guilty of an offence.

(2) A requirement is within this subsection if it is imposed—

(a) by section 163 or by virtue of section 166(4) (requirements to transmit annual report to Commission), taken with sections 164, 166(5) and 168(7) (documents to be supplied with annual report), as applicable,

(b) by section 169(3) (requirement to transmit annual return to Commission),

(c) by section 171(2) (supply by charity trustees of copy of most recent annual report), or

(d) by section 172(1) or by virtue of section 172(3) (supply by charity trustees of copy of most recent accounts);

and in subsection (1) "the specified date for compliance" means the date for compliance specified in the section in question.

(3) It is a defence, where a person is charged with an offence under subsection (1), to prove that the person took all reasonable steps for securing that the requirement in question would be complied with in time.

(4) A person guilty of an offence under subsection (1) is liable on summary conviction to—

(a) a fine not exceeding level 4 on the standard scale, and

(b) for continued contravention, a daily default fine not exceeding 10% of level 4 on the standard scale for so long as the person in question remains a charity trustee of the charity.

CHAPTER 5

POWERS TO SET FINANCIAL THRESHOLDS

174 Powers to alter certain sums specified in this Part

(1) The Minister may by order amend any provision listed in subsection (2)—

(a) by substituting a different sum for the sum for the time being specified in that provision, or

(b) if the provision specifies more than one sum, by substituting a different sum for any sum specified in that provision.

(2) The provisions are—

section 133 (gross income in connection with option to prepare account and statement instead of statement of accounts);

section 144(1)(a) or (b) (gross income and value of assets in connection with requirements as to audit of larger charities);

section 145(1) (gross income in connection with option to have accounts examined instead of audited);

section 145(3) (gross income in connection with requirements as to qualifications of independent examiner);

section 163(1) or (2) (gross income in connection with requirements to transmit annual report to Commission);

section 169(2) (gross income in connection with requirement to prepare annual return).

175 Aggregate gross income of group

The Minister may by regulations make provision for determining for the purposes of this Part the amount of the aggregate gross income for a financial year of a group consisting of a parent charity and its subsidiary undertaking or undertakings.

176 Larger groups: "relevant income threshold" and "relevant assets threshold"

(1) The reference to the relevant income threshold in paragraph (a) or (b) of section 151(1) is a reference to the sum prescribed as the relevant income threshold for the purposes of that paragraph.

(2) The reference to the relevant assets threshold in paragraph (b) of section 151(1) is a reference to the sum prescribed as the relevant assets threshold for the purposes of that paragraph.

(3) "Prescribed" means prescribed by regulations made by the Minister.

PART 9

CHARITY TRUSTEES, TRUSTEES AND AUDITORS ETC.

Meaning of "charity trustees"

177 Meaning of "charity trustees"

In this Act, except in so far as the context otherwise requires, "charity trustees" means the persons having the general control and management of the administration of a charity.

Disqualification of charity trustees and trustees

178 Persons disqualified from being charity trustees or trustees of a charity

(1) A person ("P") is disqualified from being a charity trustee or trustee for a charity in the following cases—

Case A

P has been convicted of any offence involving dishonesty or deception.

Case B

P has been adjudged bankrupt or sequestration of P's estate has been awarded and (in either case)—

(a) P has not been discharged, or

(b) P is the subject of a bankruptcy restrictions order or an interim order.

Case C

P has made a composition or arrangement with, or granted a trust deed for, creditors and has not been discharged in respect of it.

Case D

P has been removed from the office of charity trustee or trustee for a charity by an order made—

(a) by the Commission under section 79(2)(a) or by the Commission or the Commissioners under a relevant earlier enactment (as defined by section 179(5)), or

(b) by the High Court,

on the ground of any misconduct or mismanagement in the administration of the charity for which P was responsible or to which P was privy, or which P's conduct contributed to or facilitated.

Case E

P has been removed, under section 34(5)(e) of the Charities and Trustee Investment (Scotland) Act 2005 (asp 10) (powers of the Court of Session) or the relevant earlier legislation (as defined by section 179(6)), from being concerned in the management or control of any body.

Case F

P is subject to—

(a) a disqualification order or disqualification undertaking under the Company Directors Disqualification Act 1986 or the Company Directors Disqualification (Northern Ireland) Order 2002 (S.I. 2002/3150 (N.I.4)), or

(b) an order made under section 429(2) of the Insolvency Act 1986 (disabilities on revocation of county court administration order).

(2) Subsection (1) is subject to sections 179 to 181.

179 Disqualification: pre-commencement events etc.

(1) Case A—

(a) applies whether the conviction occurred before or after the commencement of section 178(1), but

(b) does not apply in relation to any conviction which is a spent conviction for the purposes of the Rehabilitation of Offenders Act 1974.

(2) Case B applies whether the adjudication of bankruptcy or the sequestration or the making of a bankruptcy restrictions order or an interim order occurred before or after the commencement of section 178(1).

(3) Case C applies whether the composition or arrangement was made, or the trust deed was granted, before or after the commencement of section 178(1).

(4) Cases D to F apply in relation to orders made and removals effected before or after the commencement of section 178(1).

(5) In Case D—

(a) "the Commissioners" means the Charity Commissioners for England and Wales, and

(b) "relevant earlier enactment" means—

(i) section 18(2)(i) of the Charities Act 1993 (power to act for protection of charities),

(ii) section 20(1A)(i) of the Charities Act 1960, or

(iii) section 20(1)(i) of the 1960 Act (as in force before the commencement of section 8 of the Charities Act 1992).

(6) In Case E, "the relevant earlier legislation" means section 7 of the Law Reform (Miscellaneous Provisions) (Scotland) Act 1990 (powers of Court of Session to deal with management of charities).

180 Disqualification: exceptions in relation to charitable companies

(1) Where (apart from this subsection) a person ("P") is disqualified under Case B from being a charity trustee or trustee for a charitable company, P is not so disqualified if leave has been granted under section 11 of the Company Directors Disqualification Act 1986 (undischarged bankrupts) for P to act as director of the company.

(2) Similarly, a person ("P") is not disqualified under Case F from being a charity trustee or trustee for a charitable company if, in a case set out in the first column of the table, leave has been granted as mentioned in the second column for P to act as director of the company—

P is subject to a disqualification order or disqualification undertaking under the Company Directors Disqualification Act 1986.	Leave has been granted for the purposes of section 1(1)(a) or 1A(1)(a) of the 1986 Act.
P is subject to a disqualification order or disqualification undertaking under the Company Directors Disqualification (Northern Ireland) Order 2002 (S.I. 2002/3150 (N.I.4)).	Leave has been granted by the High Court in Northern Ireland.
P is subject to an order under section 429(2) of the Insolvency Act 1986.	Leave has been granted by the court which made the order.

181 Power to waive disqualification

(1) This section applies where a person ("P') is disqualified under section 178(1).

(2) The Commission may, if P makes an application under this subsection, waive P's disqualification—

(a) generally, or

(b) in relation to a particular charity or a particular class of charities.

(3) If—

(a) P is disqualified under Case D or E and makes an application under subsection (2) 5 years or more after the date on which the disqualification took effect, and

(b) the Commission is not prevented from granting the application by subsection (5),

the Commission must grant the application unless satisfied that, because of any special circumstances, it should be refused.

(4) Any waiver under subsection (2) must be notified in writing to P.

(5) No waiver may be granted under subsection (2) in relation to any charitable company if—

(a) P is for the time being prohibited from acting as director of the company, by virtue of—

(i) a disqualification order or disqualification undertaking under the Company Directors Disqualification Act 1986, or

(ii) a provision of the 1986 Act mentioned in subsection (6), and

(b) leave has not been granted for P to act as director of any other company.

(6) The provisions of the 1986 Act are—

section 11(1) (undischarged bankrupts);

section 12(2) (failure to pay under county court administration order);

section 12A (Northern Irish disqualification orders);

section 12B (Northern Irish disqualification undertakings).

182 Records of persons removed from office

(1) For the purposes of sections 178 to 181 the Commission must keep, in such manner as it thinks fit, a register of all persons who have been removed from office as mentioned in Case D—

(a) by an order of the Commission or the Commissioners made before or after the commencement of section 178(1), or

(b) by an order of the High Court made after the commencement of section 45(1) of the Charities Act 1992;

and, where any person is so removed from office by an order of the High Court, the court must notify the Commission of the person's removal.

(2) The entries in the register kept under subsection (1) must be available for public inspection in legible form at all reasonable times.

(3) In this section "the Commissioners" means the Charity Commissioners for England and Wales.

183 Criminal consequences of acting while disqualified

(1) Subject to subsection (2), it is an offence for any person to act as a charity trustee or trustee for a charity while disqualified from being such a trustee by virtue of section 178.

(2) Subsection (1) does not apply if—

(a) the charity concerned is a company, and

(b) the disqualified person is disqualified by virtue only of Case B or F.

(3) A person guilty of an offence under subsection (1) is liable—

(a) on summary conviction, to imprisonment for a term not exceeding 12 months or to a fine not exceeding the statutory maximum, or both;

(b) on conviction on indictment, to imprisonment for a term not exceeding 2 years or to a fine, or both.

184 Civil consequences of acting while disqualified

(1) Any acts done as charity trustee or trustee for a charity by a person disqualified from being such a trustee by virtue of section 178 are not invalid merely because of that disqualification.

(2) Subsection (3) applies if the Commission is satisfied that any person—

(a) has acted as charity trustee or trustee for a charity while disqualified from being such a trustee by virtue of section 178, and

(b) while so acting, has received from the charity any sums by way of remuneration or expenses, or any benefit in kind, in connection with acting as charity trustee or trustee for the charity.

(3) The Commission may by order direct the person—

(a) to repay to the charity the whole or part of any such sums, or

(b) (as the case may be) to pay to the charity the whole or part of the monetary value (as determined by the Commission) of any such benefit.

(4) Subsection (3) does not apply to any sums received by way of remuneration or expenses in respect of any time when the person concerned was not disqualified from being a charity trustee or trustee for the charity.

Remuneration of charity trustees and trustees etc.

185 Remuneration of charity trustees or trustees etc. providing services to charity

(1) This section applies to remuneration for services provided by a person ("P") to or on behalf of a charity where—

(a) P is a charity trustee or trustee for the charity, or

(b) P is connected with a charity trustee or trustee for the charity and the remuneration might result in that trustee obtaining any benefit.

This is subject to subsection (3).

(2) If Conditions A to D are met in relation to remuneration within subsection (1), P is entitled to receive the remuneration out of the funds of the charity.

Condition A

Condition A is that the amount or maximum amount of the remuneration—

(a) is set out in an agreement in writing between the charity or its charity trustees (as the case may be) and P under which P is to provide the services in question to or on behalf of the charity, and

(b) does not exceed what is reasonable in the circumstances for the provision by P of the services in question.

Condition B

Condition B is that, before entering into that agreement, the charity trustees decided that they were satisfied that it would be in the best interests of the charity for the services to be provided by P to or on behalf of the charity for the amount or maximum amount of remuneration set out in the agreement.

Condition C

Condition C is that if immediately after the agreement is entered into there is, in the case of the charity, more than one person who is a charity trustee and is—

(a) a person in respect of whom an agreement within Condition A is in force,

(b) a person who is entitled to receive remuneration out of the funds of the charity otherwise than by virtue of such an agreement, or

(c) a person connected with a person falling within paragraph (a) or (b),

the total number of them constitute a minority of the persons for the time being holding office as charity trustees of the charity.

Condition D

Condition D is that the trusts of the charity do not contain any express provision that prohibits P from receiving the remuneration.

(3) Nothing in this section applies to—

(a) any remuneration for services provided by a person in the person's capacity as a charity trustee or trustee for a charity or under a contract of employment, or

(b) any remuneration not within paragraph (a) which a person is entitled to receive out of the funds of a charity by virtue of—

(i) any provision contained in the trusts of the charity;

(ii) any order of the court or the Commission;

(iii) any statutory provision contained in or having effect under an Act other than this section.

(4) Before entering into an agreement within Condition A the charity trustees must have regard to any guidance given by the Commission concerning the making of such agreements.

(5) The duty of care in section 1(1) of the Trustee Act 2000 applies to a charity trustee when making such a decision as is mentioned in Condition B.

(6) For the purposes of Condition C an agreement within Condition A is in force so long as any obligations under the agreement have not been fully discharged by a party to it.

(7) Sections 187 and 188 (interpretation) apply for the purposes of this section.

186 Disqualification of charity trustee or trustee receiving remuneration under s.185

(1) This section applies to any charity trustee or trustee for a charity—

(a) who is or would be entitled to remuneration under an agreement or proposed agreement within Condition A, or

(b) who is connected with a person who is or would be so entitled.

(2) The charity trustee or trustee for a charity is disqualified from acting as such in relation to any decision or other matter connected with the agreement.

(3) But if an act is done by a person who is disqualified from doing it by virtue of subsection (2), the act is not invalid merely because of that disqualification.

(4) If the Commission is satisfied—

(a) that a person ("P") has done any act which P was disqualified from doing by virtue of subsection (2), and

(b) that P or a person connected with P has received or is to receive from the charity any remuneration under the agreement in question,

it may make an order under subsection (5) or (6) (as appropriate).

(5) An order under this subsection is one requiring P—

(a) to reimburse to the charity the whole or part of the remuneration received as mentioned in subsection (4)(b);

(b) to the extent that the remuneration consists of a benefit in kind, to reimburse to the charity the whole or part of the monetary value (as determined by the Commission) of the benefit in kind.

(6) An order under this subsection is one directing that P or (as the case may be) the connected person is not to be paid the whole or part of the remuneration mentioned in subsection (4)(b).

(7) If the Commission makes an order under subsection (5) or (6), P or (as the case may be) the connected person accordingly ceases to have any entitlement under the agreement to so much of the remuneration (or its monetary value) as the order requires P to reimburse to the charity or (as the case may be) as it directs is not to be paid to P.

(8) Sections 187 and 188 (interpretation) apply for the purposes of this section.

187 Meaning of "benefit", "remuneration", "services" etc.

In sections 185 and 186—

"benefit" means a direct or indirect benefit of any nature;

"maximum amount", in relation to remuneration, means the maximum amount of the remuneration whether specified in or ascertainable under the terms of the agreement in question;

"remuneration" includes any benefit in kind (and "amount" accordingly includes monetary value);

"services", in the context of remuneration for services, includes goods that are supplied in connection with the provision of services.

188 Meaning of "connected person"

(1) For the purposes of sections 185 and 186, the following persons are connected with a charity trustee or trustee for a charity—

(a) a child, parent, grandchild, grandparent, brother or sister of the trustee;

(b) the spouse or civil partner of the trustee or of any person falling within paragraph (a);

(c) a person carrying on business in partnership with the trustee or with any person falling within paragraph (a) or (b);

(d) an institution which is controlled—

(i) by the trustee or by any person falling within paragraph (a), (b) or (c), or

(ii) by two or more persons falling within sub-paragraph (i), when taken together.

(e) a body corporate in which—

(i) the trustee or any connected person falling within any of paragraphs (a) to (c) has a substantial interest, or

(ii) two or more persons falling within sub-paragraph (i), when taken together, have a substantial interest.

(2) Sections 350 to 352 (meaning of child, spouse and civil partner, controlled institution and substantial interest) apply for the purposes of subsection (1).

Indemnity insurance for charity trustees and trustees

189 Indemnity insurance for charity trustees and trustees

(1) The charity trustees of a charity may arrange for the purchase, out of the funds of the charity, of insurance designed to indemnify the charity trustees or any trustees for the charity against any personal liability in respect of—

(a) any breach of trust or breach of duty committed by them in their capacity as charity trustees or trustees for the charity, or

(b) any negligence, default, breach of duty or breach of trust committed by them in their capacity as directors or officers of—

(i) the charity (if it is a body corporate), or

(ii) any body corporate carrying on any activities on behalf of the charity.

(2) But the terms of such insurance must be so framed as to exclude the provision of any indemnity for a person ("P") in respect of—

(a) any liability incurred by P to pay—

(i) a fine imposed in criminal proceedings, or

(ii) a sum payable to a regulatory authority by way of a penalty in respect of non-compliance with any requirement of a regulatory nature (however arising),

(b) any liability incurred by P in defending any criminal proceedings in which P is convicted of an offence arising out of any fraud or dishonesty, or wilful or reckless misconduct, by P, or

(c) any liability incurred by P to the charity that arises out of any conduct—

(i) which P knew (or must reasonably be assumed to have known) was not in the interests of the charity, or

(ii) in the case of which P did not care whether it was in the best interests of the charity or not.

(3) For the purposes of subsection (2)(b)—

(a) the reference to any such conviction is a reference to one that has become final,

(b) a conviction becomes final—

(i) if not appealed against, at the end of the period for bringing an appeal, or

(ii) if appealed against, at the time when the appeal (or any further appeal) is disposed of, and

(c) an appeal is disposed of—

(i) if it is determined and the period for bringing any further appeal has ended, or

(ii) if it is abandoned or otherwise ceases to have effect.

(4) The charity trustees of a charity may not purchase insurance under this section unless they decide that they are satisfied that it is in the best interests of the charity for them to do so.

(5) The duty of care in section 1(1) of the Trustee Act 2000 applies to a charity trustee when making such a decision.

(6) This section—

(a) does not authorise the purchase of any insurance whose purchase is expressly prohibited by the trusts of the charity, but

(b) has effect despite any provision prohibiting the charity trustees or trustees for the charity receiving any personal benefit out of the funds of the charity.

190 Power to amend s.189

The Minister may by order make such amendments of section 189(2) and (3) as the Minister considers appropriate.

Powers to relieve trustees and auditors etc. from liability

191 Commission's power to relieve trustees and auditors etc. from liability

(1) This section applies to a person ("P") who is or has been—

(a) a charity trustee or trustee for a charity,

(b) a person appointed to audit a charity's accounts (whether appointed under an enactment or otherwise), or

(c) an independent examiner or other person appointed to examine or report on a charity's accounts (whether appointed under an enactment or otherwise).

(2) If the Commission considers—

(a) that P is or may be personally liable for a breach of trust or breach of duty committed in P's capacity as a person within subsection (1)(a), (b) or (c), but

(b) that P has acted honestly and reasonably and ought fairly to be excused for the breach of trust or duty,

the Commission may make an order relieving P wholly or partly from any such liability.

(3) An order under subsection (2) may grant the relief on such terms as the Commission thinks fit.

(4) Subsection (2) does not apply in relation to any personal contractual liability of a charity trustee or trustee for a charity.

(5) For the purposes of this section and section 192—

(a) subsection (1)(b) is to be read as including a reference to the Auditor General for Wales acting as auditor under Part 8, and

(b) subsection (1)(c) is to be read as including a reference to the Auditor General for Wales acting as examiner under Part 8;

and in subsection (1)(b) and (c) any reference to a charity's accounts is to be read as including any group accounts prepared by the charity trustees of a charity.

(6) This section does not affect the operation of—

(a) section 61 of the Trustee Act 1925 (power of court to grant relief to trustees),
(b) section 1157 of the Companies Act 2006 (power of court to grant relief to officers or auditors of companies), or
(c) section 192 (which extends section 1157 to auditors etc. of charities which are not companies).

192 Court's power to grant relief to apply to all auditors etc. of charities which are not companies

(1) Section 1157 of the Companies Act 2006 (power of court to grant relief to officers or auditors of companies) has effect in relation to a person to whom this section applies as it has effect in relation to a person employed as an auditor by a company.

(2) This section applies to—
(a) a person acting in a capacity within section 191(1)(b) or (c) in a case where, apart from this section, section 1157 of the 2006 Act would not apply in relation to that person as a person so acting, and
(b) a charity trustee of a CIO.

PART 10

CHARITABLE COMPANIES ETC.

Introductory

193 Meaning of "charitable company"

In this Act "charitable company" means a charity which is a company.

Disclosure of charitable status by companies

194 Requirement to disclose charitable status

(1) Where a charitable company's name does not include the word "charity" or "charitable", the fact that the company is a charity must be stated in legible characters—
(a) in every location, and in every description of document or communication, in which it is required by regulations under section 82 of the Companies Act 2006 to state its registered name, and
(b) in all conveyances purporting to be executed by the company.

(2) Where a company's name includes the word "elusen" or "elusennol" (the Welsh equivalents of "charity" and "charitable"), subsection (1) does not apply in relation to any document that is wholly in Welsh.

(3) The statement required by subsection (1) must be in English, except that, in the case of a document that is otherwise wholly in Welsh, the statement may be in Welsh if it consists of or includes the word "elusen" or "elusennol".

(4) In subsection (1)(b) "conveyance" means any instrument creating, transferring, varying or extinguishing an interest in land.

195 Civil consequences of failure to make required disclosure

(1) This section applies to any legal proceedings brought by a charitable company to which section 194 applies to enforce a right arising out of a contract or conveyance in connection with which there was a failure to comply with that section.

(2) The proceedings must be dismissed if it is shown that the defendant to the proceedings—

(a) has a claim against the company arising out of the contract or conveyance that the defendant has been unable to pursue because of the company's failure to comply with section 194, or

(b) has suffered some financial loss in connection with the contract or conveyance because of the company's failure to comply with that section,

unless the court before which the proceedings are brought is satisfied that it is just and equitable to permit the proceedings to continue.

(3) This section does not affect the right of any person to enforce such rights as that person may have against another in any proceedings brought by the other.

196 Criminal consequences of failure to make required disclosure

(1) Where a charitable company fails, without reasonable excuse, to comply with section 194, an offence is committed by—

(a) the company, and

(b) every officer of the company who is in default.

(2) For this purpose a shadow director of the company is treated as an officer of the company if the failure is to comply with section 194(1)(a) and that person would be treated as an officer of the company for the purposes of the corresponding requirement of regulations under section 82 of the Companies Act 2006.

(3) A person guilty of such an offence is liable on summary conviction to a fine not exceeding level 3 on the standard scale and, for continued contravention, a daily default fine not exceeding 10% of level 3 on the standard scale.

(4) Expressions used in this section have the same meaning as in section 84 of the Companies Act 2006 (criminal consequences of failure to disclose company's registered name).

Restrictions on alteration of objects

197 Alteration of objects by bodies corporate and charitable status

(1) Subsection (2) applies where a charity—

(a) is a company or other body corporate, and

(b) has power to alter the instruments establishing or regulating it as a body corporate.

(2) No exercise of the power which has the effect of the body ceasing to be a charity is valid so as to affect the application of—

(a) any property acquired under any disposition or agreement previously made otherwise than for full consideration in money or money's worth, or any property representing property so acquired,

(b) any property representing income which has accrued before the alteration is made, or

(c) the income from any such property.

198 Alteration of objects by companies and Commission's consent

(1) Any regulated alteration by a charitable company—

(a) requires the prior written consent of the Commission, and

(b) is ineffective if such consent has not been obtained.

(2) The following are regulated alterations—

(a) an amendment of the company's articles of association adding, removing or altering a statement of the company's objects,

(b) any alteration of any provision of its articles of association directing the application of property of the company on its dissolution, and

(c) any alteration of any provision of its articles of association where the alteration would provide authorisation for any benefit to be obtained by directors or members of the company or persons connected with them.

(3) Where a company that has made a regulated alteration in accordance with subsection (1) is required—

(a) by section 26 of the Companies Act 2006 to send to the registrar of companies a copy of its articles as amended,

(b) by section 30 of that Act to forward to the registrar a copy of the special resolution effecting the alteration, or

(c) by section 31 of that Act to give notice to the registrar of the amendment,

the copy or notice must be accompanied by a copy of the Commission's consent.

(4) If more than one of those provisions applies and they are complied with at different times, the company need not send a further copy of the Commission's consent if a copy was sent on an earlier occasion.

(5) Subsections (2) to (4) of section 30 of that Act (offence of failing to comply with section 30) apply in relation to a failure to comply with subsection (3) as in relation to a failure to comply with that section.

199 Meaning of "benefit" in s.198(2)

For the purposes of section 198(2)(c) "benefit" means a direct or indirect benefit of any nature, except that it does not include any remuneration (within the meaning of section 185) whose receipt may be authorised under that section.

200 Meaning of "connected person" in s.198(2)

(1) For the purposes of section 198(2)(c), the following persons are connected with a director or member of a charitable company—

(a) a child, parent, grandchild, grandparent, brother or sister of the director or member;

(b) the spouse or civil partner of the director or member or of any person falling within paragraph (a);

(c) a person carrying on business in partnership with the director or member or with any person falling within paragraph (a) or (b);

(d) an institution which is controlled—

(i) by the director or member or by any person falling within paragraph (a), (b) or (c), or

(ii) by two or more persons falling within sub-paragraph (i), when taken together.

(e) a body corporate in which—

(i) the director or member or any connected person falling within any of paragraphs (a) to (c) has a substantial interest, or

(ii) two or more persons falling within sub-paragraph (i), when taken together, have a substantial interest.

(2) Sections 350 to 352 (meaning of child, spouse, civil partner, controlled institution and substantial interest) apply for the purposes of subsection (1).

Acts requiring Commission consent

201 Consent of Commission required for approval etc. by members of charitable companies

(1) In the case of a charitable company, each of the following is ineffective without the prior written consent of the Commission—

(a) any approval given by the members of the company under any provision of Chapter 4 of Part 10 of the Companies Act 2006 (transactions with directors requiring approval by members) listed in subsection (2), and

(b) any affirmation given by members of the company under section 196 or 214 of the 2006 Act (affirmation of unapproved property transactions and loans).

(2) The provisions of the 2006 Act are—

(a) section 188 (directors' long-term service contracts);

(b) section 190 (substantial property transactions with directors etc.);

(c) section 197, 198 or 200 (loans and quasi-loans to directors etc.);

(d) section 201 (credit transactions for benefit of directors etc.);

(e) section 203 (related arrangements);

(f) section 217 (payments to directors for loss of office);

(g) section 218 (payments to directors for loss of office: transfer of undertaking etc.).

202 Consent of Commission required for certain acts of charitable company

(1) A charitable company may not do an act to which this section applies without the prior written consent of the Commission.

(2) This section applies to an act that—

(a) does not require approval under a listed provision of Chapter 4 of Part 10 of the Companies Act 2006 (transactions with directors) by the members of the company, but

(b) would require such approval but for an exemption in the provision in question that disapplies the need for approval on the part of the members of a body corporate which is a wholly-owned subsidiary of another body corporate.

(3) The reference to a listed provision is a reference to a provision listed in section 201(2).

(4) If a company acts in contravention of this section, the exemption referred to in subsection (2)(b) is to be treated as being of no effect in relation to the act.

Restoration of charitable company to register

203 Application for restoration of charitable company to register

(1) The Commission may make an application under section 1029 of the Companies Act 2006 (application to court for restoration to the register of companies) to restore a charitable company to the register of companies.

(2) The power exercisable by the Commission by virtue of this section is exercisable—

(a) by the Commission of its own motion, but

(b) only with the agreement of the Attorney General on each occasion.

PART 11

CHARITABLE INCORPORATED ORGANISATIONS (CIOS)

CHAPTER 1

GENERAL

Nature and constitution

204 Meaning of "CIO"

In this Act "CIO" means charitable incorporated organisation.

205 Nature

(1) A CIO is a body corporate.

(2) A CIO must have—

(a) a constitution;

(b) a principal office, which must be in England or in Wales;

(c) one or more members.

(3) The members may be—

(a) not liable to contribute to the assets of the CIO if it is wound up, or

(b) liable to do so up to a maximum amount each.

206 Constitution

(1) A CIO's constitution must state—
(a) its name,
(b) its purposes,
(c) whether its principal office is in England or in Wales, and
(d) whether or not its members are liable to contribute to its assets if it is wound up, and (if they are) up to what amount.

(2) A CIO's constitution must make provision—
(a) about who is eligible for membership, and how a person becomes a member,
(b) about the appointment of one or more persons who are to be charity trustees of the CIO, and about any conditions of eligibility for appointment, and
(c) containing directions about the application of property of the CIO on its dissolution.

(3) A CIO's constitution must also provide for such other matters, and comply with such requirements, as are specified in CIO regulations.

(4) A CIO's constitution—
(a) must be in English if its principal office is in England;
(b) may be in English or in Welsh if its principal office is in Wales.

(5) A CIO's constitution must be in the form specified in regulations made by the Commission, or as near to that form as the circumstances admit.

(6) Subject to anything in a CIO's constitution—
(a) a charity trustee of the CIO may, but need not, be a member of it,
(b) a member of the CIO may, but need not, be one of its charity trustees, and
(c) those who are members of the CIO and those who are its charity trustees may, but need not, be identical.

Formation and registration of CIO

207 Application for CIO to be constituted and registered

(1) Any one or more persons ("the applicants") may apply to the Commission for a CIO to be constituted and for its registration as a charity.

(2) The applicants must supply the Commission with—
(a) a copy of the proposed constitution of the CIO,
(b) such other documents or information as may be prescribed by CIO regulations, and
(c) such other documents or information as the Commission may require for the purposes of the application.

208 Cases where application must or may be refused

(1) The Commission must refuse an application under section 207 if—

(a) it is not satisfied that the CIO would be a charity at the time it would be registered, or

(b) the CIO's proposed constitution does not comply with one or more of the requirements of section 206 (constitution of CIOs) and any regulations made under that section.

(2) The Commission may refuse such an application if—

(a) the proposed name of the CIO—

(i) is the same as, or

(ii) is in the opinion of the Commission too like,

the name of any other charity (whether registered or not), or

(b) the Commission is of the opinion referred to in any of paragraphs (b) to (e) of section 42(2) (power to require charity's name to be changed) in relation to the proposed name of the CIO (reading paragraph (b) as referring to the proposed purposes of the CIO and to the activities which it is proposed it should carry on).

209 Registration of CIO

(1) If the Commission grants an application under section 207 it must register the CIO to which the application relates as a charity in the register of charities.

(2) The entry relating to the charity's registration in the register of charities must include—

(a) the date of the charity's registration, and

(b) a note saying that it is constituted as a CIO.

(3) A copy of the entry in the register must be sent to the charity at the principal office of the CIO.

210 Effect of registration of CIO

(1) Upon the registration of the CIO in the register of charities, it becomes by virtue of the registration a body corporate—

(a) whose constitution is that proposed in the application,

(b) whose name is that specified in the constitution, and

(c) whose first member is, or first members are, the applicants referred to in section 207.

(2) All property for the time being vested in the applicants (or, if more than one, any of them) on trust for the charitable purposes of the CIO (when incorporated) by virtue of this subsection becomes vested in the CIO upon its registration.

Name and status

211 Name

(1) The name of a CIO must appear in legible characters—

(a) in every location, and in every description of document or communication, in which a charitable company would be required by regulations under section 82 of the Companies Act 2006 to state its registered name, and

(b) in all conveyances purporting to be executed by the CIO.

(2) In subsection (1)(b), "conveyance" means any instrument creating, transferring, varying or extinguishing an interest in land.

212 Status

(1) Subsection (3) applies if the name of a CIO does not include—

- (a) "charitable incorporated organisation",
- (b) "CIO", with or without full stops after each letter, or
- (c) a Welsh equivalent mentioned in subsection (2) (but this option applies only if the CIO's constitution is in Welsh),

and it is irrelevant, in any such case, whether or not capital letters are used.

(2) The Welsh equivalents referred to in subsection (1)(c) are—

- (a) "sefydliad elusennol corfforedig", or
- (b) "SEC", with or without full stops after each letter.

(3) If this subsection applies, the fact that a CIO is a CIO must be stated in legible characters in all the locations, documents, communications and conveyances mentioned in section 211(1).

(4) The statement required by subsection (3) must be in English, except that in the case of a document which is otherwise wholly in Welsh, the statement may be in Welsh.

213 Civil consequences of failure to disclose name or status

(1) This section applies to any legal proceedings brought by a CIO to enforce a right arising out of a contract or conveyance in connection with which there was a failure to comply with section 211 or 212.

(2) The proceedings must be dismissed if it is shown that the defendant to the proceedings—

- (a) has a claim against the CIO arising out of the contract or conveyance that the defendant has been unable to pursue because of the failure to comply with section 211 or 212, or
- (b) has suffered some financial loss in connection with the contract or conveyance because of the failure to comply with section 211 or 212,

unless the court before which the proceedings are brought is satisfied that it is just and equitable to permit the proceedings to continue.

(3) This section does not affect the right of any person to enforce such rights as that person may have against another in any proceedings brought by the other.

214 Offence of failing to disclose name or status

(1) In the case of failure, without reasonable excuse, to comply with section 211 or 212 an offence is committed by—

- (a) every charity trustee of the CIO who is in default, and
- (b) any other person who on the CIO's behalf—
  - (i) signs or authorises the signing of the offending document, communication or conveyance, or
  - (ii) otherwise commits or authorises the offending act or omission.

(2) A person guilty of an offence under subsection (1) is liable on summary conviction to a fine not exceeding level 3 on the standard scale and, for continued contravention, a daily default fine not exceeding 10% of level 3 on the standard scale.

(3) The reference in subsection (1) to a charity trustee being in default, and the reference in subsection (2) to a daily default fine, have the same meaning as in the Companies Acts (see sections 1121 to 1123 and 1125 of the Companies Act 2006).

215 Offence of holding out that a body is a CIO

(1) It is an offence for a person (in whatever way) to hold any body out as being a CIO when it is not.

(2) It is a defence where a person is charged with an offence under subsection (1) to prove that the person believed on reasonable grounds that the body was a CIO.

(3) A person guilty of an offence under subsection (1) is liable on summary conviction to a fine not exceeding level 3 on the standard scale.

CHAPTER 2

POWERS, CAPACITY AND PROCEDURE ETC.

216 Powers of CIO

(1) Subject to anything in its constitution, a CIO may do anything which is calculated to further its purposes or is conducive or incidental to doing so.

(2) The CIO's charity trustees are to manage the affairs of the CIO and may for that purpose exercise all the powers of the CIO.

217 Constitutional requirements

(1) A CIO must use and apply its property in furtherance of its purposes and in accordance with its constitution.

(2) If the CIO is one whose members are liable to contribute to its assets if it is wound up, its constitution binds the CIO and its members for the time being to the same extent as if its provisions were contained in a contract—
  (a) to which the CIO and each of its members was a party, and
  (b) which contained obligations on the part of the CIO and each member to observe all the provisions of the constitution.

(3) Money payable by a member to the CIO under the constitution is a debt due from that member to the CIO, and is of the nature of an ordinary contract debt.

218 Third parties

(1) Subject to subsection (3), the validity of an act done (or purportedly done) by a CIO is not to be called into question on the ground that the CIO lacked constitutional capacity.

(2) Subject to subsection (3), the power of the charity trustees of a CIO to act so as to bind the CIO (or authorise others to do so) is not to be called into question on the ground of any constitutional limitations on their powers.

(3) Subsections (1) and (2) apply only in favour of a person who gives full consideration in money or money's worth in relation to the act in question, and does not know—

(a) in a subsection (1) case, that the act is beyond the CIO's constitutional capacity, or

(b) in a subsection (2) case, that the act is beyond the constitutional powers of its charity trustees,

and (in addition) subsection (2) applies only if the person dealt with the CIO in good faith (which the person is presumed to have done unless the contrary is proved).

(4) A party to an arrangement or transaction with a CIO is not bound to inquire—

(a) whether it is within the CIO's constitutional capacity, or

(b) as to any constitutional limitations on the powers of its charity trustees to bind the CIO or authorise others to do so.

(5) If a CIO purports to transfer or grant an interest in property, the fact—

(a) that the act was beyond its constitutional capacity, or

(b) that its charity trustees in connection with the act exceeded their constitutional powers,

does not affect the title of a person who subsequently acquires the property or any interest in it for full consideration without actual notice of any such circumstances affecting the validity of the CIO's act.

(6) In any proceedings arising out of subsections (1) to (3), the burden of proving that a person knew that an act—

(a) was beyond the CIO's constitutional capacity, or

(b) was beyond the constitutional powers of its charity trustees,

lies on the person making that allegation.

(7) In this section and section 219—

(a) references to a CIO's lack of constitutional capacity are to lack of capacity because of anything in its constitution, and

(b) references to constitutional limitations on the powers of a CIO's charity trustees are to limitations on their powers under its constitution, including limitations deriving from a resolution of the CIO in general meeting, or from an agreement between the CIO's members, and the references to constitutional powers are to be read accordingly.

219 Limits to s.218

(1) Nothing in section 218 prevents a person from bringing proceedings to restrain the doing of an act which would be—

(a) beyond the CIO's constitutional capacity, or

(b) beyond the constitutional powers of the CIO's charity trustees.

(2) But no such proceedings may be brought in respect of an act to be done in fulfilment of a legal obligation arising from a previous act of the CIO.

(3) Subsection (2) does not prevent the Commission from exercising any of its powers.

(4) Nothing in section 218(2) affects any liability incurred by the CIO's charity trustees (or any one of them) for acting beyond their (or that charity trustee's) constitutional powers.

(5) Nothing in section 218 absolves the CIO's charity trustees from their duty to act within the CIO's constitution and in accordance with any constitutional limitations on their powers.

220 Duty of CIO members

Each member of a CIO must exercise the powers that the member has in that capacity in the way that the member decides, in good faith, would be most likely to further the purposes of the CIO.

221 Duties of charity trustees

(1) Each charity trustee of a CIO must exercise the powers and perform the functions that the charity trustee has in that capacity in the way that the charity trustee decides, in good faith, would be most likely to further the purposes of the CIO.

(2) Each charity trustee of a CIO must in the performance of functions in that capacity exercise such care and skill as is reasonable in the circumstances, having regard in particular—

(a) to any special knowledge or experience that the charity trustee has or purports to have, and

(b) if the charity trustee acts as such in the course of a business or profession, to any special knowledge or experience that it is reasonable to expect of a person acting in the course of that kind of business or profession.

But this is subject to any provision of a CIO's constitution permitted by virtue of regulations made under subsection (3).

(3) CIO regulations may permit a CIO's constitution to provide that the duty in subsection (2)—

(a) does not apply, or

(b) does not apply in so far as is specified in the constitution.

(4) Regulations under subsection (3) may provide for limits on the extent to which, or the cases in which, a CIO's constitution may disapply the duty in subsection (2).

222 Personal benefit and payments

(1) A charity trustee of a CIO may not benefit personally from an arrangement or transaction entered into by the CIO if, before the arrangement or transaction was entered into, the charity trustee did not disclose to all the charity trustees of the CIO any material interest (whether direct or indirect) which the charity trustee had in it or in any other person or body party to it.

(2) Nothing in subsection (1) confers authority for a charity trustee of a CIO to benefit personally from any arrangement or transaction entered into by the CIO.

(3) A charity trustee of a CIO—

(a) is entitled to be reimbursed by the CIO, or

(b) may pay out of the CIO's funds,

expenses properly incurred by the charity trustee in the performance of that charity trustee's functions as such.

223 Regulations about procedure of CIOs

(1) CIO regulations may make provision about the procedure of CIOs.

(2) Subject to—

(a) any such regulations,

(b) any other requirement imposed by or by virtue of this Act or any other enactment, and

(c) anything in the CIO's constitution,

a CIO may regulate its own procedure.

(3) But a CIO's procedure must include provision for the holding of a general meeting of its members, and the regulations referred to in subsection (1) may in particular make provision about such meetings.

CHAPTER 3

AMENDMENT OF CONSTITUTION

224 Amendment of constitution and procedure

(1) A CIO may by resolution of its members amend its constitution (and a single resolution may provide for more than one amendment).

(2) Such a resolution must be passed—

(a) by a 75% majority of those voting at a general meeting of the CIO (including those voting by proxy or by post, if voting that way is permitted), or

(b) unanimously by the CIO's members, otherwise than at a general meeting.

(3) The date of passing of such a resolution is—

(a) the date of the general meeting at which it was passed, or

(b) if it was passed otherwise than at a general meeting, the date on which provision in the CIO's constitution or in regulations made under section 223 treats it as having been passed (but that date may not be earlier than that on which the last member agreed to it).

225 Amendment of constitution and charitable status

The power of a CIO to amend its constitution is not exercisable in any way which would result in the CIO's ceasing to be a charity.

226 Amendment of constitution and Commission's consent

(1) Subject to section 227(5), a resolution containing an amendment which would make any regulated alteration is to that extent ineffective unless the prior written consent of the Commission has been obtained to the making of the amendment.

(2) The following are regulated alterations—

(a) any alteration of the CIO's purposes,

(b) any alteration of any provision of the CIO's constitution directing the application of property of the CIO on its dissolution, and

(c) any alteration of any provision of the CIO's constitution where the alteration would provide authorisation for any benefit to be obtained by charity trustees or members of the CIO or persons connected with them.

(3) Sections 248 (meaning of "benefit") and 249 (meaning of "connected person") apply for the purposes of this section.

227 Registration and coming into effect of amendments

(1) A CIO must send to the Commission a copy of a resolution containing an amendment to its constitution, together with—

(a) a copy of the constitution as amended, and

(b) such other documents and information as the Commission may require,

by the end of the period of 15 days beginning with the date of passing of the resolution (see section 224(3)).

(2) An amendment to a CIO's constitution does not take effect until it has been registered.

(3) The Commission must refuse to register an amendment if—

(a) in the opinion of the Commission the CIO had no power to make it (for example, because the effect of making it would be that the CIO ceased to be a charity, or that the CIO or its constitution did not comply with any requirement imposed by or by virtue of this Act or any other enactment), or

(b) the amendment would change the name of the CIO, and the Commission could have refused an application under section 207 for the constitution and registration of a CIO with the name specified in the amendment on a ground set out in section 208(2).

(4) The Commission may refuse to register an amendment if—

(a) the amendment would make a regulated alteration, and

(b) the consent referred to in section 226(1) had not been obtained.

(5) But if the Commission does register such an amendment, section 226(1) does not apply.

CHAPTER 4

CONVERSION, AMALGAMATION AND TRANSFER

Conversion of certain bodies to CIO

228 Application for conversion by charitable company

(1) A charitable company may apply to the Commission to be converted into a CIO, and for the CIO's registration as a charity, in accordance with this section.

(2) But such an application may not be made by—

(a) a company having a share capital if any of the shares are not fully paid up, or
(b) an exempt charity.

(3) The company must supply the Commission with—
(a) a copy of a resolution of the company that it be converted into a CIO,
(b) a copy of the proposed constitution of the CIO,
(c) a copy of a resolution of the company adopting the proposed constitution of the CIO,
(d) such other documents or information as may be prescribed by CIO regulations, and
(e) such other documents or information as the Commission may require for the purposes of the application.

(4) The resolution referred to in subsection (3)(a) must be—
(a) a special resolution of the company, or
(b) a unanimous written resolution signed by or on behalf of all the members of the company who would be entitled to vote on a special resolution.

(5) Chapter 3 of Part 3 of the Companies Act 2006 (resolutions and agreements affecting a company's constitution) does not apply to such a resolution.

(6) In the case of a company limited by guarantee which makes an application under this section (whether or not it also has a share capital), the proposed constitution of the CIO must (unless subsection (8) applies) provide—
(a) for the CIO's members to be liable to contribute to its assets if it is wound up, and
(b) for the amount up to which they are so liable.

(7) That amount must not be less than the amount up to which they were liable to contribute to the assets of the company if it was wound up.

(8) If the amount each member of the company is liable to contribute to its assets on its winding up is £10 or less—
(a) the guarantee is extinguished on the conversion of the company into a CIO, and
(b) the requirements of subsections (6) and (7) do not apply.

229 Application for conversion by registered society

(1) A charity which is a registered society may apply to the Commission to be converted into a CIO, and for the CIO's registration as a charity, in accordance with this section.

"Registered society" has the same meaning as in the Co-operative and Community Benefit Societies and Credit Unions Act 1965.

(2) But such an application may not be made by—
(a) a registered society having a share capital if any of the shares are not fully paid up, or
(b) an exempt charity.

(3) The registered society must supply the Commission with—
(a) a copy of a resolution of the registered society that it be converted into a CIO,
(b) a copy of the proposed constitution of the CIO,

(c) a copy of a resolution of the registered society adopting the proposed constitution of the CIO,

(d) such other documents or information as may be prescribed by CIO regulations, and

(e) such other documents or information as the Commission may require for the purposes of the application.

(4) The resolution referred to in subsection (3)(a) must be—

(a) a special resolution of the registered society, or

(b) a unanimous written resolution signed by or on behalf of all the members of the registered society who would be entitled to vote on a special resolution.

(5) In subsection (4), "special resolution" has the meaning given in section 52(3) of the Co-operative and Community Benefit Societies and Credit Unions Act 1965.

230 Commission to consult appropriate registrar and others

(1) The Commission must notify the following of an application for conversion—

(a) the appropriate registrar, and

(b) such other persons (if any) as the Commission thinks appropriate in the particular case,

and must consult those notified about whether the application should be granted.

(2) In subsection (1) and sections 231 to 233, "the appropriate registrar" means—

(a) in the case of an application by a charitable company, the registrar of companies;

(b) in the case of an application by a registered society, the Financial Services Authority.

(3) In this section and sections 231 to 233, "application for conversion" means an application under section 228 or 229.

231 Cases where application must or may be refused

(1) The Commission must refuse an application for conversion if—

(a) it is not satisfied that the CIO would be a charity at the time it would be registered,

(b) the CIO's proposed constitution does not comply with one or more of the requirements of section 206 (constitution of CIOs) and any regulations made under that section, or

(c) in the case of an application for conversion made by a company limited by guarantee, the CIO's proposed constitution does not comply with the requirements of section 228(6) and (7).

(2) The Commission may refuse an application for conversion if—

(a) the proposed name of the CIO—

(i) is the same as, or

(ii) is in the opinion of the Commission too like,

the name of any other charity (whether registered or not),

(b) the Commission is of the opinion referred to in any of paragraphs (b) to (e) of section 42(2) (power to require charity's name to be changed) in relation to the proposed name of the CIO (reading paragraph (b) as referring to the proposed purposes of the CIO and to the activities which it is proposed it should carry on), or

(c) having considered any representations received from those whom it has consulted under section 230(1), the Commission considers (having regard to any regulations made under subsection (3)) that it would not be appropriate to grant the application.

(3) CIO regulations may make provision about circumstances in which it would not be appropriate to grant an application for conversion.

(4) If the Commission refuses an application for conversion, it must so notify the appropriate registrar.

232 Provisional and final registration of converting body

(1) If the Commission grants an application for conversion, it must—

(a) register the CIO to which the application related in the register of charities, and

(b) send to the appropriate registrar a copy of—

(i) each of the relevant resolutions of the converting company or registered society, and

(ii) the entry in the register relating to the CIO.

(2) In subsection (1)(b), "the relevant resolutions" means—

(a) in the case of a converting company, the resolutions referred to in section 228(3)(a) and (c), and

(b) in the case of a converting society, the resolutions referred to in section 229(3)(a) and (c).

(3) The registration of the CIO in the register is provisional only until the appropriate registrar cancels the registration of the company or society as required by subsection (4)(b).

(4) The appropriate registrar must—

(a) register the documents sent under subsection (1)(b), and

(b) cancel the registration of the company in the register of companies, or of the society in the mutual societies register,

and must notify the Commission that this action has been taken.

(5) The entry relating to the charity's registration in the register must include—

(a) a note that it is constituted as a CIO,

(b) the date on which it became so constituted, and

(c) a note of the name of the company or society which was converted into the CIO.

(6) But the matters mentioned in subsections (5)(a) and (b) are to be included only when the appropriate registrar has notified the Commission as required by subsection (4).

(7) A copy of the entry in the register must be sent to the charity at the principal office of the CIO.

233 Effect of registration becoming final

(1) Upon the cancellation by the appropriate registrar of the registration of the company or of the registered society, the company or society is converted into a CIO, a body corporate—

(a) whose constitution is that proposed in the application for conversion,

(b) whose name is that specified in the constitution, and

(c) whose first members are the members of the converting company or society immediately before the moment of conversion.

(2) If the converting company or society had a share capital—

(a) upon the conversion of the company or society all the shares are by virtue of this subsection cancelled, and

(b) no former holder of any cancelled share has any right in respect of it after its cancellation.

(3) Subsection (2) does not affect any right which accrued in respect of a share before its cancellation.

(4) The conversion of a company or society into a CIO does not affect, in particular, any liability to which the company or society was subject by virtue of its being a charitable company or registered society.

234 Conversion of community interest company

(1) CIO regulations may make provision for—

(a) the conversion of a community interest company into a CIO, and

(b) the CIO's registration as a charity.

(2) The regulations may, in particular, apply, or apply with modifications specified in the regulations, or disapply, anything in—

(a) sections 53 to 55 of the Companies (Audit, Investigations and Community Enterprise) Act 2004, or

(b) sections 228 to 233.

Amalgamation of CIOs

235 Application for amalgamation of CIOs

(1) Any two or more CIOs ("the old CIOs") may, in accordance with this section, apply to the Commission to be amalgamated, and for the incorporation and registration as a charity of a new CIO ("the new CIO") as their successor.

(2) The old CIOs must supply the Commission with—

(a) a copy of the proposed constitution of the new CIO,

(b) such other documents or information as may be prescribed by CIO regulations, and

(c) such other documents or information as the Commission may require for the purposes of the application.

(3) In addition to the documents and information referred to in subsection (2), the old CIOs must supply the Commission with—

(a) a copy of a resolution of each of the old CIOs approving the proposed amalgamation, and

(b) a copy of a resolution of each of the old CIOs adopting the proposed constitution of the new CIO.

(4) The resolutions referred to in subsection (3) must have been passed—

(a) by a 75% majority of those voting at a general meeting of the CIO (including those voting by proxy or by post, if voting that way is permitted), or

(b) unanimously by the CIO's members, otherwise than at a general meeting.

(5) The date of passing of such a resolution is—

(a) the date of the general meeting at which it was passed, or

(b) if it was passed otherwise than at a general meeting, the date on which provision in the CIO's constitution or in regulations made under section 223 treats it as having been passed (but that date may not be earlier than that on which the last member agreed to it).

236 Notice of application for amalgamation

(1) Each old CIO must—

(a) give notice of the proposed amalgamation in the way (or ways) that in the opinion of its charity trustees will make it most likely to come to the attention of those who would be affected by the amalgamation, and

(b) send a copy of the notice to the Commission.

(2) The notice must invite any persons who consider that they would be affected by the proposed amalgamation to make written representations to the Commission no later than a date determined by the Commission and specified in the notice.

237 Cases where application must or may be refused

(1) The Commission must refuse an application for amalgamation if—

(a) it is not satisfied that the new CIO would be a charity at the time it would be registered, or

(b) the new CIO's proposed constitution does not comply with one or more of the requirements of section 206 and any regulations made under that section.

(2) In addition to being required to refuse it on one of the grounds mentioned in subsection (1), the Commission must refuse an application for amalgamation if it considers that there is a serious risk that the new CIO would be unable properly to pursue its purposes.

(3) The Commission may refuse an application for amalgamation if—

(a) the proposed name of the new CIO—

(i) is the same as, or

(ii) is in the opinion of the Commission too like,

the name of any other charity (whether registered or not), or

(b) the Commission is of the opinion referred to in any of paragraphs (b) to (e) of section 42(2) (power to require charity's name to be changed) in relation to the proposed name of the new CIO (reading paragraph (b) as referring to the proposed purposes of the new CIO and to the activities which it is proposed it should carry on).

(4) The Commission may refuse an application for amalgamation if it is not satisfied that the provision in the constitution of the new CIO about the matters mentioned in subsection (5) is—

(a) the same, or

(b) substantially the same,

as the provision about those matters in the constitutions of each of the old CIOs.

(5) The matters are—

(a) the purposes of the CIO,

(b) the application of property of the CIO on its dissolution, and

(c) authorisation for any benefit to be obtained by charity trustees or members of the CIO or persons connected with them.

(6) Sections 248 (meaning of "benefit") and 249 (meaning of "connected person") apply for the purposes of this section.

(7) In this section and sections 238 and 239, "application for amalgamation" means an application under section 235.

238 Registration of amalgamated CIO

(1) If the Commission grants an application for amalgamation, it must register the new CIO in the register of charities.

(2) The entry relating to the registration in the register of the charity constituted as the new CIO must include—

(a) a note that it is constituted as a CIO,

(b) the date of the charity's registration, and

(c) a note that the CIO was formed following amalgamation, and of the name of each of the old CIOs.

(3) A copy of the entry in the register must be sent to the charity at the principal office of the new CIO.

239 Effect of registration

(1) Upon the registration of the new CIO it becomes by virtue of the registration a body corporate—

(a) whose constitution is that proposed in the application for amalgamation,

(b) whose name is that specified in the constitution, and

(c) whose first members are the members of the old CIOs immediately before the new CIO was registered.

(2) Upon the registration of the new CIO—

(a) all the property, rights and liabilities of each of the old CIOs become by virtue of this subsection the property, rights and liabilities of the new CIO, and

(b) each of the old CIOs is dissolved.

(3) Any gift which—

(a) is expressed as a gift to one of the old CIOs, and

(b) takes effect on or after the date of registration of the new CIO, takes effect as a gift to the new CIO.

Transfer of CIO's undertaking to another CIO

240 Resolutions about transfer of CIO's undertaking to another CIO

(1) A CIO may resolve that all its property, rights and liabilities should be transferred to another CIO specified in the resolution.

(2) Where a CIO has passed such a resolution, it must send to the Commission—
 (a) a copy of the resolution, and
 (b) a copy of a resolution of the transferee CIO agreeing to the transfer to it.

(3) The resolutions referred to in subsections (1) and (2)(b) must have been passed—
 (a) by a 75% majority of those voting at a general meeting of the CIO (including those voting by proxy or by post, if voting that way is permitted), or
 (b) unanimously by the CIO's members, otherwise than at a general meeting.

(4) The date of passing of such a resolution is—
 (a) the date of the general meeting at which it was passed, or
 (b) if it was passed otherwise than at a general meeting, the date on which provision in the CIO's constitution or in regulations made under section 223 treats it as having been passed (but that date may not be earlier than that on which the last member agreed to it).

(5) The resolution of the transferor CIO does not take effect until confirmed by the Commission.

241 Notice of transfer of CIO's undertaking to another CIO

Having received the copy resolutions referred to in section 240(2), the Commission—
 (a) may direct the transferor CIO to give public notice of its resolution in such manner as is specified in the direction, and
 (b) if it gives such a direction, must take into account any representations made to it by persons appearing to it to be interested in the transferor CIO, where those representations are made to it within the period of 28 days beginning with the date when public notice of the resolution is given by the transferor CIO.

242 Cases where confirmation of resolution must or may be refused

(1) The Commission must refuse to confirm the resolution of the transferor CIO if it considers that there is a serious risk that the transferee CIO would be unable properly to pursue the purposes of the transferor CIO.

(2) The Commission may refuse to confirm the resolution if it is not satisfied that the provision in the constitution of the transferee CIO about the matters mentioned in subsection (3) is—
 (a) the same, or
 (b) substantially the same,

as the provision about those matters in the constitution of the transferor CIO.

(3) The matters are—

(a) the purposes of the CIO,

(b) the application of property of the CIO on its dissolution, and

(c) authorisation for any benefit to be obtained by charity trustees or members of the CIO or persons connected with them.

(4) Sections 248 (meaning of "benefit") and 249 (meaning of "connected person") apply for the purposes of this section.

243 Confirmation of resolution

(1) If the Commission does not notify the transferor CIO within the relevant period that it is either confirming or refusing to confirm the transferor CIO's resolution, the resolution is to be treated as confirmed by the Commission on the day after the end of that period.

(2) Subject to subsection (3), "the relevant period" means—

(a) if the Commission directs the transferor CIO under section 241 to give public notice of its resolution, the period of 6 months beginning with the date when that notice is given, or

(b) otherwise, the period of 6 months beginning with the date when both of the copy resolutions referred to in section 240(2) have been received by the Commission.

(3) The Commission may at any time within the period of 6 months mentioned in subsection (2)(a) or (b) give the transferor CIO a notice extending the relevant period by such period (not exceeding 6 months) as is specified in the notice.

(4) A notice under subsection (3) must set out the Commission's reasons for the extension.

244 Effect of confirmation of resolution

(1) If the resolution of the transferor CIO is confirmed (or treated as confirmed) by the Commission—

(a) all the property, rights and liabilities of the transferor CIO become by virtue of this subsection the property, rights and liabilities of the transferee CIO in accordance with the resolution, and

(b) the transferor CIO is dissolved.

(2) Any gift which—

(a) is expressed as a gift to the transferor CIO, and

(b) takes effect on or after the date on which the resolution is confirmed (or treated as confirmed),

takes effect as a gift to the transferee CIO.

CHAPTER 5

SUPPLEMENTARY

245 Regulations about winding up, insolvency and dissolution

(1) CIO regulations may make provision about—

(a) the winding up of CIOs,
(b) their insolvency,
(c) their dissolution, and
(d) their revival and restoration to the register following dissolution.

(2) The regulations may, in particular, make provision—
(a) about the transfer on the dissolution of a CIO of its property and rights (including property and rights held on trust for the CIO) to the official custodian or another person or body;
(b) requiring any person in whose name any stocks, funds or securities are standing in trust for a CIO to transfer them into the name of the official custodian or another person or body;
(c) about the disclaiming, by the official custodian or other transferee of a CIO's property, of title to any of that property;
(d) about the application of a CIO's property cy-près;
(e) about circumstances in which charity trustees may be personally liable for contributions to the assets of a CIO or for its debts;
(f) about the reversal on a CIO's revival of anything done on its dissolution.

(3) The regulations may—
(a) apply any enactment which would not otherwise apply, either without modification or with modifications specified in the regulations,
(b) disapply, or modify (in ways specified in the regulations) the application of, any enactment which would otherwise apply.

(4) In subsection (3), "enactment" includes a provision of subordinate legislation within the meaning of the Interpretation Act 1978.

246 Power to make further provision about CIOs

(1) CIO regulations may make further provision about applications for registration of CIOs, the administration of CIOs, the conversion of charitable companies, registered societies and community interest companies into CIOs, the amalgamation of CIOs, and in relation to CIOs generally.

(2) The regulations may, in particular, make provision about—
(a) the execution of deeds and documents;
(b) the electronic communication of messages or documents relevant to a CIO or to any dealing with the Commission in relation to one;
(c) the maintenance of registers of members and of charity trustees;
(d) the maintenance of other registers (for example, a register of charges over the CIO's assets).

(3) The regulations may—
(a) apply any enactment which would not otherwise apply, either without modification or with modifications specified in the regulations,
(b) disapply, or modify (in ways specified in the regulations) the application of, any enactment which would otherwise apply.

(4) The regulations may, in relation to charities constituted as CIOs—
(a) disapply any of sections 29 to 38 (registration of charities),

(b) modify the application of any of those sections in ways specified in the regulations.

(5) In subsection (3), "enactment" includes a provision of subordinate legislation within the meaning of the Interpretation Act 1978.

247 Meaning of "CIO regulations"

In this Part "CIO regulations" means regulations made by the Minister.

248 Meaning of "benefit"

(1) This section applies for the purposes of sections 226(2)(c), 237(5)(c) and 242(3)(c) (cases where Commission may refuse to consent to amendment of constitution, to grant an application for amalgamation or to confirm a resolution transferring a CIO's undertaking).

(2) "Benefit" means a direct or indirect benefit of any nature, except that it does not include any remuneration (within the meaning of section 185) whose receipt may be authorised under that section.

249 Meaning of "connected person"

(1) This section applies for the purposes of sections 226(2)(c), 237(5)(c) and 242(3)(c).

(2) The following persons are connected with a charity trustee or member of a CIO—

(a) a child, parent, grandchild, grandparent, brother or sister of the trustee or member;

(b) the spouse or civil partner of the trustee or member or of any person falling within paragraph (a);

(c) a person carrying on business in partnership with the trustee or member or with any person falling within paragraph (a) or (b);

(d) an institution which is controlled—

(i) by the trustee or member or by any person falling within paragraph (a), (b) or (c), or

(ii) by two or more persons falling within sub-paragraph (i), when taken together.

(e) a body corporate in which—

(i) the trustee or member or any connected person falling within any of paragraphs (a) to (c) has a substantial interest, or

(ii) two or more persons falling within sub-paragraph (i), when taken together, have a substantial interest.

(3) Sections 350 to 352 (meaning of child, spouse, civil partner, controlled institution and substantial interest) apply for the purposes of subsection (2).

250 Effect of provisions relating to vesting or transfer of property

No vesting or transfer of any property in pursuance of any provision of this Part operates as a breach of a covenant or condition against alienation or gives rise to a forfeiture.

PART 12

INCORPORATION OF CHARITY TRUSTEES

General

251 Incorporation of charity trustees

(1) The Commission may grant a certificate of incorporation of the charity trustees of a charity as a body corporate if—

(a) the charity trustees of the charity, in accordance with section 256, apply to the Commission for such a certificate, and

(b) the Commission considers that the incorporation of the charity trustees would be in the interests of the charity.

(2) Such a certificate is subject to such conditions or directions as the Commission thinks fit to insert in it.

(3) But the Commission must not grant such a certificate if the charity—

(a) appears to the Commission to be required to be registered in accordance with section 30, but

(b) is not so registered.

(4) On the grant of such a certificate—

(a) the charity trustees of the charity become a body corporate by such name as is specified in the certificate, and

(b) any rights or liabilities of those trustees in connection with any property vesting in the body under section 252 become rights or liabilities of that body.

Paragraph (b) does not affect the operation of section 254 (liability of charity trustees not affected by incorporation).

(5) After their incorporation the charity trustees—

(a) may sue and be sued in their corporate name, and

(b) have the same powers, and are subject to the same restrictions and limitations, as respects the holding, acquisition and disposal of property for or in connection with the purposes of the charity as they had or were subject to while unincorporated;

and any relevant legal proceedings that might have been continued or commenced by or against the charity trustees may be continued or commenced by or against them in their corporate name.

(6) In subsection (5) "relevant legal proceedings" means legal proceedings in connection with any property vesting in the incorporated body under section 252.

(7) An incorporated body need not have a common seal.

252 Estate to vest in incorporated body

(1) The certificate of incorporation vests in the incorporated body all real and personal estate, of whatever nature or tenure, belonging to or held by any person or persons in trust for the relevant charity.

(2) On the vesting of all real and personal estate under subsection (1), any person or persons in whose name or names any stocks, funds or securities are standing in trust for the relevant charity must transfer them into the name of the incorporated body.

(3) Subsections (1) and (2) do not apply to property vested in the official custodian.

253 Gifts to take effect as gifts to incorporated body

(1) After the incorporation under this Part of the charity trustees of any charity, every relevant donation, gift and disposition of property made—

(a) to or in favour of the charity, or the charity trustees of the charity, or

(b) otherwise for the purposes of the charity,

takes effect as if made to or in favour of the incorporated body or otherwise for the same purposes.

(2) For the purposes of subsection (1), a donation, gift or disposition of property is a relevant one if (whether of real or personal property and whether made by deed, will or otherwise)—

(a) it was lawfully made before the incorporation but has not actually taken effect, or

(b) it is lawfully made after the incorporation.

254 Liability of charity trustees not affected by incorporation

After a certificate of incorporation has been granted under this Part, all charity trustees of the charity are, despite their incorporation—

(a) chargeable for such property as comes into their hands, and

(b) answerable and accountable for their own acts, receipts, neglects, and defaults, and for the due administration of the charity and its property,

in the same manner and to the same extent as if no such incorporation had been effected.

255 Charity trustees bound by conditions in certificate etc.

(1) All conditions and directions inserted in any certificate of incorporation are binding upon and must be performed or observed by the charity trustees as trusts of the charity.

(2) Section 336 (enforcement of orders of Commission) applies to any charity trustee who fails to perform or observe any such condition or direction as it applies to a person guilty of disobedience to any such order of the Commission as is mentioned in that section.

Application procedure

256 Applications for incorporation

(1) Every application to the Commission for a certificate of incorporation under this Part must be—

(a) in writing and signed by the charity trustees of the charity concerned, and

(b) accompanied by such documents or information as the Commission may require for the purpose of the application.

(2) The Commission may require—

(a) any statement contained in any such application, or

(b) any document or information supplied under subsection (1)(b),

to be verified in such manner as it may specify.

257 Requirement to be met before certificate is granted

Before a certificate of incorporation is granted under this Part, charity trustees of the charity must have been effectually appointed to the satisfaction of the Commission.

258 Certificate conclusive as to compliance with incorporation requirements etc.

(1) A certificate of incorporation granted under this Part is conclusive evidence that all the preliminary requirements for incorporation under this Part have been complied with.

(2) The date of incorporation mentioned in the certificate is to be treated as being the date at which incorporation has taken place.

Administration etc. of charity whose charity trustees are incorporated

259 Filling up of vacancies in charity trustees

(1) This section applies where a certificate of incorporation is granted under this Part.

(2) Vacancies in the number of the charity trustees of the charity must from time to time be filled up so far as required by the constitution or settlement of the charity, or by any conditions or directions in the certificate—

(a) by such legal means as would have been available for the appointment of new charity trustees of the charity if no certificate of incorporation had been granted, or

(b) otherwise as required by such conditions or directions.

260 Execution of documents by incorporated body: general

(1) This section and section 261 have effect as respects the execution of documents by an incorporated body.

(2) If an incorporated body has a common seal, a document may be executed by the body by the affixing of its common seal.

(3) Whether or not it has a common seal, a document may be executed by an incorporated body by being—

(a) signed by a majority of the charity trustees of the relevant charity and expressed (in whatever form of words) to be executed by the body, or

(b) executed in pursuance of an authority given under section 261(1).

(4) A document duly executed by an incorporated body which makes it clear on its face that it is intended by the person or persons making it to be a deed has effect, upon

delivery, as a deed; and it is presumed, unless a contrary intention is proved, to be delivered upon its being so executed.

(5) In favour of a purchaser a document is to be treated as having been duly executed by an incorporated body if it purports to be signed by—

(a) a majority of the charity trustees of the relevant charity, or

(b) such of the charity trustees of the relevant charity as are authorised by the charity trustees of that charity to execute it in the name and on behalf of the body,

and, if the document makes it clear on its face that it is intended by the person or persons making it to be a deed, it is to be treated as having been delivered upon its being executed.

(6) For the purposes of subsection (5) "purchaser"—

(a) means a purchaser in good faith for valuable consideration, and

(b) includes a lessee, mortgagee or other person who for valuable consideration acquires an interest in property.

261 Conferral of authority to execute documents

(1) For the purposes of section 260(3)(b) the charity trustees of the relevant charity in the case of an incorporated body may, subject to the trusts of the charity, confer on any two or more of their number—

(a) a general authority, or

(b) an authority limited in such manner as the charity trustees think fit,

to execute in the name and on behalf of the body documents for giving effect to transactions to which the body is a party.

(2) An authority under subsection (1)—

(a) suffices for any document if it is given in writing or by resolution of a meeting of the charity trustees of the relevant charity, despite the want of any formality that would be required in giving an authority apart from that subsection;

(b) may be given so as to make the powers conferred exercisable by any of the charity trustees, or may be restricted to named persons or in any other way;

(c) subject to any such restriction, and until it is revoked, has effect, despite any change in the charity trustees of the relevant charity, as a continuing authority given by the charity trustees from time to time of the charity and exercisable by such charity trustees.

(3) In any authority under subsection (1) to execute a document in the name and on behalf of an incorporated body there is, unless the contrary intention appears, implied authority also to execute it for the body in the name and on behalf of the official custodian or of any other person, in any case in which the charity trustees could do so.

Commission's powers to amend certificate or dissolve body

262 Amendment of certificate of incorporation

(1) The Commission may amend a certificate of incorporation—

(a) on the application of the incorporated body to which it relates, or

(b) of its own motion.

(2) Before making any such amendment of its own motion, the Commission must by notice in writing—

(a) inform the charity trustees of the relevant charity of its proposals, and

(b) invite those charity trustees to make representations to it within a time specified in the notice.

(3) The time so specified must be not less than one month from the date of the notice.

(4) The Commission—

(a) must take into consideration any representations made by those charity trustees within the time so specified, and

(b) may then (without further notice) proceed with its proposals either without modification or with such modifications as appear to it to be desirable.

(5) The Commission may amend a certificate of incorporation by—

(a) making an order specifying the amendment, or

(b) issuing a new certificate of incorporation taking account of the amendment.

263 Dissolution of incorporated body

(1) The Commission may of its own motion make an order dissolving an incorporated body from such date as is specified in the order, if the Commission is satisfied—

(a) that the body has no assets or does not operate,

(b) that the relevant charity has ceased to exist,

(c) that the institution previously constituting, or treated by the Commission as constituting, the relevant charity has ceased to be, or (as the case may be) was not at the time of the body's incorporation, a charity, or

(d) that the purposes of the relevant charity—

(i) have been achieved so far as is possible, or

(ii) are in practice incapable of being achieved.

(2) The Commission may make an order dissolving an incorporated body from such date as is specified in the order, if the Commission is satisfied, on the application of the charity trustees of the relevant charity, that it would be in the interests of the charity for the body to be dissolved.

(3) Subject to subsection (4), an order made under this section with respect to an incorporated body has the effect of vesting in the charity trustees of the relevant charity, in trust for that charity, all property for the time being vested—

(a) in the body, or

(b) in any other person (apart from the official custodian),

in trust for that charity.

(4) If the Commission so directs in the order—

(a) all or any specified part of that property, instead of vesting in the charity trustees of the relevant charity, vests in—

(i) a specified person as trustee for, or nominee of, that charity, or

(ii) such persons (other than the charity trustees of the relevant charity) as may be specified;

(b) any specified investments, or any specified class or description of investments, held by any person in trust for the relevant charity are to be transferred to—

(i) the charity trustees of that charity, or

(ii) any such person or persons as is or are mentioned in paragraph (a)(i) or (ii).

For this purpose "specified" means specified by the Commission in the order.

(5) Where an order to which this subsection applies is made with respect to an incorporated body—

(a) any rights or liabilities of the body become rights or liabilities of the charity trustees of the relevant charity, and

(b) any legal proceedings that might have been continued or commenced by or against the body may be continued or commenced by or against those trustees.

(6) Subsection (5) applies to any order under this section by virtue of which—

(a) any property vested as mentioned in subsection (3) is vested—

(i) in the charity trustees of the relevant charity, or

(ii) in any person as trustee for, or nominee of, that charity, or

(b) any investments held by any person in trust for the relevant charity are required to be transferred—

(i) to the charity trustees of that charity, or

(ii) to any person as trustee for, or nominee of, that charity.

Supplementary

264 Records of applications and certificates

(1) The Commission must keep a record of all applications for, and certificates of, incorporation under this Part.

(2) Documents sent to the Commission under this Part are to be kept by the Commission for such period as it thinks fit.

(3) Documents kept under this section are to be open to public inspection at all reasonable times.

(4) Any person who is provided with a copy or extract of any document kept under this section may require it to be certified by a certificate signed by a member of the staff of the Commission.

265 Meaning of "incorporated body" and "relevant charity"

In this Part—

"incorporated body" means a body incorporated under section 251;

"the relevant charity", in relation to an incorporated body, means the charity the charity trustees of which have been incorporated as that body.

266 Effect of provisions relating to vesting or transfer of property

No vesting or transfer of any property in pursuance of any provision of this Part operates as a breach of a covenant or condition against alienation or gives rise to a forfeiture.

PART 13

UNINCORPORATED CHARITIES

Power to transfer all property of unincorporated charity

267 Introduction

(1) Section 268 (resolution to transfer all property) applies to a charity if—

- (a) (subject to subsection (2)) its gross income in its last financial year did not exceed £10,000,
- (b) it does not hold any designated land, and
- (c) it is not a company or other body corporate.

"Designated land" means land held on trusts which stipulate that it is to be used for the purposes, or any particular purposes, of the charity.

(2) Subsection (1)(a) does not apply in relation to a resolution by the charity trustees of a charity—

- (a) to transfer all its property to a CIO, or
- (b) to divide its property between two or more CIOs.

(3) Where a charity has a permanent endowment, sections 268 to 272 have effect in accordance with sections 273 and 274.

(4) In sections 268 to 274 references to the transfer of property to a charity are references to its transfer—

- (a) to the charity,
- (b) to the charity trustees,
- (c) to any trustee for the charity, or
- (d) to a person nominated by the charity trustees to hold it in trust for the charity,

as the charity trustees may determine.

268 Resolution to transfer all property

(1) The charity trustees of a charity to which this section applies (see section 267) may resolve for the purposes of this section—

- (a) that all the property of the charity should be transferred to another charity specified in the resolution, or
- (b) that all the property of the charity should be transferred to two or more charities specified in the resolution in accordance with such division of the property between them as is so specified.

(2) Any charity so specified may be either a registered charity or a charity which is not required to be registered.

(3) But the charity trustees of a charity ("the transferor charity") do not have power to pass a resolution under subsection (1) unless they are satisfied—

(a) that it is expedient in the interests of furthering the purposes for which the property is held by the transferor charity for the property to be transferred in accordance with the resolution, and

(b) that the purposes (or any of the purposes) of any charity to which property is to be transferred under the resolution are substantially similar to the purposes (or any of the purposes) of the transferor charity.

(4) Any resolution under subsection (1) must be passed by a majority of not less than two-thirds of the charity trustees who vote on the resolution.

(5) Where charity trustees have passed a resolution under subsection (1), they must send a copy of it to the Commission, together with a statement of their reasons for passing it.

269 Notice of, and information about, resolution to transfer property

(1) Having received the copy of the resolution under section 268(5), the Commission—

(a) may direct the charity trustees to give public notice of the resolution in such manner as is specified in the direction, and

(b) if it gives such a direction, must take into account any representations made to it—

(i) by persons appearing to it to be interested in the charity, and

(ii) within the period of 28 days beginning with the date when public notice of the resolution is given by the charity trustees.

(2) The Commission may also direct the charity trustees to provide the Commission with additional information or explanations relating to—

(a) the circumstances in and by reference to which they have decided to act under section 268, or

(b) their compliance with any obligation imposed on them by or under section 268 or this section in connection with the resolution.

270 General rule as to when s.268 resolution takes effect

Subject to section 271, a resolution under section 268(1) takes effect at the end of the period of 60 days beginning with the date on which the copy of it was received by the Commission.

271 S.268 resolution not to take effect or to take effect at later date

(1) A resolution does not take effect under section 270 if before the end of—

(a) the 60-day period, or

(b) that period as modified by subsection (4) or (5),

the Commission notifies the charity trustees in writing that it objects to the resolution, either on procedural grounds or on the merits of the proposals contained in the resolution.

(2) "The 60-day period" means the period of 60 days mentioned in section 270.

(3) "On procedural grounds" means on the grounds that any obligation imposed on the charity trustees by or under section 268 or 269 has not been complied with in connection with the resolution.

(4) If under section 269(1) the Commission directs the charity trustees to give public notice of a resolution, the running of the 60-day period is suspended by virtue of this subsection—

(a) as from the date on which the direction is given to the charity trustees, and

(b) until the end of the period of 42 days beginning with the date on which public notice of the resolution is given by the charity trustees.

(5) If under section 269(2) the Commission directs the charity trustees to provide any information or explanations, the running of the 60-day period is suspended by virtue of this subsection—

(a) as from the date on which the direction is given to the charity trustees, and

(b) until the date on which the information or explanations is or are provided to the Commission.

(6) Subsection (7) applies once the period of time, or the total period of time, during which the 60-day period is suspended by virtue of either or both of subsections (4) and (5) exceeds 120 days.

(7) At that point the resolution (if not previously objected to by the Commission) is to be treated as if it had never been passed.

272 Transfer of property in accordance with s.268 resolution

(1) Subsection (2) applies where a resolution under section 268(1) has taken effect.

(2) The charity trustees must arrange for all the property of the transferor charity to be transferred in accordance with the resolution, and on terms that any property so transferred—

(a) is to be held by the charity to which it is transferred ("the transferee charity") in accordance with subsection (3), but

(b) when so held is nevertheless to be subject to any restrictions on expenditure to which it was subject as property of the transferor charity;

and the charity trustees must arrange for the property to be so transferred by such date after the resolution takes effect as they agree with the charity trustees of the transferee charity or charities concerned.

(3) The charity trustees of any charity to which property is transferred under this section must secure, so far as is reasonably practicable, that the property is applied for such of its purposes as are substantially similar to those of the transferor charity.

But this requirement does not apply if those charity trustees consider that complying with it would not result in a suitable and effective method of applying the property.

(4) For the purpose of enabling any property to be transferred to a charity under this section, the Commission may, at the request of the charity trustees of that charity, make orders vesting any property of the transferor charity—

(a) in the transferee charity, in its charity trustees or in any trustee for that charity, or

(b) in any other person nominated by those charity trustees to hold property in trust for that charity.

273 Transfer where charity has permanent endowment: general

(1) This section and section 274 provide for the operation of sections 268 to 272 where a charity within section 267(1) has a permanent endowment (whether or not the charity's trusts contain provision for the termination of the charity).

(2) If the charity has both a permanent endowment and other property ("unrestricted property")—

(a) a resolution under section 268(1) must relate to both its permanent endowment and its unrestricted property, and

(b) sections 268 to 272 apply—

(i) in relation to its unrestricted property, as if references in those sections to all or any of the property of the charity were references to all or any of its unrestricted property, and

(ii) in relation to its permanent endowment, in accordance with section 274.

(3) If all of the property of the charity is comprised in its permanent endowment, sections 268 to 272 apply in relation to its permanent endowment in accordance with section 274.

274 Requirements relating to permanent endowment

(1) Sections 268 to 272 apply in relation to the permanent endowment of the charity (as mentioned in section 273(2)(b)(ii) and (3)) with the following modifications.

(2) References in sections 268 to 272 to all or any of the property of the charity are references to all or any of the property comprised in its permanent endowment.

(3) If the property comprised in its permanent endowment is to be transferred to a single charity, the charity trustees must (instead of being satisfied as mentioned in section 268(3)(b)) be satisfied that the proposed transferee charity has purposes which are substantially similar to all of the purposes of the transferor charity.

(4) If the property comprised in its permanent endowment is to be transferred to two or more charities, the charity trustees must (instead of being satisfied as mentioned in section 268(3)(b)) be satisfied—

(a) that the proposed transferee charities, taken together, have purposes which are substantially similar to all of the purposes of the transferor charity, and

(b) that each of the proposed transferee charities has purposes which are substantially similar to one or more of the purposes of the transferor charity.

(5) In the case of a transfer to which subsection (4) applies, the resolution under section 268(1) must provide for the property comprised in the permanent endowment of the charity to be divided between the transferee charities in such a way as to take account of such guidance as may be given by the Commission for the purposes of this section.

(6) For the purposes of sections 268 to 272, the references in sections 269(2)(b) and 271(3) to any obligation imposed on the charity trustees by or under section 268 or 269

includes a reference to any obligation imposed on them by virtue of any of subsections (3) to (5).

(7) The requirement in section 272(3) applies in the case of every such transfer, and in complying with that requirement the charity trustees of a transferee charity must secure that the application of property transferred to the charity takes account of such guidance as may be given by the Commission for the purposes of this section.

(8) Any guidance given by the Commission for the purposes of this section may take such form and be given in such manner as the Commission considers appropriate.

Powers to alter purposes or powers etc. of unincorporated charity

275 Resolution to replace purposes of unincorporated charity

(1) This section applies to a charity if—

(a) its gross income in its last financial year did not exceed £10,000,

(b) it does not hold any designated land, and

(c) it is not a company or other body corporate.

"Designated land" means land held on trusts which stipulate that it is to be used for the purposes, or any particular purposes, of the charity.

(2) The charity trustees of such a charity may resolve for the purposes of this section that the trusts of the charity should be modified by replacing all or any of the purposes of the charity with other purposes specified in the resolution.

(3) The other purposes so specified must be charitable purposes.

(4) But the charity trustees of a charity do not have power to pass a resolution under subsection (2) unless they are satisfied—

(a) that it is expedient in the interests of the charity for the purposes in question to be replaced, and

(b) that, so far as is reasonably practicable, the new purposes consist of or include purposes that are similar in character to those that are to be replaced.

(5) Any resolution under subsection (2) must be passed by a majority of not less than two-thirds of the charity trustees who vote on the resolution.

(6) Where charity trustees have passed a resolution under subsection (2), they must send a copy of it to the Commission, together with a statement of their reasons for passing it.

276 Notice of, and information about, s.275 resolution

(1) Having received the copy of the resolution under section 275(6), the Commission—

(a) may direct the charity trustees to give public notice of the resolution in such manner as is specified in the direction, and

(b) if it gives such a direction, must take into account any representations made to it—

(i) by persons appearing to it to be interested in the charity, and

(ii) within the period of 28 days beginning with the date when public notice of the resolution is given by the charity trustees.

(2) The Commission may also direct the charity trustees to provide the Commission with additional information or explanations relating to—

(a) the circumstances in and by reference to which they have decided to act under section 275, or

(b) their compliance with any obligation imposed on them by or under section 275 or this section in connection with the resolution.

277 General rule as to when s.275 resolution takes effect

Subject to section 278, a resolution under section 275(2) takes effect at the end of the period of 60 days beginning with the date on which the copy of it was received by the Commission.

278 S.275 resolution not to take effect or to take effect at a later date

(1) A resolution does not take effect under section 277 if before the end of—

(a) the 60-day period, or

(b) that period as modified by subsection (4) or (5),

the Commission notifies the charity trustees in writing that it objects to the resolution, either on procedural grounds or on the merits of the proposals contained in the resolution.

(2) "The 60-day period" means the period of 60 days mentioned in section 277.

(3) "On procedural grounds" means on the grounds that any obligation imposed on the charity trustees by or under section 275 or 276 has not been complied with in connection with the resolution.

(4) If under section 276(1) the Commission directs the charity trustees to give public notice of a resolution, the running of the 60-day period is suspended by virtue of this subsection—

(a) as from the date on which the direction is given to the charity trustees, and

(b) until the end of the period of 42 days beginning with the date on which public notice of the resolution is given by the charity trustees.

(5) If under section 276(2) the Commission directs the charity trustees to provide any information or explanations, the running of the 60-day period is suspended by virtue of this subsection—

(a) as from the date on which the direction is given to the charity trustees, and

(b) until the date on which the information or explanations is or are provided to the Commission.

(6) Subsection (7) applies once the period of time, or the total period of time, during which the 60-day period is suspended by virtue of either or both of subsections (4) and (5) exceeds 120 days.

(7) At that point the resolution (if not previously objected to by the Commission) is to be treated as if it had never been passed.

279 Replacement of purposes in accordance with s.275

As from the time when a resolution takes effect under section 277, the trusts of the charity concerned are to be taken to have been modified in accordance with the terms of the resolution.

280 Power to modify powers or procedures of unincorporated charity

(1) This section applies to any charity which is not a company or other body corporate.

(2) The charity trustees of such a charity may resolve for the purposes of this section that any provision of the trusts of the charity—

(a) relating to any of the powers exercisable by the charity trustees in the administration of the charity, or

(b) regulating the procedure to be followed in any respect in connection with its administration,

should be modified in such manner as is specified in the resolution.

(3) Subsection (4) applies if the charity is an unincorporated association with a body of members distinct from the charity trustees.

(4) Any resolution of the charity trustees under subsection (2) must be approved by a further resolution which is passed at a general meeting of the body—

(a) by a majority of not less than two-thirds of the members entitled to attend and vote at the meeting who vote on the resolution, or

(b) by a decision taken without a vote and without any expression of dissent in response to the question put to the meeting.

(5) Where—

(a) the charity trustees have passed a resolution under subsection (2), and

(b) (if subsection (4) applies) a further resolution has been passed under that subsection,

the trusts of the charity are to be taken to have been modified in accordance with the terms of the resolution.

(6) The trusts are to be taken to have been so modified as from—

(a) such date as is specified for this purpose in the resolution under subsection (2), or

(b) (if later) the date when any such further resolution was passed under subsection (4).

Powers of unincorporated charities to spend capital

281 Power of unincorporated charities to spend capital: general

(1) This section applies to any available endowment fund of a charity which is not a company or other body corporate.

(2) But this section does not apply to a fund if sections 282 to 284 (power to spend larger fund given for particular purpose) apply to it.

(3) If the condition in subsection (4) is met in relation to the charity, the charity trustees may resolve for the purposes of this section that the fund, or a portion of it, ought to be freed from the restrictions with respect to expenditure of capital that apply to it.

(4) The condition is that the charity trustees are satisfied that the purposes set out in the trusts to which the fund is subject could be carried out more effectively if the capital of the fund, or the relevant portion of the capital, could be expended as well as income accruing to it, rather than just such income.

(5) Once the charity trustees have passed a resolution under subsection (3), the fund or portion may by virtue of this section be expended in carrying out the purposes set out in the trusts to which the fund is subject without regard to the restrictions mentioned in that subsection.

(6) The fund or portion may be so expended as from such date as is specified for this purpose in the resolution.

(7) In this section "available endowment fund", in relation to a charity, means—
- (a) the whole of the charity's permanent endowment if it is all subject to the same trusts, or
- (b) any part of its permanent endowment which is subject to any particular trusts that are different from those to which any other part is subject.

282 Resolution to spend larger fund given for particular purpose

(1) This section applies to any available endowment fund of a charity which is not a company or other body corporate if—
- (a) the capital of the fund consists entirely of property given—
  - (i) by a particular individual,
  - (ii) by a particular institution (by way of grant or otherwise), or
  - (iii) by two or more individuals or institutions in pursuit of a common purpose, and
- (b) the charity's gross income in its last financial year exceeded £1,000 and the market value of the endowment fund exceeds £10,000.

(2) If the condition in subsection (3) is met in relation to the charity, the charity trustees may resolve for the purposes of this section that the fund, or a portion of it, ought to be freed from the restrictions with respect to expenditure of capital that apply to it.

(3) The condition is that the charity trustees are satisfied that the purposes set out in the trusts to which the fund is subject could be carried out more effectively if the capital of the fund, or the relevant portion of the capital, could be expended as well as income accruing to it, rather than just such income.

(4) The charity trustees—
- (a) must send a copy of any resolution under subsection (2) to the Commission, together with a statement of their reasons for passing it, and
- (b) may not implement the resolution except in accordance with sections 283 and 284.

(5) In this section—

"available endowment fund" has the same meaning as in section 281;

"market value", in relation to an endowment fund, means—

(a) the market value of the fund as recorded in the accounts for the last financial year of the relevant charity, or

(b) if no such value was so recorded, the current market value of the fund as determined on a valuation carried out for the purpose.

(6) In subsection (1), the reference to the giving of property by an individual includes the individual's giving it by will.

283 Notice of, and information about, s.282 resolution

(1) Having received the copy of the resolution under section 282(4), the Commission may—

(a) direct the charity trustees to give public notice of the resolution in such manner as is specified in the direction, and

(b) if it gives such a direction, must take into account any representations made to it—

(i) by persons appearing to it to be interested in the charity, and

(ii) within the period of 28 days beginning with the date when public notice of the resolution is given by the charity trustees.

(2) The Commission may also direct the charity trustees to provide the Commission with additional information or explanations relating to—

(a) the circumstances in and by reference to which they have decided to act under section 282, or

(b) their compliance with any obligation imposed on them by or under section 282 or this section in connection with the resolution.

284 When and how s.282 resolution takes effect

(1) When considering whether to concur with the resolution under section 282(2), the Commission must take into account—

(a) any evidence available to it as to the wishes of the donor or donors mentioned in section 282(1)(a), and

(b) any changes in the circumstances relating to the charity since the making of the gift or gifts (including, in particular, its financial position, the needs of its beneficiaries, and the social, economic and legal environment in which it operates).

(2) The Commission must not concur with the resolution unless it is satisfied—

(a) that its implementation would accord with the spirit of the gift or gifts mentioned in section 282(1)(a) (even though it would be inconsistent with the restrictions mentioned in section 282(2)), and

(b) that the charity trustees have complied with the obligations imposed on them by or under section 282 or 283 in connection with the resolution.

(3) Before the end of the period of 3 months beginning with the relevant date, the Commission must notify the charity trustees in writing—

(a) that the Commission concurs with the resolution, or

(b) that it does not concur with it.

(4) In subsection (3) "the relevant date" means—

(a) if the Commission directs the charity trustees under section 283(1) to give public notice of the resolution, the date when that notice is given, and

(b) otherwise, the date on which the Commission receives the copy of the resolution in accordance with section 282(4).

(5) Where—

(a) the charity trustees are notified by the Commission that it concurs with the resolution, or

(b) the period of 3 months mentioned in subsection (3) has elapsed without the Commission notifying them that it does not concur with the resolution,

the fund or portion may, by virtue of this section, be expended in carrying out the purposes set out in the trusts to which the fund is subject without regard to the restrictions mentioned in section 282(2).

Supplementary

285 Power to alter sums specified in this Part

(1) The Minister may by order amend any provision listed in subsection (2)—

(a) by substituting a different sum for the sum for the time being specified in that provision, or

(b) if the provision specifies more than one sum, by substituting a different sum for any sum specified in that provision.

(2) The provisions are—

section 267(1) (income level for purposes of resolution to transfer property of unincorporated charity);

section 275(1) (income level for purposes of resolution to replace purposes of unincorporated charity);

section 282(1) (income level and market value of fund for purposes of resolution to spend larger fund given for particular purpose).

286 Effect of provisions relating to vesting or transfer of property

No vesting or transfer of any property in pursuance of any provision of this Part operates as a breach of a covenant or condition against alienation or gives rise to a forfeiture.

PART 14

SPECIAL TRUSTS

287 Meaning of "special trust"

(1) In this Act, "special trust" means property which—

(a) is held and administered by or on behalf of a charity for any special purposes of the charity, and

(b) is so held and administered on separate trusts relating only to that property.

(2) But a special trust does not, by itself, constitute a charity for the purposes of Part 8 (charity accounts, reports and returns).

288 Power to spend capital subject to special trusts: general

(1) This section applies to any available endowment fund of a special trust which, as the result of a direction under section 12(1), is to be treated as a separate charity ("the relevant charity") for the purposes of this section and sections 289 to 292.

(2) But this section does not apply to such a fund if sections 289 to 291 (power to spend capital subject to special trusts: larger fund) apply in relation to it.

(3) If the condition in subsection (4) is met in relation to the relevant charity, the charity trustees may resolve for the purposes of this section that the fund, or a portion of it, ought to be freed from the restrictions with respect to expenditure of capital that apply to it.

(4) The condition is that the charity trustees are satisfied that the purposes set out in the trusts to which the fund is subject could be carried out more effectively if the capital of the fund, or the relevant portion of the capital, could be expended as well as income accruing to it, rather than just such income.

(5) Once the charity trustees have passed a resolution under subsection (3), the fund or portion may, by virtue of this section, be expended in carrying out the purposes set out in the trusts to which the fund is subject without regard to the restrictions mentioned in that subsection.

(6) The fund or portion may be so expended as from such date as is specified for this purpose in the resolution.

(7) In this section, "available endowment fund" has the same meaning as in section 281 (power of unincorporated charities to spend capital: general).

289 Resolution to spend capital subject to special trusts: larger fund

(1) This section applies to a fund within section 288(1) if—

- (a) the capital of the fund consists entirely of property given—
  - (i) by a particular individual,
  - (ii) by a particular institution (by way of grant or otherwise), or
  - (iii) by two or more individuals or institutions in pursuit of a common purpose, and
- (b) the market value of the fund exceeds £10,000.

(2) If the condition in subsection (3) is met in relation to the relevant charity, the charity trustees may resolve for the purposes of this section that the fund, or a portion of it, ought to be freed from the restrictions with respect to expenditure of capital that apply to it.

(3) The condition is that the charity trustees are satisfied that the purposes set out in the trusts to which the fund is subject could be carried out more effectively if the capital of the fund, or the relevant portion of the capital, could be expended as well as income accruing to it, rather than just such income.

(4) The charity trustees—

(a) must send a copy of any resolution under subsection (2) to the Commission, together with a statement of their reasons for passing it, and
(b) may not implement the resolution except in accordance with sections 290 and 291.

(5) In this section, "market value" has the same meaning as in section 282 (resolution to spend larger fund for given for particular purpose).

(6) In subsection (1), the reference to the giving of property by an individual includes the individual's giving it by will.

290 Notice of, and information about, s.289 resolution

(1) Having received the copy of the resolution under section 289(4), the Commission may—
(a) direct the charity trustees to give public notice of the resolution in such manner as is specified in the direction, and
(b) if it gives such a direction, must take into account any representations made to it—
(i) by persons appearing to it to be interested in the relevant charity, and
(ii) within the period of 28 days beginning with the date when public notice of the resolution is given by the charity trustees.

(2) The Commission may also direct the charity trustees to provide the Commission with additional information or explanations relating to—
(a) the circumstances in and by reference to which they have decided to act under section 289, or
(b) their compliance with any obligation imposed on them by or under section 289 or this section in connection with the resolution.

291 When and how s.289 resolution takes effect

(1) When considering whether to concur with the resolution under section 289(2), the Commission must take into account—
(a) any evidence available to it as to the wishes of the donor or donors mentioned in section 289(1)(a), and
(b) any changes in the circumstances relating to the relevant charity since the making of the gift or gifts (including, in particular, its financial position, the needs of its beneficiaries, and the social, economic and legal environment in which it operates).

(2) The Commission must not concur with the resolution unless it is satisfied—
(a) that its implementation would accord with the spirit of the gift or gifts mentioned in section 289(1)(a) (even though it would be inconsistent with the restrictions mentioned in section 289(2)), and
(b) that the charity trustees have complied with the obligations imposed on them by or under section 289 or 290 in connection with the resolution.

(3) Before the end of the period of 3 months beginning with the relevant date, the Commission must notify the charity trustees in writing—
(a) that the Commission concurs with the resolution, or
(b) that it does not concur with it.

(4) In subsection (3) "the relevant date" means—

(a) if the Commission directs the charity trustees under section 290(1) to give public notice of the resolution, the date when that notice is given, and

(b) otherwise, the date on which the Commission receives the copy of the resolution in accordance with section 289(4).

(5) Where—

(a) the charity trustees are notified by the Commission that it concurs with the resolution, or

(b) the period of 3 months mentioned in subsection (3) has elapsed without the Commission notifying them that it does not concur with the resolution,

the fund or portion may, by virtue of this section, be expended in carrying out the purposes set out in the trusts to which the fund is subject without regard to the restrictions mentioned in section 289(2).

(6) The fund or portion may be so expended as from such date as is specified for this purpose in the resolution.

292 Power to alter sum specified in s.289

The Minister may by order amend section 289(1) (market value of fund for purposes of resolution to spend capital subject to special trusts: larger fund) by substituting a different sum for the sum for the time being specified there.

PART 15

LOCAL CHARITIES

Indexes and reviews etc.

293 Meaning of "local charity"

In this Act, except in so far as the context otherwise requires, "local charity" means, in relation to any area, a charity established for purposes which are—

(a) by their nature, or

(b) by the trusts of the charity,

directed wholly or mainly to the benefit of that area or of part of it.

294 Local authority's index of local charities

(1) A council may maintain an index of local charities or of any class of local charities in the council's area, and may publish information contained in the index, or summaries or extracts taken from it.

(2) A council proposing to establish or maintaining under this section an index of local charities or of any class of local charities must, on request, be supplied by the Commission free of charge—

(a) with copies of such entries in the register of charities as are relevant to the index, or

(b) with particulars of any changes in the entries of which copies have been supplied before;

and the Commission may arrange that it will without further request supply a council with particulars of any such changes.

(3) An index maintained under this section must be open to public inspection at all reasonable times.

295 Reviews of local charities by local authority

(1) A council may—

(a) subject to the following provisions of this section, initiate, and carry out in co-operation with the charity trustees, a review of the working of any group of local charities with the same or similar purposes in the council's area, and

(b) make to the Commission such report on the review and such recommendations arising from it as the council, after consultation with the trustees, think fit.

(2) A council having power to initiate reviews under this section may—

(a) co-operate with other persons in any review by them of the working of local charities in the council's area (with or without other charities), or

(b) join with other persons in initiating and carrying out such a review.

(3) No review initiated by a council under this section is to extend—

(a) to any charity without the consent of the charity trustees, or

(b) to any ecclesiastical charity.

(4) No review initiated under this section by a district council is to extend to the working in any county of a local charity established for purposes similar or complementary to any services provided by county councils unless the review so extends with the consent of the council of that county.

(5) Subsection (4) does not apply in relation to Wales.

296 S.294 and s.295: supplementary

(1) In sections 294 and 295 and this section "council" means—

(a) a district council,

(b) a county council,

(c) a county borough council,

(d) a London borough council, or

(e) the Common Council of the City of London.

(2) A council may employ any voluntary organisation as their agent for the purposes of sections 294 and 295, on such terms and within such limits (if any) or in such cases as they may agree.

(3) In subsection (2), "voluntary organisation" means any body—

(a) whose activities are carried on otherwise than for profit, and

(b) which is not a public or local authority.

(4) A joint board discharging any of a council's functions has the same powers under sections 294 and 295 and this section as the council as respects local charities in the

council's area which are established for purposes similar or complementary to any services provided by the board.

297 Co-operation between charities, and between charities and local authorities

(1) Any local council and any joint board discharging any functions of a local council—

(a) may make, with any charity established for purposes similar or complementary to services provided by the council or board, arrangements for co-ordinating—

(i) the activities of the council or board, and

(ii) those of the charity,

in the interests of persons who may benefit from those services or from the charity, and

(b) is at liberty to disclose to any such charity in the interests of those persons any information obtained in connection with the services provided by the council or board, whether or not arrangements have been made with the charity under this subsection.

(2) In subsection (1), "local council" means—

(a) in relation to England—

(i) a district council,

(ii) a county council,

(iii) a London borough council,

(iv) a parish council,

(v) the Common Council of the City of London, or

(vi) the Council of the Isles of Scilly, and

(b) in relation to Wales—

(i) a county council,

(ii) a county borough council, or

(iii) a community council.

(3) Charity trustees may, regardless of anything in the trusts of the charity, by virtue of this subsection do all or any of the following things, if it appears to them likely to promote or make more effective the work of the charity—

(a) they may co-operate in any review undertaken under section 295 or otherwise of the working of charities or any class of charities;

(b) they may make arrangements with an authority acting under subsection (1) or with another charity for co-ordinating their activities and those of the authority or of the other charity;

(c) they may publish information of other charities with a view to bringing them to the notice of those for whose benefit they are intended.

(4) Charity trustees may defray the expense of acting under subsection (3) out of any income or money applicable as income of the charity.

Parochial charities

298 Transfer of property to parish or community council or its appointees

(1) This section applies where trustees hold any property—

(a) for the purposes of a public recreation ground, or of allotments (whether under inclosure Acts or otherwise), for the benefit of inhabitants of a parish having a parish council or (in Wales) community having a community council, or

(b) for other charitable purposes connected with such a parish or community;

and it applies to property held for any public purposes as it applies to property held for charitable purposes.

But it does not apply where trustees hold property for an ecclesiastical charity.

(2) The trustees may, with the approval of the Commission and with the consent of the parish or community council, transfer the property to—

(a) the parish or community council, or

(b) persons appointed by the parish or community council;

and the council or their appointees must hold the property on the same trusts and subject to the same conditions as the trustees did.

299 Local authorities' power to appoint representative trustees

(1) This section applies where a parochial charity in a parish or (in Wales) a community is not—

(a) an ecclesiastical charity, or

(b) a charity founded within the preceding 40 years.

(2) If the charity trustees do not include persons—

(a) elected by the local government electors or inhabitants of the parish or community, or

(b) appointed by the parish council or parish meeting or (in Wales) by the community council or the county council or (as the case may be) county borough council,

the parish council or parish meeting or the community council or the county council or county borough council may appoint additional charity trustees, to such number as the Commission may allow.

(3) If there is a sole charity trustee not elected or appointed as mentioned in subsection (2), the number of the charity trustees may, with the approval of the Commission, be increased to 3, of whom—

(a) one may be nominated by the person holding the office of the sole trustee, and

(b) one may be nominated by the parish council or parish meeting or by the community council or the county council or county borough council.

300 Powers of appointment deriving from pre-1894 powers

(1) Subsection (2) applies where, under the trusts of a charity other than an ecclesiastical charity—

(a) the inhabitants of a rural parish (whether in vestry or not), or

(b) a select vestry,

were formerly (in 1894) entitled to appoint charity trustees for, or trustees or beneficiaries of, the charity.

(2) The appointment is to be made—

(a) in a parish having a parish council or (in Wales) a community having a community council, by the parish or community council, or in the case of beneficiaries, by persons appointed by the parish or community council;

(b) in a parish not having a parish council or (in Wales) a community not having a community council, by the parish meeting or by the county council or (as the case may be) county borough council.

(3) Subsection (4) applies where—

(a) overseers as such, or

(b) except in the case of an ecclesiastical charity, churchwardens as such,

were formerly (in 1894) charity trustees of or trustees for a parochial charity in a rural parish, either alone or jointly with other persons.

(4) Instead of the former overseer or church warden trustees there are to be trustees (to a number not greater than that of the former overseer or churchwarden trustees) appointed—

(a) by the parish council or, if there is no parish council, by the parish meeting, or

(b) by the community council or, if there is no community council, by the county council or (as the case may be) county borough council.

(5) In this section "formerly (in 1894)" relates to the period immediately before the passing of the Local Government Act 1894 and "former" is to be read accordingly.

301 Powers of appointment deriving from pre-1927 powers

(1) Subsection (2) applies where, outside Greater London (other than the outer London boroughs), overseers of a parish as such were formerly (in 1927) charity trustees of or trustees for any charity, either alone or jointly with other persons.

(2) Instead of the former overseer trustees there are to be trustees (to a number not greater than that of the former overseer trustees) appointed—

(a) by the parish council or, if there is no parish council, by the parish meeting, or

(b) (in Wales) by the community council or, if there is no community council, by the county council or (as the case may be) county borough council.

(3) In the case of an urban parish existing immediately before the passing of the Local Government Act 1972 which after 1st April 1974 is not comprised in a parish, the power of appointment under subsection (2) is exercisable by the district council.

(4) In this section "formerly (in 1927)" relates to the period immediately before 1 April 1927 and "former" is to be read accordingly.

302 Term of office of trustees appointed under s.299 to s.301

(1) Any appointment of a charity trustee or trustee for a charity which is made by virtue of sections 299 to 301 must be for a term of 4 years, and a retiring trustee is eligible for re-appointment.

But this is subject to subsections (2) and (3).

(2) On an appointment under section 299, where—

(a) no previous appointments have been made by virtue of—

(i) section 299, or

(ii) the corresponding provision of the Local Government Act 1894, the Charities Act 1960 or the Charities Act 1993, and

(b) more than one trustee is appointed,

half of those appointed (or as nearly as may be) must be appointed for a term of 2 years.

(3) An appointment made to fill a casual vacancy must be for the remainder of the term of the previous appointment.

303 S.298 to s.302: supplementary

(1) In sections 299 and 300, "parochial charity" means, in relation to any parish or (in Wales) community, a charity the benefits of which are, or the separate distribution of the benefits of which is, confined to inhabitants of—

(a) the parish or community,

(b) a single ancient ecclesiastical parish which included that parish or community or part of it, or

(c) an area consisting of that parish or community with not more than 4 neighbouring parishes or communities.

(2) Sections 298 to 302 do not affect the trusteeship, control or management of any foundation or voluntary school within the meaning of the School Standards and Framework Act 1998.

(3) Sections 298 to 302—

(a) do not apply to the Isles of Scilly, and

(b) have effect subject to any order (including any future order) made under any enactment relating to local government with respect to local government areas or the powers of local authorities.

Supplementary

304 Effect of provisions relating to vesting or transfer of property

No vesting or transfer of any property in pursuance of any provision of this Part operates as a breach of a covenant or condition against alienation or gives rise to a forfeiture.

PART 16

CHARITY MERGERS

Registration

305 Register of charity mergers

(1) There continues to be a register of charity mergers, to be kept by the Commission in such manner as it thinks fit and maintained by it.

(2) The register must contain an entry in respect of every relevant charity merger which is notified to the Commission in accordance with section 307 and such procedures as it may determine.

306 Meaning of "relevant charity merger" etc.

(1) In this Part "relevant charity merger" means—

(a) a merger of two or more charities in connection with which one of them ("the transferee") has transferred to it all the property of the other or others, each of which (a "transferor") ceases to exist, or is to cease to exist, on or after the transfer of its property to the transferee, or

(b) a merger of two or more charities ("transferors") in connection with which both or all of them cease to exist, or are to cease to exist, on or after the transfer of all of their property to a new charity ("the transferee").

(2) In the case of a merger involving the transfer of property of any charity—

(a) which has both a permanent endowment and other property ("unrestricted property"), and

(b) whose trusts do not contain provision for the termination of the charity,

subsection (1)(a) or (b) applies subject to the modifications in subsection (3).

(3) The modifications in relation to any such charity are—

(a) the reference to all of its property is to be treated as a reference to all of its unrestricted property, and

(b) any reference to its ceasing to exist is to be treated as omitted.

(4) In this section and sections 307 and 308—

(a) any reference to a transfer of property includes a transfer effected by a vesting declaration, and

(b) "vesting declaration" means a declaration to which section 310(2) applies.

307 Notification of charity mergers

(1) A notification under section 305(2) may be given in respect of a relevant charity merger at any time after—

(a) the transfer of property involved in the merger has taken place, or

(b) (if more than one transfer of property is so involved) the last of those transfers has taken place.

(2) If a vesting declaration is made in connection with a relevant charity merger, a notification under section 305(2) must be given in respect of the merger once the transfer, or the last of the transfers, mentioned in subsection (1) has taken place.

(3) A notification under section 305(2) is to be given by the charity trustees of the transferee and must—

(a) specify the transfer or transfers of property involved in the merger and the date or dates on which it or they took place,

(b) include a statement that appropriate arrangements have been made with respect to the discharge of any liabilities of the transferor charity or charities, and

(c) in the case of a notification required by subsection (2), set out the matters mentioned in subsection (4).

(4) The matters are—

(a) the fact that the vesting declaration in question has been made,

(b) the date when the declaration was made, and

(c) the date on which the vesting of title under the declaration took place by virtue of section 310(2).

308 Details to be entered in register of charity mergers

(1) Subsection (2) applies to the entry to be made in the register of charity mergers in respect of a relevant charity merger, as required by section 305(2).

(2) The entry must—

(a) specify the date when the transfer or transfers of property involved in the merger took place,

(b) if a vesting declaration was made in connection with the merger, set out the matters mentioned in section 307(4), and

(c) contain such other particulars of the merger as the Commission thinks fit.

309 Right to inspect register of charity mergers

(1) The register of charity mergers must be open to public inspection at all reasonable times.

(2) Where any information contained in the register is not in documentary form, subsection (1) is to be read as requiring the information to be available for public inspection in legible form at all reasonable times.

Vesting declarations and effect of merger on certain gifts

310 Pre-merger vesting declarations

(1) Subsection (2) applies to a declaration which—

(a) is made by deed for the purposes of this section by the charity trustees of the transferor,

(b) is made in connection with a relevant charity merger, and

(c) is to the effect that (subject to subsections (3) and (4)) all of the transferor's property is to vest in the transferee on such date as is specified in the declaration ("the specified date").

(2) The declaration operates on the specified date to vest the legal title to all of the transferor's property in the transferee, without the need for any further document transferring it.

This is subject to subsections (3) and (4).

(3) Subsection (2) does not apply to—

(a) any land held by the transferor as security for money subject to the trusts of the transferor (other than land held on trust for securing debentures or debenture stock),

(b) any land held by the transferor under a lease or agreement which contains any covenant (however described) against assignment of the transferor's interest without the consent of some other person, unless that consent has been obtained before the specified date, or

(c) any shares, stock, annuity or other property which is only transferable in books kept by a company or other body or in a manner directed by or under any enactment.

(4) In its application to registered land within the meaning of the Land Registration Act 2002, subsection (2) is subject to section 27 of that Act (dispositions required to be registered).

311 Effect of registering charity merger on gifts to transferor

(1) This section applies where a relevant charity merger is registered in the register of charity mergers.

(2) Any gift which—

(a) is expressed as a gift to the transferor, and

(b) takes effect on or after the date of registration of the merger,

takes effect as a gift to the transferee, unless it is an excluded gift.

(3) A gift is an excluded gift if—

(a) the transferor is a charity within section 306(2), and

(b) the gift is intended to be held subject to the trusts on which the whole or part of the charity's permanent endowment is held.

312 "Transferor" and "transferee" etc. in s.310 and s.311

(1) In sections 310 and 311—

(a) any reference to the transferor, in relation to a relevant charity merger, is a reference to the transferor (or one of the transferors) within the meaning of section 306, and

(b) any reference to all of the transferor's property, where the transferor is a charity within section 306(2), is a reference to all of the transferor's unrestricted property (within the meaning of section 306(2)(a)).

(2) In sections 310 and 311, any reference to the transferee, in relation to a relevant charity merger, is a reference to—

(a) the transferee (within the meaning of section 306), if it is a company or other body corporate, and

(b) otherwise, the charity trustees of the transferee (within the meaning of section 306).

Supplementary

313 Effect of provisions relating to vesting or transfer of property

No vesting or transfer of any property in pursuance of any provision of this Part operates as a breach of a covenant or condition against alienation or gives rise to a forfeiture.

314 Exception for CIOs

Nothing in this Part applies in a case where section 235 (amalgamation of CIOs) or 240 (transfer of CIO's undertaking to another CIO) applies.

PART 17

THE TRIBUNAL

CHAPTER 1

GENERAL

315 The Tribunal

(1) In this Act, "the Tribunal" in relation to any appeal, application or reference, means—

(a) the Upper Tribunal, in any case where it is determined by or under Tribunal Procedure Rules that the Upper Tribunal is to hear the appeal, application or reference, or

(b) the First-tier Tribunal, in any other case.

(2) The Tribunal has jurisdiction to hear and determine—

(a) such appeals and applications as may be made to the Tribunal in accordance with Chapter 2, or any other enactment, in respect of decisions, orders or directions of the Commission, and

(b) such matters as may be referred to the Tribunal in accordance with Chapter 3 by the Commission or the Attorney General.

(3) Such appeals, applications and matters are to be heard and determined by the Tribunal in accordance with Chapters 2 and 3, or any such enactment, taken with—

(a) rules made under section 316(2), and

(b) Tribunal Procedure Rules.

316 Rules relating to appeals, applications or references

(1) This section applies in relation to appeals, applications or references to the Tribunal which are mentioned in section 315(2).

(2) The Lord Chancellor may make rules—

(a) specifying steps which must be taken before appeals, applications or references are made to the Tribunal (and the period within which any such steps must be taken);

(b) requiring the Commission to inform persons of their right to appeal or apply to the Tribunal following a final decision, direction or order of the Commission.

(3) Tribunal Procedure Rules may make any other provision regulating the exercise of rights to appeal or to apply to the Tribunal and matters relating to the making of references to it.

(4) Rules under subsection (2) or (3) may confer a discretion on—

(a) the Tribunal, or

(b) any other person.

(5) Rules of the Lord Chancellor under this section—

(a) are to be made by statutory instrument, and

(b) are subject to annulment in pursuance of a resolution of either House of Parliament.

(6) Rules of the Lord Chancellor under this section may make—

(a) different provision for different cases, and

(b) such supplemental, incidental, consequential or transitional provision or savings as the Lord Chancellor considers appropriate.

317 Appeal from Tribunal

(1) For the purposes of sections 11(2)and 13(2) of the Tribunals, Courts and Enforcement Act 2007, the Commission and the Attorney General are to be treated as parties to cases before the Tribunal in respect of any such appeal, application or reference as is mentioned in section 315(2).

(2) In the case of an appeal under section 11 or 13 of the Tribunals, Courts and Enforcement Act 2007 against a decision of the Tribunal which determines a question referred to it by the Commission or the Attorney General, the tribunal or court hearing the appeal—

(a) must consider afresh the question referred to the Tribunal, and

(b) may take into account evidence which was not available to the Tribunal.

318 Intervention by Attorney General

(1) This section applies to any proceedings—

(a) before the Tribunal, or

(b) on an appeal from the Tribunal,

to which the Attorney General is not a party.

(2) The appropriate body may at any stage of the proceedings direct that all the necessary papers in the proceedings be sent to the Attorney General.

(3) A direction under subsection (2) may be made by the appropriate body—

(a) of its own motion, or

(b) on the application of any party to the proceedings.

(4) The Attorney General may—

(a) intervene in the proceedings in such manner as the Attorney General thinks necessary or expedient, and

(b) argue before the appropriate body any question in relation to the proceedings which the appropriate body considers it necessary to have fully argued.

(5) Subsection (4) applies whether or not a direction is given under subsection (2).

(6) In this section "the appropriate body" means the Tribunal or, in the case of an appeal from the Tribunal, the tribunal or court hearing the appeal.

CHAPTER 2

APPEALS AND APPLICATIONS TO TRIBUNAL

319 Appeals: general

(1) Except in the case of a reviewable matter (see section 322) an appeal may be brought to the Tribunal against any decision, direction or order mentioned in column 1 of Schedule 6.

(2) Such an appeal may be brought by—

(a) the Attorney General, or

(b) any person specified in the corresponding entry in column 2 of Schedule 6.

(3) The Commission is to be the respondent to such an appeal.

(4) In determining such an appeal the Tribunal—

(a) must consider afresh the decision, direction or order appealed against, and

(b) may take into account evidence which was not available to the Commission.

(5) The Tribunal may—

(a) dismiss the appeal, or

(b) if it allows the appeal, exercise any power specified in the corresponding entry in column 3 of Schedule 6.

320 Appeals: orders under s.52

(1) Section 319(4)(a) does not apply in relation to an appeal against an order made under section 52 (power to call for documents).

(2) On such an appeal the Tribunal must consider whether the information or document in question—

(a) relates to a charity;

(b) is relevant to the discharge of the functions of the Commission or the official custodian.

(3) The Tribunal may allow such an appeal only if it is satisfied that the information or document in question does not fall within subsection (2)(a) or (b).

321 Reviews

(1) An application may be made to the Tribunal for the review of a reviewable matter.

(2) Such an application may be made by—

(a) the Attorney General, or

(b) any person mentioned in the entry in column 2 of Schedule 6 which corresponds to the entry in column 1 which relates to the reviewable matter.

(3) The Commission is to be the respondent to such an application.

(4) In determining such an application the Tribunal must apply the principles which would be applied by the High Court on an application for judicial review.

(5) The Tribunal may—

(a) dismiss the application, or

(b) if it allows the application, exercise any power mentioned in the entry in column 3 of Schedule 6 which corresponds to the entry in column 1 which relates to the reviewable matter.

322 Reviewable matters

(1) In this Chapter references to reviewable matters are to—

(a) decisions to which subsection (2) applies, and

(b) orders to which subsection (3) applies.

(2) This subsection applies to decisions of the Commission—

(a) to institute an inquiry under section 46 with regard to a particular institution;

(b) to institute an inquiry under section 46 with regard to a class of institutions;

(c) not to make a common investment scheme under section 96;

(d) not to make a common deposit scheme under section 100;

(e) not to make an order under section 105 (power to authorise dealings with charity property etc.) in relation to a charity;

(f) not to make an order under section 117 (restrictions on dispositions of land) in relation to land held by or in trust for a charity;

(g) not to make an order under section 124 (restrictions on mortgages) in relation to a mortgage of land held by or in trust for a charity.

(3) This subsection applies to an order made by the Commission under section 147(2) (investigation and audit) in relation to a charitable company.

323 Remission of matters to Commission

References in column 3 of Schedule 6 to the power to remit a matter to the Commission are to the power to remit the matter—

(a) generally, or

(b) for determination in accordance with a finding made or direction given by the Tribunal.

324 Power to amend provisions relating to appeals and applications to Tribunal

(1) The Minister may by order—

(a) amend or otherwise modify an entry in Schedule 6,

(b) add an entry to Schedule 6, or

(c) remove an entry from Schedule 6.

(2) An order under subsection (1) may make such amendments, repeals or other modifications of—

(a) sections 319 to 323, or

(b) an enactment which applies this Chapter and Schedule 6,

as the Minister considers appropriate in consequence of any change in Schedule 6 made by the order.

(3) Subsections (1) and (2) apply (with the necessary modifications) in relation to section 57 of the Charities Act 2006 as if—

(a) that section were contained in this Chapter, and
(b) the reference in subsection (2) to sections 319 to 323 included a reference to any other provision relating to appeals to the Tribunal which is contained in Chapter 1 of Part 3 of the Charities Act 2006.

CHAPTER 3

REFERENCES TO TRIBUNAL

325 References by Commission

(1) A question which—
  (a) has arisen in connection with the exercise by the Commission of any of its functions, and
  (b) involves either the operation of charity law in any respect or its application to a particular state of affairs,

may be referred to the Tribunal by the Commission if the Commission considers it desirable to refer the question to the Tribunal.

(2) The Commission may make such a reference only with the consent of the Attorney General.

(3) The Commission is to be a party to proceedings before the Tribunal on the reference.

(4) The following are entitled to be parties to proceedings before the Tribunal on the reference—
  (a) the Attorney General, and
  (b) with the Tribunal's permission—
    (i) the charity trustees of any charity which is likely to be affected by the Tribunal's decision on the reference,
    (ii) any such charity which is a body corporate, and
    (iii) any other person who is likely to be so affected.

326 References by Attorney General

(1) A question which involves—
  (a) the operation of charity law in any respect, or
  (b) the application of charity law to a particular state of affairs,

may be referred to the Tribunal by the Attorney General if the Attorney General considers it desirable to refer the question to the Tribunal.

(2) The Attorney General is to be a party to proceedings before the Tribunal on the reference.

(3) The following are entitled to be parties to proceedings before the Tribunal on the reference—
  (a) the Commission, and
  (b) with the Tribunal's permission—
    (i) the charity trustees of any charity which is likely to be affected by the Tribunal's decision on the reference,

(ii) any such charity which is a body corporate, and

(iii) any other person who is likely to be so affected.

327 Powers of Commission in relation to matters referred to Tribunal

(1) This section applies where a question which involves the application of charity law to a particular state of affairs has been referred to the Tribunal under section 325 or 326.

(2) The Commission must not take any steps in reliance on any view as to the application of charity law to that state of affairs until—

(a) proceedings on the reference (including any proceedings on appeal) have been concluded, and

(b) any period during which an appeal (or further appeal) may ordinarily be made has ended.

(3) Where—

(a) paragraphs (a) and (b) of subsection (2) are satisfied, and

(b) the question has been decided in proceedings on the reference,

the Commission must give effect to that decision when dealing with the particular state of affairs to which the reference related.

328 Suspension of time limits while reference is in progress

(1) Subsection (2) applies if—

(a) section 327(2) prevents the Commission from taking any steps which it would otherwise be permitted or required to take, and

(b) the steps in question may be taken only during a period specified in an enactment ("the specified period").

(2) The running of the specified period is suspended for the period which—

(a) begins with the date on which the question is referred to the Tribunal, and

(b) ends with the date on which paragraphs (a) and (b) of section 327(2) are satisfied.

(3) Nothing in—

(a) this section, or

(b) section 271 or 278 (suspension of period during which Commission may object to resolution of unincorporated charity),

prevents the specified period being suspended concurrently by virtue of subsection (2) and any of the provisions of sections 271 and 278.

329 Agreement for Commission to act while reference is in progress

(1) Section 327(2) does not apply in relation to any steps taken by the Commission with the agreement of—

(a) the persons who are parties to the proceedings on the reference at the time when those steps are taken, and

(b) (if not within paragraph (a)) the charity trustees of any charity which—

(i) is likely to be directly affected by the taking of those steps, and

(ii) is not a party to the proceedings at that time.

(2) The Commission may take those steps despite the suspension in accordance with section 328(2) of any period during which it would otherwise be permitted or required to take them.

(3) Section 327(3) does not require the Commission to give effect to a decision as to the application of charity law to a particular state of affairs to the extent that the decision is inconsistent with any steps already taken by the Commission in relation to that state of affairs in accordance with this section.

330 Appeals and applications in respect of matters determined on references

(1) No appeal or application may be made to the Tribunal by a person to whom subsection (2) applies in respect of an order or decision made, or direction given, by the Commission in accordance with section 327(3).

(2) This subsection applies to a person who was at any stage a party to the proceedings in which the question referred to the Tribunal was decided.

(3) Any enactment (including one contained in this Act) which provides for an appeal or application to be made to the Tribunal has effect subject to subsection (1).

331 Interpretation

(1) In this Chapter—

"charity law" means—

(a) any enactment contained in, or made under, this Act or the Charities Act 2006,

(b) any other enactment specified in regulations made by the Minister, and

(c) any rule of law which relates to charities, and

"enactment" includes an enactment comprised in subordinate legislation (within the meaning of the Interpretation Act 1978), and includes an enactment whenever passed or made.

(2) The exclusions contained in section 10(2) (ecclesiastical corporations etc.) do not have effect for the purposes of this Chapter.

PART 18

MISCELLANEOUS AND SUPPLEMENTARY

Administrative provisions about charities

332 Manner of giving notice of charity meetings, etc.

(1) All notices which are required or authorised by the trusts of a charity to be given to a charity trustee, member or subscriber—

(a) may be sent by post, and

(b) if sent by post, may be addressed to any address given as the address of the charity trustee, member or subscriber in the list of such persons for the time being in use at the office or principal office of the charity.

(2) Subsections (3) and (4) apply where a notice is required by the trusts of the charity to be given to a charity trustee, member or subscriber.

(3) If the notice is given by post, it is to be treated as having been given by the time at which the letter containing it would be delivered in the ordinary course of post.

(4) If the notice is a notice of any meeting or election, the notice need not be given to any charity trustee, member or subscriber who, in the list mentioned in subsection (1)(b), has no address in the United Kingdom.

333 Conferral of authority to execute documents

(1) Charity trustees may, subject to the trusts of the charity, confer on any two or more of their body—

(a) a general authority, or

(b) an authority limited in such manner as the charity trustees think fit,

to execute in the names and on behalf of the charity trustees documents for giving effect to transactions to which the charity trustees are a party.

(2) Any document executed in pursuance of an authority under subsection (1) is of the same effect as if executed by the whole body.

(3) An authority under subsection (1)—

(a) suffices for any document if it is given in writing or by resolution of a meeting of the charity trustees, despite the want of any formality that would be required in giving an authority apart from that subsection;

(b) may be given so as to make the powers conferred exercisable by any of the charity trustees, or may be restricted to named persons or in any other way;

(c) subject to any such restriction, and until it is revoked, has effect, despite any change in the charity trustees, as a continuing authority given by the charity trustees from time to time of the charity and exercisable by such charity trustees.

(4) In any authority under this section to execute a document in the names and on behalf of charity trustees there is, unless the contrary intention appears, implied authority also to execute it for them in the name and on behalf of the official custodian or of any other person, in any case in which the charity trustees could do so.

(5) Where a document purports to be executed in pursuance of this section, then in favour of a person who (then or afterwards) in good faith acquires for money or money's worth—

(a) an interest in or charge on property, or

(b) the benefit of any covenant or agreement expressed to be entered into by the charity trustees,

it is conclusively presumed to have been duly executed by virtue of this section.

(6) The powers conferred by this section are in addition to and not in derogation of any other powers.

334 Transfer and evidence of title to property vested in trustees

(1) Subsection (2) applies where, under the trusts of a charity, trustees of property held for the purposes of the charity may be appointed or discharged by resolution of a meeting of the charity trustees, members or other persons.

(2) A memorandum declaring a trustee to have been so appointed or discharged is sufficient evidence of that fact if the memorandum—

(a) is signed either at the meeting by the person presiding or in some other manner directed by the meeting, and

(b) is attested by two persons present at the meeting.

(3) A memorandum evidencing the appointment or discharge of a trustee under subsection (2), if executed as a deed, has the same operation under section 40 of the Trustee Act 1925 (vesting declarations as respects trust property in deeds appointing or discharging trustees) as if the appointment or discharge were effected by the deed.

(4) For the purposes of this section, where a document purports to have been signed and attested as mentioned in subsection (2), then on proof (whether by evidence or as a matter of presumption) of the signature the document is presumed to have been so signed and attested, unless the contrary is shown.

(5) This section applies to a memorandum made at any time, except that subsection (3) applies only to those made on or after 1 January 1961.

(6) This section applies in relation to any institution to which the Literary and Scientific Institutions Act 1854 applies as it applies in relation to a charity.

(7) No vesting or transfer of any property in pursuance of any provision of this section operates as a breach of a covenant or condition against alienation or gives rise to a forfeiture.

Enforcement powers of Commission etc.

335 Enforcement of requirements by order of Commission

(1) If a person fails to comply with any requirement imposed by or under this Act then (subject to subsection (2)) the Commission may by order give that person such directions as it considers appropriate for securing that the default is made good.

(2) Subsection (1) does not apply to any such requirement if—

(a) a person who fails to comply with, or is persistently in default in relation to, the requirement is liable to any criminal penalty, or

(b) the requirement is imposed by—

(i) an order of the Commission to which section 336 applies, or

(ii) a direction of the Commission to which section 336 applies by virtue of section 338(2).

336 Enforcement of orders of Commission

(1) A person guilty of disobedience to an order mentioned in subsection (2) may on the application of the Commission to the High Court be dealt with as for disobedience to an order of the High Court.

(2) The orders are—

(a) an order of the Commission under—

section 52(1) (power to call for documents),

section 84 (power to direct specified action to be taken),

section 85 (power to direct application of charity property),

section 87 (supervision of certain Scottish charities),

section 155 (power to direct compliance with regulations giving auditors etc. access to information etc.),

section 184 (civil consequences of acting while disqualified),

section 186 (disqualification of charity trustee or trustee receiving remuneration under section 185),

section 263 (dissolution of incorporated body),

(b) an order of the Commission under—

section 69 (concurrent jurisdiction with High Court for certain purposes), or

any of sections 76 and 79 to 81 (powers to act for protection of charities etc.),

requiring a transfer of property or payment to be called for or made, or

(c) an order of the Commission requiring a default under this Act to be made good.

337 Other provisions as to orders of Commission

(1) Any order made by the Commission under this Act may include such incidental or supplementary provisions as the Commission thinks expedient for carrying into effect the objects of the order.

(2) Where the Commission exercises any jurisdiction to make an order under this Act on an application or reference to it, it may insert any such provisions in the order even though the application or reference does not propose their insertion.

(3) Where the Commission makes an order under this Act, the Commission—

(a) may itself give such public notice as it thinks fit of the making or contents of the order, or

(b) may require it to be given by—

(i) any person on whose application the order is made, or

(ii) any charity affected by the order.

(4) The Commission may, with or without any application or reference to it, discharge an order in whole or in part, and subject or not to any savings or other transitional provisions, if—

(a) it made the order under any provision of this Act other than section 263 (dissolution of incorporated body), and

(b) at any time within 12 months after it made the order, it is satisfied that the order was made by mistake or on misrepresentation or otherwise than in conformity with this Act.

(5) Except for the purposes of subsection (4) or an appeal under this Act, an order made by the Commission under this Act—

(a) is to be treated as having been duly and formally made, and

(b) is not to be called in question on the ground only of irregularity or informality,

but (subject to any further order) has effect according to its tenor.

(6) Any order made by the Commission under any provision of this Act may be varied or revoked by a subsequent order so made and may include transitional provisions or savings.

338 Directions of the Commission or person conducting inquiry

(1) Any direction given by the Commission under any provision of this Act—

(a) may be varied or revoked by a further direction given under that provision, and

(b) must be given in writing.

(2) Sections 336 (enforcement of orders) and 337(1) to (3) and (5) (other provisions as to orders) apply to any such directions as they apply to an order of the Commission.

(3) In subsection (1) the reference to the Commission includes, in relation to a direction under section 47(2) (obtaining evidence etc. for the purposes of an inquiry), a reference to any person conducting an inquiry under section 46.

(4) Nothing in this section is to be read as applying to any directions contained in an order made by the Commission under section 335(1) (directions for securing that default is made good).

339 Service of orders and directions

(1) This section applies to any order or direction made or given by the Commission under this Act.

(2) Any such order or direction may be served on a person (other than a body corporate) by—

(a) delivering it to that person,

(b) leaving it at that person's last known address in the United Kingdom, or

(c) sending it by post to that person at that address.

(3) Any such order or direction may be served on a body corporate by delivering it or sending it by post—

(a) to the registered or principal office of the body in the United Kingdom, or

(b) if it has no such office in the United Kingdom, to any place in the United Kingdom where it carries on business or conducts its activities (as the case may be).

(4) Any such order or direction may also be served on a person (including a body corporate) by sending it by post to that person at an address notified by that person to the Commission for the purposes of this subsection.

(5) In this section any reference to the Commission includes, in relation to a direction under section 47(2) (obtaining evidence etc. for the purposes of an inquiry), a reference to any person conducting an inquiry under section 46.

Documents and evidence etc.

340 Enrolment and deposit of documents etc.

(1) The Commission may provide books in which any deed, will or other document relating to a charity may be enrolled.

(2) The Commission may accept for safe keeping any document of or relating to a charity, and the charity trustees or other persons having the custody of documents of or relating to a charity (including a charity which has ceased to exist) may with the consent of the Commission deposit them with the Commission for safe keeping, except in the case of documents required by some other enactment to be kept elsewhere.

(3) Regulations made by the Minister may make provision for such documents deposited with the Commission under this section as may be prescribed by the regulations to be destroyed or otherwise disposed of after such period or in such circumstances as may be so prescribed.

(4) Subsection (3) applies to any document—

(a) transmitted to the Commission under section 52, and

(b) kept by the Commission under section 52(3),

as if the document had been deposited with the Commission for safe keeping under this section.

(5) Subsections (3) and (4) apply (with any necessary adaptations) to documents enrolled by, deposited with or transmitted to the Charity Commissioners for England and Wales under corresponding previous enactments, including in particular the Charitable Trusts Act 1853 to 1939.

341 Evidence of documents received by Commission etc.

(1) Subsection (2) applies where a document is enrolled by the Commission or is for the time being deposited with the Commission under section 340.

(2) Evidence of the document's contents may be given by means of a copy certified by any member of the staff of the Commission generally or specially authorised by the Commission to act for this purpose.

(3) A document purporting to be such a copy is to be received in evidence without proof—

(a) of the official position, authority or handwriting of the person certifying it, or

(b) of the original document being enrolled or deposited.

(4) Subsections (2) and (3) apply to any document—

(a) transmitted to the Commission under section 52, and

(b) kept by the Commission under section 52(3),

as if the document had been deposited with the Commission for safe keeping under section 340.

(5) Subsections (2) to (4) apply (with any necessary adaptations) to documents enrolled by, deposited with or transmitted to the Charity Commissioners for England and Wales under corresponding previous enactments, including in particular the Charitable Trusts Act 1853 to 1939.

342 Report of inquiry to be evidence in certain proceedings

(1) A copy of the report of the person conducting an inquiry under section 46, if certified by the Commission to be a true copy, is admissible in any proceedings to which this section applies—

(a) as evidence of any fact stated in the report, and

(b) as evidence of the opinion of that person as to any matter referred to in it.

(2) This section applies to—

(a) any legal proceedings instituted by the Commission under Part 6, and

(b) any legal proceedings instituted by the Attorney General in respect of a charity.

(3) A document purporting to be a certificate issued for the purposes of subsection (1) is to be—

(a) received in evidence, and

(b) treated as such a certificate,

unless the contrary is proved.

343 Evidence of documents issued by Commission etc.

(1) Evidence of any order, certificate or other document issued by the Commission may be given by means of a copy retained by it, or taken from a copy so retained, if the copy is certified to be a true copy by any member of the staff of the Commission generally or specially authorised by the Commission to act for this purpose.

(2) Evidence of an entry in any register kept by the Commission may be given by means of a copy of the entry, if the copy is certified to be a true copy by any member of the staff of the Commission generally or specially authorised by the Commission to act for this purpose.

(3) A document purporting to be such a copy as is mentioned in subsection (1) or (2) is to be received in evidence without proof of the official position, authority or handwriting of the person certifying it.

(4) Subsections (1) and (3) apply to any order, certificate or other document issued by the Charity Commissioners for England and Wales as they apply to any order, certificate or other document issued by the Commission.

344 Other miscellaneous provisions as to evidence

(1) Subsection (2) applies to proceedings to recover or compel payment of any rentcharge or other periodical payment claimed by or on behalf of a charity out of land or of the rents, profits or other income of land, otherwise than as rent incident to a reversion.

(2) If it is shown in any proceedings to which this subsection applies that the rentcharge or other periodical payment has at any time been paid for 12 consecutive years to or for the benefit of the charity—

(a) that is prima facie evidence of the perpetual liability to it of the land or income, and

(b) no proof of its origin is necessary.

(3) In any proceedings, the following documents are admissible as evidence of the documents and facts stated in them—

(a) the printed copies of the reports of the Commissioners for enquiring concerning charities, 1818 to 1837, who were appointed under the Act 58 Geo. 3 c. 91 and subsequent Acts, and

(b) the printed copies of the reports which were made for various counties and county boroughs to the Charity Commissioners by their assistant commissioners and presented to the House of Commons as returns to orders of various dates beginning with 8 December 1890, and ending with 9 September 1909.

Offences

345 Restriction on institution of proceedings for certain offences

(1) No proceedings for an offence to which this section applies are to be instituted except by or with the consent of the Director of Public Prosecutions.

(2) This section applies to any offence under—

(a) section 41 (offences in connection with statements required in official publications etc.),

(b) section 60 (supply of false or misleading information to Commission etc.),

(c) section 77(1) (offence of contravening certain orders made for protection of charities),

(d) section 173 (offences of failing to supply certain documents), or

(e) section 183(1) (criminal consequences of acting while disqualified).

346 Offences by bodies corporate

(1) If an offence under this Act—

(a) is committed by a body corporate, and

(b) is proved to have been committed with the consent or connivance of, or to be attributable to any neglect on the part of, an officer of the body corporate,

the officer as well as the body corporate is guilty of the offence and liable to be proceeded against and punished accordingly.

(2) In this section, "officer", in relation to a body corporate, means—

(a) any director, manager, secretary or other similar officer of the body corporate, or

(b) any person who was purporting to act in any such capacity,

and, in relation to a body corporate whose affairs are managed by its members, "director" means a member of the body corporate.

Regulations and orders

347 Regulations and orders: general

(1) Any power of the Minister to make any regulations or order under this Act is exercisable by statutory instrument.

(2) Subject to sections 348(1) and 349(1), regulations or orders of the Minister under this Act are subject to annulment in pursuance of a resolution of either House of Parliament.

(3) Any regulations of the Minister or the Commission and any order of the Minister under this Act may make—

(a) different provision for different cases or descriptions of case or different purposes or areas, and

(b) such supplemental, incidental, consequential, transitory or transitional provision or savings as the Minister or, as the case may be, the Commission considers appropriate.

(4) Nothing in this section applies to an order under paragraph 29 of Schedule 9 (transitory modifications).

348 Regulations subject to affirmative procedure etc.

(1) Section 347(2) (negative procedure) does not apply to—

(a) regulations under section 19 (fees and other amounts payable to Commission) which require the payment of a fee in respect of any matter for which no fee was previously payable;

(b) regulations under section 25 (meaning of "principal regulator") which amend any provision of an Act;

(c) regulations under section 245 (regulations about winding up, insolvency and dissolution of CIOs).

(2) No regulations within subsection (1)(a) or (c) may be made unless a draft of the regulations has been laid before and approved by a resolution of each House of Parliament.

(3) No regulations within subsection (1)(b) may be made (whether alone or with other provisions) unless a draft of the regulations has been laid before and approved by a resolution of each House of Parliament.

(4) Before making any regulations under—

(a) Part 8 (charity accounts, reports and returns), or

(b) section 245 or 246 (certain powers to make regulations about CIOs),

the Minister must consult such persons or bodies of persons as the Minister considers appropriate.

349 Orders subject to affirmative procedure etc.

(1) Section 347(2) (negative procedure) does not apply to—

(a) an order under section 23 (power to amend Schedule 3 so as to add or remove exempt charities);

(b) an order under section 73(2) (powers to make schemes altering provision made by Acts etc.);

(c) an order under section 190 (power to amend provisions relating to indemnity insurance for charity trustees and trustees);

(d) an order under section 324 (power to amend provisions relating to appeals and applications to Tribunal).

(2) No order within subsection (1)(a) may be made (whether alone or with other provisions) unless a draft of the order has been laid before and approved by a resolution of each House of Parliament.

(3) No order within subsection (1)(c) or (d) may be made unless a draft of the order has been laid before and approved by a resolution of each House of Parliament.

(4) If a draft of an instrument containing an order under section 23 would, apart from this subsection, be treated for the purposes of the Standing Orders of either House of Parliament as a hybrid instrument, it is to proceed in that House as if it were not such an instrument.

Interpretation

350 Connected person: child, spouse and civil partner

(1) In sections 118(2)(c), 188(1)(a), 200(1)(a) and 249(2)(a), "child" includes a stepchild and an illegitimate child.

(2) For the purposes of sections 118(2)(e), 188(1)(b), 200(1)(b) and 249(2)(b)—
- (a) a person living with another as that person's husband or wife is to be treated as that person's spouse;
- (b) where two people of the same sex are not civil partners but live together as if they were, each of them is to be treated as the civil partner of the other.

351 Connected person: controlled institution

For the purposes of sections 118(2)(g), 157(1)(a), 188(1)(d), 200(1)(d) and 249(2)(d), a person controls an institution if the person is able to secure that the affairs of the institution are conducted in accordance with the person's wishes.

352 Connected person: substantial interest in body corporate

(1) For the purposes of sections 118(2)(h), 157(1)(b), 188(1)(e), 200(1)(e) and 249(2)(e), any such connected person as is there mentioned has a substantial interest in a body corporate if the person or institution in question—
- (a) is interested in shares comprised in the equity share capital of that body of a nominal value of more than one-fifth of that share capital, or
- (b) is entitled to exercise, or control the exercise of, more than one-fifth of the voting power at any general meeting of that body.

(2) The rules set out in Schedule 1 to the Companies Act 2006 (rules for interpretation of certain provisions of that Act) apply for the purposes of subsection (1) as they apply for the purposes of section 254 of that Act ("connected persons" etc.).

(3) In this section "equity share capital" and "share" have the same meaning as in that Act.

353 Minor definitions

(1) In this Act, except in so far as the context otherwise requires—

"company" means a company registered under the Companies Act 2006 in England and Wales or Scotland;

"the court" means—

(a) the High Court, and

(b) within the limits of its jurisdiction, any other court in England and Wales having a jurisdiction in respect of charities concurrent (within any limit of area or amount) with that of the High Court,

and includes any judge or officer of the court exercising the jurisdiction of the court;

"ecclesiastical charity" has the same meaning as in the Local Government Act 1894;

"financial year"—

(a) in relation to a charitable company, is to be construed in accordance with section 390 of the Companies Act 2006, and

(b) in relation to any other charity, is to be construed in accordance with regulations made by virtue of section 132(3);

but this is subject to any provision of regulations made by virtue of section 142(3) (financial years of subsidiary undertakings);

"gross income", in relation to a charity, means its gross recorded income from all sources including special trusts;

"independent examiner", in relation to a charity, means such a person as is mentioned in section 145(1)(a);

"members", in relation to a charity with a body of members distinct from the charity trustees, means any of those members;

"the Minister" means the Minister for the Cabinet Office;

"trusts"—

(a) in relation to a charity, means the provisions establishing it as a charity and regulating its purposes and administration, whether those provisions take effect by way of trust or not, and

(b) in relation to other institutions has a corresponding meaning.

(2) In this Act, except in so far as the context otherwise requires, "document" includes information recorded in any form, and, in relation to information recorded otherwise than in legible form—

(a) any reference to its production is to be read as a reference to the provision of a copy of it in legible form, and

(b) any reference to the provision of a copy of, or extract from, it is accordingly to be read as a reference to the provision of a copy of, or extract from, it in legible form.

(3) A charity is to be treated for the purposes of this Act as having a permanent endowment unless all property held for the purposes of the charity may be expended for those purposes without distinction between—

(a) capital, and

(b) income;

and in this Act "permanent endowment" means, in relation to any charity, property held subject to a restriction on its being expended for the purposes of the charity.

PART 19

FINAL PROVISIONS

354 Amendments etc.

(1) Schedule 7 contains consequential amendments.

(2) Schedule 8 contains transitional provisions and savings.

(3) Schedule 9 contains transitory modifications.

(4) Schedule 10 contains repeals and revocations.

355 Commencement

This Act comes into force at the end of the period of 3 months beginning with the day on which it is passed.

356 Extent

(1) Subject to subsections (2) to (7), this Act extends to England and Wales only.

(2) Chapter 1 of Part 1 (meaning of "charity" and "charitable purpose": general)—

(a) extends also to Scotland, but affects the law of Scotland only so far as mentioned in section 7;

(b) extends also to Northern Ireland, but affects the law of Northern Ireland only so far as mentioned in section 8.

(3) In Part 5 (information powers), sections 54 to 59 (disclosure of information to and by Commission) extend to the whole of the United Kingdom.

(4) In Part 6 (application of property cy-près etc.)—

(a) section 68(3) and (4) (amendment of Royal charters by Order in Council where body corporate the subject of a scheme), and

(b) sections 96 to 104 (common investment or deposit funds),

extend also to Northern Ireland.

(5) Paragraph 2 of Schedule 7 (construction of references in enactments and documents to Charity Commissioners for England and Wales) extends also to Scotland and Northern Ireland.

(6) Subject to any provision made by Schedule 7, any amendment, repeal or revocation made by Schedule 7 or 10 has the same extent as the enactment or provision to which it relates.

(7) In Part 2 of Schedule 8 (transitionals and savings: recreational etc. purposes)—

(a) paragraphs 9 to 12 extend also to Scotland but paragraphs 10 and 12 affect the law of Scotland only so far as mentioned in those paragraphs;

(b) paragraphs 9 to 11 and 13 extend also to Northern Ireland but paragraphs 10 and 13 affect the law of Northern Ireland only so far as mentioned in those paragraphs.

357 Index of defined expressions

Schedule 11 lists the places where some of the expressions used in this Act are defined or otherwise explained.

358 Short title

This Act may be cited as the Charities Act 2011.

SCHEDULES

SCHEDULE 1

Section 13

THE CHARITY COMMISSION

Membership

1 (1) The Commission is to consist of—
(a) a person appointed by the Minister to chair the Commission, and
(b) at least 4, but not more than 8, other members appointed by the Minister.

(2) The Minister must exercise the power in sub-paragraph (1) so as to secure that—
(a) the knowledge and experience of the members of the Commission (taken together) includes knowledge and experience of the matters mentioned in sub-paragraph (3),
(b) at least two members have a 7 year general qualification within the meaning of section 71 of the Courts and Legal Services Act 1990, and
(c) at least one member—
(i) knows about conditions in Wales, and
(ii) has been appointed following consultation with the Welsh Ministers.

(3) The matters are—
(a) the law relating to charities,
(b) charity accounts and the financing of charities, and
(c) the operation and regulation of charities of different sizes and descriptions.

(4) In sub-paragraph (2)(c) "member" does not include the person appointed to chair the Commission.

Terms of appointment and remuneration

2 The members of the Commission hold and vacate office as such in accordance with the terms of their respective appointments.

3 (1) An appointment of a person to hold office as a member of the Commission must be for a term of no more than 3 years.

(2) A person holding office as a member of the Commission—
(a) may resign that office by giving notice in writing to the Minister, and
(b) may be removed from office by the Minister on the ground of incapacity or misbehaviour.

(3) Before removing a member of the Commission the Minister must consult—
(a) the Commission, and
(b) if the member was appointed following consultation with the Welsh Ministers, the Welsh Ministers.

(4) No person may hold office as a member of the Commission for more than 10 years in total.

(5) For the purposes of sub-paragraph (4), time spent holding office as a Charity Commissioner for England and Wales counts as time spent holding office as a member of the Commission.

4 (1) The Commission must pay to its members such remuneration, and such other allowances, as may be determined by the Minister.

(2) The Commission must, if required to do so by the Minister—

- (a) pay such pension, allowances or gratuities as may be determined by the Minister to or in respect of a person who is or has been a member of the Commission, or
- (b) make such payments as may be so determined towards provision for the payment of a pension, allowances or gratuities to or in respect of such a person.

(3) Sub-paragraph (4) applies if the Minister determines that there are special circumstances which make it right for a person ceasing to hold office as a member of the Commission to receive compensation.

(4) The Commission must pay to the person a sum by way of compensation of such amount as may be determined by the Minister.

Staff

5 (1) The Commission—

- (a) must appoint a chief executive, and
- (b) may appoint such other staff as it may determine.

(2) The terms and conditions of service of persons appointed under sub-paragraph (1) are to be such as the Commission may determine with the approval of the Minister for the Civil Service.

Committees

6 (1) The Commission may establish committees and any committee of the Commission may establish sub-committees.

(2) The members of a committee of the Commission may include persons who are not members of the Commission (and the members of a sub-committee may include persons who are not members of the committee or of the Commission).

Procedure etc.

7 (1) The Commission may regulate its own procedure (including quorum).

(2) The validity of anything done by the Commission is not affected by—

- (a) a vacancy among its members, or
- (b) a defect in the appointment of a member.

Performance of functions

8 Anything authorised or required to be done by the Commission may be done by—

(a) any member or member of staff of the Commission who is authorised for that purpose by the Commission, whether generally or specially;

(b) any committee of the Commission which has been so authorised.

Evidence

9 The Documentary Evidence Act 1868 has effect as if—

(a) the Commission were mentioned in the first column of the Schedule to that Act,

(b) any member or member of staff of the Commission authorised to act on behalf of the Commission were specified in the second column of that Schedule in connection with the Commission, and

(c) the regulations referred to in that Act included any document issued by or under the authority of the Commission.

Execution of documents

10 (1) A document is executed by the Commission by the fixing of its common seal to the document.

(2) But the fixing of that seal to a document must be authenticated by the signature of—

(a) any member of the Commission, or

(b) any member of its staff,

who is authorised for the purpose by the Commission.

(3) A document which is expressed (in whatever form of words) to be executed by the Commission and is signed by—

(a) any member of the Commission, or

(b) any member of its staff,

who is authorised for the purpose by the Commission has the same effect as if executed in accordance with sub-paragraphs (1) and (2).

(4) A document executed by the Commission which makes it clear on its face that it is intended to be a deed has effect, upon delivery, as a deed; and it is to be presumed (unless a contrary intention is proved) to be delivered upon its being executed.

(5) In favour of a purchaser a document is to be treated as having been duly executed by the Commission if it purports to be signed on its behalf by—

(a) any member of the Commission, or

(b) any member of its staff;

and, if it makes it clear on its face that it is intended to be a deed, it is to be treated as having been delivered upon its being executed.

(6) For the purposes of this paragraph—

"authorised" means authorised whether generally or specially, and

"purchaser"—

(a) means a purchaser in good faith for valuable consideration, and

(b) includes a lessee, mortgagee or other person who for valuable consideration acquired an interest in property.

Annual report

11 (1) As soon as practicable after the end of each financial year the Commission must publish a report on—

(a) the discharge of its functions,

(b) the extent to which, in its opinion, its objectives (see section 14) have been met,

(c) the performance of its general duties (see section 16), and

(d) the management of its affairs,

during that year.

(2) The Commission must lay a copy of each such report before Parliament.

(3) "Financial year" means the 12 months ending with 31 March in any year.

Annual public meeting

12 (1) The Commission must hold a public meeting ("the annual meeting") for the purpose of enabling a report under paragraph 11 to be considered.

(2) The annual meeting must be held within the period of 3 months beginning with the day on which the report is published.

(3) The Commission must organise the annual meeting so as to allow—

(a) a general discussion of the contents of the report which is being considered, and

(b) a reasonable opportunity for those attending the meeting to put questions to the Commission about matters to which the report relates.

(4) But subject to sub-paragraph (3) the annual meeting is to be organised and conducted in such a way as the Commission considers appropriate.

(5) The Commission must—

(a) take such steps as are reasonable in the circumstances to ensure that notice of the annual meeting is given to every registered charity, and

(b) publish notice of the annual meeting in the way appearing to it to be best calculated to bring it to the attention of members of the public.

(6) Each such notice must—

(a) give details of the time and place at which the meeting is to be held,

(b) set out the proposed agenda for the meeting,

(c) indicate the proposed duration of the meeting, and

(d) give details of the Commission's arrangements for enabling persons to attend.

(7) If the Commission proposes to alter any of the arrangements which have been included in notices given or published under sub-paragraph (5) it must—

(a) give reasonable notice of the alteration, and

(b) publish the notice in the way appearing to it to be best calculated to bring it to the attention of registered charities and members of the public.

Status: *This is the original version (as it was originally enacted).*

SCHEDULE 2

Section 21

THE OFFICIAL CUSTODIAN

Status and official seal

1 The official custodian is a corporation sole whose official seal is to be officially and judicially noticed.

Expenses

2 The expenses of the official custodian (except those reimbursed to, or recovered by, the official custodian as trustee for any charity) are to be defrayed by the Commission.

Performance of functions and liability for loss or misapplication of property

3 Anything which is required to or may be done by, to or before the official custodian may be done by, to or before any member of the staff of the Commission generally or specially authorised by it to act for the official custodian during a vacancy in the official custodian's office or otherwise.

4 (1) The official custodian is not liable as trustee for any charity in respect of any loss or of the misapplication of any property unless it is occasioned by or through the wilful neglect or default of—

(a) the official custodian, or

(b) any person acting for the official custodian.

(2) But the Consolidated Fund is liable to make good to a charity any sums for which the official custodian may be liable because of any such neglect or default.

Accounts

5 The official custodian must—

(a) keep such books of account and such records in relation to them as may be directed by the Treasury, and

(b) prepare accounts, in such form, in such manner and at such times as may be directed by the Treasury.

6 The Comptroller and Auditor General must—

(a) examine, certify and report on the accounts so prepared, and

(b) send a copy of the certified accounts and the report to the Commission.

7 The Commission must publish and lay before Parliament a copy of the documents sent to it under paragraph 6(b).

SCHEDULE 3

Section 22

EXEMPT CHARITIES

Institutions with an exemption from the Charitable Trusts Acts 1853 to 1939

1 (1) Any institution which, if the Charities Act 1960 had not been passed, would be exempted from the powers and jurisdiction, under the Charitable Trusts Acts 1853 to 1939, of—

(a) the Charity Commissioners for England and Wales, or

(b) the Minister of Education,

(apart from any power of the Commissioners or Minister to apply those Acts in whole or in part to charities otherwise exempt) by the terms of any enactment not contained in the Charitable Trusts Acts 1853 to 1939 other than section 9 of the Places of Worship Registration Act 1855.

(2) Sub-paragraph (1) does not include—

(a) any Investment Fund or Deposit Fund within the meaning of the Church Funds Investment Measure 1958,

(b) any investment fund or deposit fund within the meaning of the Methodist Church Funds Act 1960, or

(c) the representative body of the Welsh Church or property administered by it.

Educational institutions

2 The universities of Oxford, Cambridge, London, Durham, Newcastle and Manchester.

3 King's College London and Queen Mary and Westfield College in the University of London.

4 (1) Any of the following, if Her Majesty declares it by Order in Council to be an exempt charity for the purposes of this Act—

(a) a university in England,

(b) a university college in England, or

(c) an institution which is connected with a university in England or a university college in England.

(2) Sub-paragraph (1) does not include—

(a) any college in the university of Oxford;

(b) any college or hall in the university of Cambridge or Durham;

(c) any students' union.

(3) For the purposes of this paragraph—

(a) a university or university college is in England if its activities are carried on, or principally carried on, in England;

(b) the Open University is to be treated as a university in England.

5 (1) An English higher education corporation.

(2) For the purposes of this paragraph a higher education corporation is an English higher education corporation if the activities of the institution conducted by that corporation are carried on, or principally carried on, in England.

6 (1) A successor company to a higher education corporation at a time when the institution conducted by the company is eligible, by virtue of an order made under section 129 of the 1988 Act, to receive support from funds administered by the Higher Education Funding Council for England.

(2) In this paragraph "the 1988 Act" means the Education Reform Act 1988 and "successor company to a higher education corporation" has the meaning given by section 129(5) of the 1988 Act.

7 A further education corporation.

8 A qualifying Academy proprietor (as defined in section 12(2) of the Academies Act 2010).

9 The governing body of any foundation, voluntary or foundation special school.

10 Any foundation body established under section 21 of the School Standards and Framework Act 1998.

11 A sixth form college corporation (within the meaning of the Further and Higher Education Act 1992).

Museums, galleries etc.

12 The Board of Trustees of the Victoria and Albert Museum.

13 The Board of Trustees of the Science Museum.

14 The Board of Trustees of the Armouries.

15 The Board of Trustees of the Royal Botanic Gardens, Kew.

16 The Board of Trustees of the National Museums and Galleries on Merseyside.

17 The trustees of the British Museum.

18 The trustees of the Natural History Museum.

19 The Board of Trustees of the National Gallery.

20 The Board of Trustees of the Tate Gallery.

21 The Board of Trustees of the National Portrait Gallery.

22 The Board of Trustees of the Wallace Collection.

23 The Trustees of the Imperial War Museum.

24 The Trustees of the National Maritime Museum.

25 The British Library Board.

Housing

26 Any registered society within the meaning of the Co-operative and Community Benefit Societies and Credit Unions Act 1965, if the society is also a non-profit registered provider of social housing.

27 Any registered society within the meaning of the Co-operative and Community Benefit Societies and Credit Unions Act 1965, if the society is also registered in the register of social landlords under Part 1 of the Housing Act 1996.

Connected institutions

28 (1) Any institution which—

(a) is administered by or on behalf of an institution included in any of paragraphs 1 to 8 and 11 to 25, and

(b) is established for the general purposes of, or for any special purpose of or in connection with, the institution mentioned in paragraph (a).

(2) Sub-paragraph (1) does not include—

(a) any college in the university of Oxford which is administered by or on behalf of that university;

(b) any college or hall in the university of Cambridge or Durham which is administered by or on behalf of that university;

(c) any student's union.

(3) Any institution which—

(a) is administered by or on behalf of a body included in paragraph 9 or 10, and

(b) is established for the general purposes of, or for any special purpose of or in connection with, that body or any foundation, voluntary or foundation special school or schools.

SCHEDULE 4

Section 62

ENLARGEMENT OF AREAS OF LOCAL CHARITIES

1 Existing area	*2 Permitted enlargement*
1. Greater London.	Any area which includes Greater London.
2. Any area in Greater London and not in, or partly in, the City of London.	(i) Any area in Greater London and not in, or partly in, the City of London; (ii) the area of Greater London exclusive of the City of London; (iii) any area which includes the area of Greater London, exclusive of the City of London; (iv) any area partly in Greater London and partly in any adjacent parish or parishes (civil or ecclesiastical), and not partly in the City of London.
3. A district.	Any area which includes the district.
4. A Welsh county or county borough.	Any area which includes the county or county borough.
5. Any area in a district.	(i) Any area in the district; (ii) the district; (iii) any area which includes the district; (iv) any area partly in the district and partly in any adjacent district or in any adjacent Welsh county or county borough.
6. Any area in a Welsh county or county borough.	(i) Any area in the county or county borough; (ii) the county or county borough;

1 Existing area	*2 Permitted enlargement*
	(iii) any area which includes the county or county borough; (iv) any area partly in the county or county borough and partly in any adjacent Welsh county or county borough or in any adjacent district.
7. A parish (civil or ecclesiastical), or two or more parishes, or an area in a parish, or partly in each of two or more parishes.	Any area not extending beyond the parish or parishes which— (i) includes, or include, the area in column 1, or (ii) is, or are, adjacent to the area in column 1.
8. In Wales, a community, or two or more communities, or an area in a community, or partly in each of two or more communities.	Any area not extending beyond the community or communities which— (i) includes, or include, the area in column 1, or (ii) is, or are, adjacent to the area in column 1.

SCHEDULE 5

Section 68

COURT'S JURISDICTION OVER CERTAIN CHARITIES GOVERNED BY OR UNDER STATUTE

1 The court may by virtue of section 68(5) and (6) exercise its jurisdiction with respect to charities in relation to—

(a) charities established or regulated by any provision of the Seamen's Fund Winding-up Act 1851 repealed by the Charities Act 1960;

(b) charities established or regulated by schemes under the Endowed Schools Act 1869 to 1948, or section 75 of the Elementary Education Act 1870 or by schemes given effect under section 2 of the Education Act 1973 or section 554 of the Education Act 1996;

(c) fuel allotments, that is, land which, by any enactment relating to inclosure or any instrument having effect under such an enactment, is vested in trustees upon trust that the land or the rents and profits of the land are to be used for the purpose of providing poor persons with fuel;

(d) charities established or regulated by any provision of the Municipal Corporations Act 1883 repealed by the Charities Act 1960 or by any scheme having effect under any such provision;

(e) charities regulated by schemes under the London Government Act 1899;

(f) charities established or regulated by orders or regulations under section 2 of the Regimental Charitable Funds Act 1935;

(g) charities regulated by sections 298 to 302 or by any such order as is mentioned in section 303.

2 Regardless of anything in section 19 of the Commons Act 1876 a scheme for the administration of a fuel allotment (within the meaning of paragraph 1(c)) may provide—

(a) for the sale or letting of the allotment or any part of it, for the discharge of the land sold or let from any restrictions as to the use of it imposed by or under any enactment relating to inclosure and for the application of the sums payable to the trustees of the allotment in respect of the sale or lease,

(b) for the exchange of the allotment or any part of it for other land, for the discharge from any such restrictions of the land given in exchange by the trustees of the allotment, and for the application of any money payable to those trustees for equality of exchange, or

(c) for the use of the allotment or any part of it for any purposes specified in the scheme.

SCHEDULE 6

Sections 319, 321, 323 and 324

APPEALS AND APPLICATIONS TO TRIBUNAL

1 Decision, direction or order	*2 Appellants/applicants (see sections 319(2)(b) and 321(2)(b))*	*3 Tribunal powers if appeal or application allowed*
Decision of the Commission not to give a direction under section 12(1) or (2) in relation to an institution or a charity.	The persons are the trustees of the institution or charity concerned.	Power to quash the decision and (if appropriate) remit the matter to the Commission.
Decision of the Commission under section 30 or 34— (a) to enter or not to enter an institution in the register of charities, or (b) to remove or not to remove an institution from the register.	The persons are— (a) the persons who are or claim to be the charity trustees of the institution, (b) (if a body corporate) the institution itself, and (c) any other person who is or may be affected by the decision.	Power to quash the decision and (if appropriate)— (a) remit the matter to the Commission; (b) direct the Commission to rectify the register.
Decision of the Commission not to make a determination under section 38(3) in relation to particular information contained in the register.	The persons are— (a) the charity trustees of the charity to which the information relates, (b) (if a body corporate) the charity itself, and (c) any other person who is or may be affected by the decision.	Power to quash the decision and (if appropriate) remit the matter to the Commission.
Direction given by the Commission under section 42 requiring the name of a charity to be changed.	The persons are— (a) the charity trustees of the charity to which the direction relates, (b) (if a body corporate) the charity itself, and (c) any other person who is or may be affected by the direction.	Power to— (a) quash the direction and (if appropriate) remit the matter to the Commission; (b) substitute for the direction any other direction which could have been given by the Commission.

1 Decision, direction or order	*2 Appellants/applicants (see sections 319(2)(b) and 321(2)(b))*	*3 Tribunal powers if appeal or application allowed*
Decision of the Commission to institute an inquiry under section 46 with regard to a particular institution.	The persons are— (a) the persons who have control or management of the institution, and (b) (if a body corporate) the institution itself.	Power to direct the Commission to end the inquiry.
Decision of the Commission to institute an inquiry under section 46 with regard to a class of institutions.	The persons are— (a) the persons who have control or management of any institution which is a member of the class of institutions, and (b) (if a body corporate) any such institution.	Power to— (a) direct the Commission that the inquiry should not consider a particular institution; (b) direct the Commission to end the inquiry.
Order made by the Commission under section 52 requiring a person to supply information or a document.	The persons are any person who is required to supply the information or document.	Power to— (a) quash the order; (b) substitute for all or part of the order any other order which could have been made by the Commission.
Order made by the Commission under section 69(1) (including such an order made by virtue of section 92(2)).	The persons are— (a) in a section 69(1)(a) case, the charity trustees of the charity to which the order relates or (if a body corporate) the charity itself, (b) in a section 69(1)(b) case, any person discharged or removed by the order, and (c) any other person who is or may be affected by the order.	Power to— (a) quash the order in whole or in part and (if appropriate) remit the matter to the Commission; (b) substitute for all or part of the order any other order which could have been made by the Commission; (c) add to the order anything which could have been contained in an order made by the Commission.
Order made by the Commission under section 76(3) in relation to a charity.	The persons are— (a) the charity trustees of the charity, (b) (if a body corporate) the charity itself, (c) in a section 76(3)(a) case, any person suspended by the order, and	Power to— (a) quash the order in whole or in part and (if appropriate) remit the matter to the Commission; (b) substitute for all or part of the order any other order which could

1 Decision, direction or order	*2 Appellants/applicants (see sections 319(2)(b) and 321(2)(b))*	*3 Tribunal powers if appeal or application allowed*
	(d) any other person who is or may be affected by the order.	have been made by the Commission; (c) add to the order anything which could have been contained in an order made by the Commission.
Decision of the Commission— (a) to discharge an order following a review under section 76(6), or (b) not to discharge an order following such a review.	The persons are— (a) the charity trustees of the charity to which the order relates, (b) (if a body corporate) the charity itself, (c) if the order in question was made under section 76(3)(a), any person suspended by it, and (d) any other person who is or may be affected by the order.	Power to— (a) quash the decision and (if appropriate) remit the matter to the Commission; (b) make the discharge of the order subject to savings or other transitional provisions; (c) remove any savings or other transitional provisions to which the discharge of the order was subject; (d) discharge the order in whole or in part (whether subject to any savings or other transitional provisions or not).
Order made by the Commission under section 79(2) in relation to a charity.	The persons are— (a) the charity trustees of the charity, (b) (if a body corporate) the charity itself, (c) in a section 79(2)(a) case, any person removed by the order, and (d) any other person who is or may be affected by the order.	Power to— (a) quash the order in whole or in part and (if appropriate) remit the matter to the Commission; (b) substitute for all or part of the order any other order which could have been made by the Commission; (c) add to the order anything which could have been contained in an order made by the Commission.
Order made by the Commission under section 80(1) removing a charity trustee.	The persons are— (a) the charity trustee, (b) the remaining charity trustees of the charity of	Power to— (a) quash the order in whole or in part and (if appropriate) remit

1 Decision, direction or order	*2 Appellants/applicants (see sections 319(2)(b) and 321(2)(b))*	*3 Tribunal powers if appeal or application allowed*
	which that trustee was a charity trustee, (c) (if a body corporate) the charity itself, and (d) any other person who is or may be affected by the order.	the matter to the Commission; (b) substitute for all or part of the order any other order which could have been made by the Commission; (c) add to the order anything which could have been contained in an order made by the Commission.
Order made by the Commission under section 80(2) appointing a charity trustee.	The persons are— (a) the other charity trustees of the charity, (b) (if a body corporate) the charity itself, and (c) any other person who is or may be affected by the order.	Power to— (a) quash the order in whole or in part and (if appropriate) remit the matter to the Commission; (b) substitute for all or part of the order any other order which could have been made by the Commission; (c) add to the order anything which could have been contained in an order made by the Commission.
Order made by the Commission under section 83(2) which suspends a person's membership of a charity.	The persons are— (a) the person whose membership is suspended by the order, and (b) any other person who is or may be affected by the order.	Power to quash the order and (if appropriate) remit the matter to the Commission.
Order made by the Commission under section 84(2) which directs a person to take action specified in the order.	The persons are any person who is directed by the order to take the specified action.	Power to quash the order and (if appropriate) remit the matter to the Commission.
Order made by the Commission under section 85(2) which directs a person to apply property in a specified manner.	The persons are any person who is directed by the order to apply the property in the specified manner.	Power to quash the order and (if appropriate) remit the matter to the Commission.

1 Decision, direction or order	*2 Appellants/applicants (see sections 319(2)(b) and 321(2)(b))*	*3 Tribunal powers if appeal or application allowed*
Order made by the Commission under section 87(3) in relation to a person holding property on behalf of a body entered in the Scottish Charity Register or of any person concerned in its management or control.	The persons are— (a) the person holding the property in question, and (b) any other person who is or may be affected by the order.	Power to quash the order and (if appropriate) remit the matter to the Commission.
Order made by the Commission under section 93(2) in relation to any land vested in the official custodian in trust for a charity.	The persons are— (a) the charity trustees of the charity, (b) (if a body corporate) the charity itself, and (c) any other person who is or may be affected by the order.	Power to— (a) quash the order and (if appropriate) remit the matter to the Commission; (b) substitute for the order any other order which could have been made by the Commission; (c) add to the order anything which could have been contained in an order made by the Commission.
Decision of the Commission not to make a common investment scheme under section 96.	The persons are— (a) the charity trustees of a charity which applied to the Commission for the scheme, (b) (if a body corporate) the charity itself, and (c) any other person who is or may be affected by the decision.	Power to quash the decision and (if appropriate) remit the matter to the Commission.
Decision of the Commission not to make a common deposit scheme under section 100.	The persons are— (a) the charity trustees of a charity which applied to the Commission for the scheme, (b) (if a body corporate) the charity itself, and (c) any other person who is or may be affected by the decision.	Power to quash the decision and (if appropriate) remit the matter to the Commission.
Decision by the Commission not to make an order under section 105 in relation to a charity.	The persons are— (a) the charity trustees of the charity, and (b) (if a body corporate) the charity itself.	Power to quash the decision and (if appropriate) remit the matter to the Commission.

1 Decision, direction or order	*2 Appellants/applicants (see sections 319(2)(b) and 321(2)(b))*	*3 Tribunal powers if appeal or application allowed*
Direction given by the Commission under section 107 in relation to an account held in the name of or on behalf of a charity.	The persons are— (a) the charity trustees of the charity, (b) (if a body corporate) the charity itself, and (c) any other person who is or may be affected by the order.	Power to— (a) quash the direction and (if appropriate) remit the matter to the Commission; (b) substitute for the direction any other direction which could have been given by the Commission; (c) add to the direction anything which could have been contained in a direction given by the Commission.
Order made by the Commission under section 112 for the assessment of a solicitor's bill.	The persons are— (a) the solicitor, (b) any person for whom the work was done by the solicitor, and (c) any other person who is or may be affected by the order.	Power to— (a) quash the order; (b) substitute for the order any other order which could have been made by the Commission; (c) add to the order anything which could have been contained in an order made by the Commission.
Decision of the Commission not to make an order under section 117 in relation to land held by or in trust for a charity.	The persons are— (a) the charity trustees of the charity, (b) (if a body corporate) the charity itself, and (c) any other person who is or may be affected by the decision.	Power to quash the decision and (if appropriate) remit the matter to the Commission.
Decision of the Commission not to make an order under section 124 in relation to a mortgage of land held by or in trust for a charity.	The persons are— (a) the charity trustees of the charity, (b) (if a body corporate) the charity itself, and (c) any other person who is or may be affected by the decision.	Power to quash the decision and (if appropriate) remit the matter to the Commission
Order made by the Commission under section 146(1) requiring the accounts of a charity to be audited.	The persons are— (a) the charity trustees of the charity, (b) (if a body corporate) the charity itself, and	Power to— (a) quash the order; (b) substitute for the order any other order which

1 Decision, direction or order	*2 Appellants/applicants (see sections 319(2)(b) and 321(2)(b))*	*3 Tribunal powers if appeal or application allowed*
	(c) any other person who is or may be affected by the order.	could have been made by the Commission; (c) add to the order anything which could have been contained in an order made by the Commission.
Order made by the Commission under section 147(2) in relation to a charitable company.	The persons are— (a) the directors of the company, (b) the company itself, and (c) any other person who is or may be affected by the order.	Power to— (a) quash the order and (if appropriate) remit the matter to the Commission; (b) substitute for the order any other order which could have been made by the Commission; (c) add to the order anything which could have been contained in an order made by the Commission.
Order made by the Commission under section 147(5) in relation to a charitable company, or a decision of the Commission not to make such an order in relation to a charitable company.	The persons are— (a) the charity trustees of the company, (b) the company itself, (c) in the case of a decision not to make an order, the auditor, and (d) any other person who is or may be affected by the order or the decision.	Power to— (a) quash the order or decision and (if appropriate) remit the matter to the Commission; (b) substitute for the order any other order of a kind the Commission could have made; (c) make any order which the Commission could have made.
Order made by the Commission under section 153(1) requiring the group accounts of a parent charity to be audited.	The persons are— (a) the charity trustees of the parent charity, (b) (if a body corporate) the parent charity itself, and (c) any other person who is or may be affected by the order.	Power to— (a) quash the order; (b) substitute for the order any other order which could have been made by the Commission; (c) add to the order anything which could have been contained in an order made by the Commission.
Order made by the Commission under	The persons are—	Power to—

1 Decision, direction or order	*2 Appellants/applicants (see sections 319(2)(b) and 321(2)(b))*	*3 Tribunal powers if appeal or application allowed*
section 155 in relation to a charity, or a decision of the Commission not to make such an order in relation to a charity.	(a) the charity trustees of the charity, (b) (if a body corporate) the charity itself, (c) in the case of a decision not to make an order, the auditor, independent examiner or examiner, and (d) any other person who is or may be affected by the order or the decision.	(a) quash the order or decision and (if appropriate) remit the matter to the Commission; (b) substitute for the order any other order of a kind the Commission could have made; (c) make any order which the Commission could have made.
Order made by the Commission under section 155 in relation to a member of a group, or a decision of the Commission not to make such an order in relation to a member of a group.	The persons are— (a) the charity trustees of the member of the group, (b) (if a body corporate) the member of the group itself, (c) in the case of a decision not to make an order, the auditor, independent examiner or examiner, and (d) any other person who is or may be affected by the order or the decision.	Power to— (a) quash the order or decision and (if appropriate) remit the matter to the Commission; (b) substitute for the order any other order of a kind the Commission could have made; (c) make any order which the Commission could have made.
Decision of the Commission under section 168(3) to request charity trustees to prepare an annual report for a charity.	The persons are— (a) the charity trustees, and (b) (if a body corporate) the charity itself.	Power to quash the decision and (if appropriate) remit the matter to the Commission.
Decision of the Commission not to dispense with the requirements of section 169(1) in relation to a charity or class of charities.	The persons are the charity trustees of any charity affected by the decision.	Power to quash the decision and (if appropriate) remit the matter to the Commission.
Decision of the Commission under section 181(2) to waive, or not to waive, a person's disqualification.	The persons are— (a) the person who applied for the waiver, and (b) any other person who is or may be affected by the decision.	Power to— (a) quash the decision and (if appropriate) remit the matter to the Commission; (b) substitute for the decision any other decision of a kind which

1 Decision, direction or order	*2 Appellants/applicants (see sections 319(2)(b) and 321(2)(b))*	*3 Tribunal powers if appeal or application allowed*
		could have been made by the Commission.
Order made by the Commission under section 184(3) in relation to a person who has acted as charity trustee or trustee for a charity.	The persons are— (a) the person subject to the order, and (b) any other person who is or may be affected by the order.	Power to— (a) quash the order and (if appropriate) remit the matter to the Commission; (b) substitute for the order any other order which could have been made by the Commission.
Order made by the Commission under section 186(5) or (6) requiring a trustee or connected person to repay, or not to receive, remuneration.	The persons are— (a) the trustee or connected person, (b) the other charity trustees of the charity concerned, and (c) any other person who is or may be affected by the order.	Power to— (a) quash the order and (if appropriate) remit the matter to the Commission; (b) substitute for the order any other order which could have been made by the Commission.
Decision of the Commission to give, or withhold, consent under section 198(1) or 201(1) in relation to a charitable company.	The persons are— (a) the charity trustees of the company, (b) the company itself, and (c) any other person who is or may be affected by the decision.	Power to quash the decision and (if appropriate) remit the matter to the Commission.
Decision of the Commission to grant an application under section 207 for the constitution of a CIO and its registration as a charity.	The persons are any person (other than the persons who made the application) who is or may be affected by the decision.	Power to quash the decision and (if appropriate)— (a) remit the matter to the Commission; (b) direct the Commission to rectify the register of charities.
Decision of the Commission under section 208 to refuse an application for the constitution of a CIO and its registration as a charity.	The persons are— (a) the persons who made the application, and (b) any other person who is or may be affected by the decision.	Power to— (a) quash the decision and (if appropriate) remit the matter to the Commission; (b) direct the Commission to grant the application.
Decision of the Commission under section 227 to refuse to register an amendment to the constitution of a CIO.	The persons are— (a) the CIO, (b) the charity trustees of the CIO, and	Power to quash the decision and (if appropriate)— (a) remit the matter to the Commission;

1 Decision, direction or order	*2 Appellants/applicants (see sections 319(2)(b) and 321(2)(b))*	*3 Tribunal powers if appeal or application allowed*
	(c) any other person who is or may be affected by the decision.	(b) direct the Commission to register the amendment.
Decision of the Commission under section 231 to refuse an application for the conversion of a charitable company or a registered society into a CIO and the CIO's registration as a charity.	The persons are— (a) the charity which made the application, (b) the charity trustees of the charity, and (c) any other person who is or may be affected by the decision.	Power to— (a) quash the decision and (if appropriate) remit the matter to the Commission; (b) direct the Commission to grant the application.
Decision of the Commission to grant an application under section 235 for the amalgamation of two or more CIOs and the incorporation and registration as a charity of a new CIO as their successor.	The persons are any creditor of any of the CIOs being amalgamated.	Power to quash the decision and (if appropriate) remit the matter to the Commission.
Decision of the Commission under section 237 to refuse an application for the amalgamation of two or more CIOs and the incorporation and registration as a charity of a new CIO as their successor.	The persons are— (a) the CIOs which applied for the amalgamation, (b) the charity trustees of the CIOs, and (c) any other person who is or may be affected by the decision.	Power to— (a) quash the decision and (if appropriate) remit the matter to the Commission; (b) direct the Commission to grant the application.
Decision of the Commission to confirm a resolution passed by a CIO under section 240(1).	The persons are any creditor of the CIO.	Power to quash the decision and (if appropriate) remit the matter to the Commission.
Decision of the Commission under section 242 to refuse to confirm a resolution passed by a CIO.	The persons are— (a) the CIO, (b) the charity trustees of the CIO, and (c) any other person who is or may be affected by the decision.	Power to— (a) quash the decision and (if appropriate) remit the matter to the Commission; (b) direct the Commission to confirm the resolution.
Decision of the Commission— (a) to grant a certificate of incorporation under section 251(1) to the charity trustees of a charity, or	The persons are— (a) the charity trustees of the charity, and (b) any other person who is or may be affected by the decision.	Power to quash— (a) the decision; (b) any conditions or directions inserted in the certificate;

1 Decision, direction or order	*2 Appellants/applicants (see sections 319(2)(b) and 321(2)(b))*	*3 Tribunal powers if appeal or application allowed*
(b) not to grant such a certificate.		
Decision of the Commission to amend a certificate of incorporation under section 262(5).	The persons are— (a) the charity trustees of the charity, and (b) any other person who is or may be affected by the amended certificate of incorporation.	Power to quash the decision and (if appropriate) remit the matter to the Commission.
Decision of the Commission not to amend a certificate of incorporation under section 262(5).	The persons are— (a) the charity trustees of the charity, and (b) any other person who is or may be affected by the decision not to amend the certificate of incorporation.	Power to— (a) quash the decision and (if appropriate) remit the matter to the Commission; (b) make any order the Commission could have made under section 262(5).
Order of the Commission under section 263(1) or (2) which dissolves an incorporated body.	The persons are— (a) the charity trustees of the charity, and (b) any other person who is or may be affected by the order.	Power to— (a) quash the order and (if appropriate) remit the matter to the Commission; (b) substitute for the order any other order which could have been made by the Commission; (c) add to the order anything which could have been contained in an order made by the Commission.
Decision of the Commission to notify charity trustees under section 271(1) that it objects to a resolution of the charity trustees under section 268(1).	The persons are— (a) the charity trustees, and (b) any other person who is or may be affected by the decision.	Power to quash the decision.
Decision of the Commission to notify charity trustees under section 278(1) that it objects to a resolution of the charity trustees under section 275(2).	The persons are— (a) the charity trustees, and (b) any other person who is or may be affected by the decision.	Power to quash the decision.
Decision of the Commission not to concur under section 284 with a resolution	The persons are— (a) the charity trustees, and	Power to quash the decision and (if appropriate) remit the matter to the Commission.

1 Decision, direction or order	*2 Appellants/applicants (see sections 319(2)(b) and 321(2)(b))*	*3 Tribunal powers if appeal or application allowed*
of charity trustees under section 282(2).	(b) any other person who is or may be affected by the decision.	
Decision of the Commission not to concur under section 291 with a resolution of charity trustees under section 289(2).	The persons are— (a) the charity trustees, (b) (if a body corporate) the charity itself, and (c) any other person who is or may be affected by the decision.	Power to quash the decision and (if appropriate) remit the matter to the Commission.
Decision of the Commission to withhold approval for the transfer of property from trustees to a parish or community council under section 298(2).	The persons are— (a) the trustees, (b) the parish or community council, and (c) any other person who is or may be affected by the decision.	Power to quash the decision and (if appropriate) remit the matter to the Commission.
Decision of the Commission to give or withhold consent under section 42(4) of the Companies Act 2006.	The persons are— (a) the charity trustees of the charitable company, (b) the company itself, and (c) any other person who is or may be affected by the decision.	Power to quash the decision and (if appropriate) remit the matter to the Commission.

SCHEDULE 7

Section 354

CONSEQUENTIAL AMENDMENTS

PART 1

GENERAL AMENDMENTS

References to the Charitable Uses Act 1601 (c. 4)

1 A reference in any enactment or document to a charity within the meaning of the Charitable Uses Act 1601 or the preamble to it is to continue to be construed as a reference to a charity as defined by section 1(1).

References to the Charity Commissioners for England and Wales

2 (1) Any enactment or document is to continue to have effect, so far as necessary in consequence of the transfer effected by section 6(4) of the Charities Act 2006, as if any reference to—

(a) the Charity Commissioners for England and Wales, or
(b) any Charity Commissioner for England and Wales,

were a reference to the Charity Commission for England and Wales.

(2) In sub-paragraph (1) "enactment" includes—
(a) any provision of subordinate legislation (within the meaning of the Interpretation Act 1978),
(b) a provision of a Measure of the Church Assembly or of the General Synod of the Church of England, and
(c) any provision made by or under an Act of the Scottish Parliament or Northern Ireland legislation.

Application of certain enactments to trust corporations

3 (1) In the definition of "trust corporation" contained in the provisions listed in sub-paragraph (2) the reference to a corporation appointed by the court in any particular case to be a trustee includes a reference to a corporation appointed by the Commission under this Act to be a trustee.

(2) The provisions are—
(a) section 117(1)(xxx) of the Settled Land Act 1925,
(b) paragraph (18) of section 68(1) of the Trustee Act 1925,
(c) section 205(1)(xxviii) of the Law of Property Act 1925,
(d) section 55(1)(xxvi) of the Administration of Estates Act 1925, and
(e) section 128 of the Senior Courts Act 1981 (c. 54).

(3) This paragraph is to be treated as always having had effect.

(4) In sub-paragraph (2), the reference to section 128 of the Senior Courts Act 1981 is to be read—
(a) in relation to any time before 1 January 1982, as a reference to section 175(1) of the Supreme Court of Judicature (Consolidation) Act 1925, and
(b) in relation to any time on or after that date but before the day on which paragraph 1(2) of Schedule 11 to the Constitutional Reform Act 2005 came into force, as a reference to section 128 of the Supreme Court Act 1981 (c. 54).

PART 2

PARTICULAR AMENDMENTS

Literary and Scientific Institutions Act 1854 (c. 112)

4 (1) In section 6, for "except with the consent of the Charity Commission or in accordance with such provisions of section 36(2) to (8) of the Charities Act 1993 as are applicable" substitute "except with the consent of the Charity Commission or in accordance with such provisions of sections 117(2) and 119 to 121 of the Charities Act 2011 as are applicable".

(2) This paragraph does not extend to Northern Ireland.

Places of Worship Registration Act 1855 (c. 81)

5 (1) In section 9(1)—

(a) for "shall, so far as it is a charity, be treated for the purposes of section 3A(4)(b) of the Charities Act 1993 (institutions to be excepted from registration under that Act) as if that provision applied to it" substitute "is, so far as it is a charity, to be treated for the purposes of section 31(3) of the Charities Act 2011 (institutions required to be excepted from registration under that Act) as if that provision applied to it", and

(b) paragraph (b) continues to have effect with the substitution, for "Charity Commissioners" of "Charity Commission".

(2) For section 9(2) substitute—

"(2) Section 337 of the 2011 Act (provisions as to orders under that Act) applies to any order under subsection (1)(b) as it applies to orders under that Act."

Places of Worship Sites Amendment Act 1882 (c. 21)

6 In section 1(d) for "except with the consent of the Charity Commission or in accordance with such provisions of section 36(2) to (8) of the Charities Act 1993 as are applicable" substitute "except with the consent of the Charity Commission or in accordance with such provisions of sections 117(2) and 119 to 121 of the Charities Act 2011 as are applicable".

Technical and Industrial Institutions Act 1892 (c. 29)

7 In section 9(1), for "with the consent of the Charity Commission or in accordance with such provisions of section 36(2) to (8) of the Charities Act 1993 as are applicable" substitute "with the consent of the Charity Commission or in accordance with such provisions of sections 117(2) and 119 to 121 of the Charities Act 2011 as are applicable".

Open Spaces Act 1906 (c. 25)

8 (1) In section 4(1A)(b), for "section 36(2) to (8) of the Charities Act 1993" substitute "sections 117(2) and 119 to 121 of the Charities Act 2011".

(2) For section 4(4) substitute—

"(4) Section 337 of the Charities Act 2011 (provisions as to orders under that Act) applies to any order of the Charity Commission under this section as it applies to orders made by it under that Act."

(3) This paragraph does not extend to Northern Ireland.

New Parishes Measure 1943 (No. 1)

9 (1) For section 14(1)(b) substitute—

"(b) any trustees for charitable purposes but (except in the case of an exempt charity within the meaning of the Charities Act 2011) only—

(i) with the sanction of an order of the Charity Commission, or

(ii) in accordance with such provisions of sections 117(2) and 119 to 121 of the Charities Act 2011 as are applicable;".

(2) For section 14(4) substitute—

"(4) Section 337 of the Charities Act 2011 (provisions as to orders under that Act) applies to any order under subsection (1)(b) as it applies to orders under that Act."

10 In section 31, for "the Charities Act 1993" substitute "section 10 of the Charities Act 2011".

London County Council (General Powers) Act 1947 (c. xlvi)

11 For section 6(3) substitute—

"(3) In relation to any disposition of land falling within section 117(1) of the Charities Act 2011, the Council or the borough council may, instead of acting with the sanction of an order of the court or of the Charity Commission, make the disposition in accordance with such provisions of sections 117(2) and 119 to 121 of that Act as are applicable."

London County Council (General Powers) Act 1955 (c. xxix)

12 For section 34(3) substitute—

"(3) In relation to any disposition of land falling within section 117(1) of the Charities Act 2011, the Council may, instead of acting with the sanction of an order of the court or of the Charity Commission, make the disposition in accordance with such provisions of sections 117(2) and 119 to 121 of that Act as are applicable."

Incumbents and Churchwardens (Trusts) Measure 1964 (No. 2)

13 In section 1, in the definition of "permanent trusts" for "section 96(3) of the Charities Act 1993" substitute "section 353(3) of the Charities Act 2011".

Co-operative and Community Benefit Societies and Credit Unions Act 1965 (c. 12)

14 In sections 5A(7)(a) and 7D(5)(a), for "as it has under section 1(1) of the Charities Act 2006" substitute "as it has under section 1(1) of the Charities Act 2011".

Leasehold Reform Act 1967 (c. 88)

15 In section 23(4), for "section 36 of the Charities Act 1993" substitute "sections 117 to 121 of the Charities Act 2011".

Co-operative and Community Benefit Societies and Credit Unions Act 1968 (c. 55)

16 In section 4A(6), for "as defined by section 1(1) of the Charities Act 2006," substitute "as defined by section 1(1) of the Charities Act 2011,".

Redundant Churches and other Religious Buildings Act 1969 (c. 22)

17 (1) In section 4, for subsections (6) to (8A) substitute—

"(6) The Charity Commission may, on the application of the acquirer of the relevant premises, by order establish a scheme under section 69 of the Charities Act 2011 (Commission's concurrent jurisdiction with the High Court for certain purposes) making provision for the restoration of the relevant premises, or part of them, to use as a place of public worship.

(7) The Charity Commission may so establish any such scheme notwithstanding—

(a) anything in section 70(2) of that Act, or

(b) that the relevant charity has ceased to exist;

and if the relevant charity has ceased to exist, any such scheme may provide for the constitution of a charity by or in trust for which the relevant premises are to be held on the restoration of those premises, or part of them, to use as a place of public worship.

(8) The Charity Commission has the same jurisdiction and powers in relation to the establishment of a scheme under subsection (2) above as it has under the provisions of sections 69 to 71 of the Charities Act 2011 (except section 70(4) and (5)) in relation to the establishment of a scheme for the administration of a charity; and section 88 of that Act (publicity relating to schemes) accordingly has effect in relation to the establishment of a scheme under subsection (2) above as it has effect in relation to the establishment of a scheme for the administration of a charity.

(8A) Chapter 2 of Part 17 of, and Schedule 6 to, the Charities Act 2011 (appeals and applications to Tribunal) apply in relation to an order made by virtue of subsection (8) above as they apply in relation to an order made under section 69(1) of that Act."

(2) In section 4(13), for the definition of "charity" substitute—

""charity" has the meaning given by section 10 of the Charities Act 2011".

(3) In section 4(13), for the definition of "the court" substitute—

""the court" has the same meaning as in the Charities Act 2011;".

18 In section 7, for subsection (2) substitute—

"(2) Nothing in this Act affects—

(a) any power of the court (within the meaning of the Charities Act 2011) or the Charity Commission to establish a scheme for the administration of a charity, or

(b) the power of the Charity Commission under section 105 of that Act to authorise dealings with trust property."

Sharing of Church Buildings Act 1969 (c. 38)

19 In section 2(4), for "the Charities Act 1993" substitute "the Charities Act 2011".

20 (1) In section 8(1), for "the Charities Act 1993" substitute "the Charities Act 2011".

(2) In section 8(2), for "section 96(2) of the Charities Act 1993" substitute "section 10(2) to (4) of the Charities Act 2011".

(3) In section 8(3), for "Section 36 of the Charities Act 1993 (restrictions on dispositions of charity land)" substitute "Sections 117 to 121 of the Charities Act 2011 (restrictions on dispositions of charity land)".

Synodical Government Measure 1969 (No. 2)

21 (1) Amend Schedule 3 as follows.

(2) In Rule 46A(a), for "section 72(1) of the Charities Act 1993 and the disqualification is not for the time being subject to a general waiver by the Charity Commission under subsection (4) of that section or to a waiver by it under that subsection" substitute "section 178 of the Charities Act 2011 and the disqualification is not for the time being subject to a general waiver by the Charity Commission under section 181 of that Act or to a waiver by it under that section".

(3) In Rule 54(1)—

(a) in the definition of "auditor", for "section 43(2) of the Charities Act 1993" substitute "section 144(2) of the Charities Act 2011", and

(b) in the definition of "independent examiner", for "Section 43(3)(a) of the Charities Act 1993" substitute "section 145(1)(a) of the Charities Act 2011".

(4) In Section 4 of Appendix I, in Note 3, for "section 72(1) of the Charities Act 1993 and the disqualification is not for the time being subject to a general waiver by the Charity Commission under subsection (4) of that section or to a waiver by it under that subsection" substitute "section 178 of the Charities Act 2011 and the disqualification is not for the time being subject to a general waiver by the Charity Commission under section 181 of that Act or to a waiver by it under that section".

(5) In Section 6 of Appendix I, in the Note, for "section 72(1) of the Charities Act 1993 and the disqualification is not for the time being subject to a general waiver by the Charity Commission under subsection (4) of that section or to a waiver by it under that subsection" substitute "section 178 of the Charities Act 2011 and the disqualification is not for the time being subject to a general waiver by the Charity Commission under section 181 of that Act or to a waiver by it under that section".

(6) In Appendix II, in paragraph 16, "the Charity Commission for an order for directions pursuant to section 44(2) of the Charities Act 1993" substitute "the Charity Commission for an order for directions pursuant to section 155 of the Charities Act 2011".

Local Government Act 1972 (c. 70)

22 In section 11(3)(c), for "section 79 of the Charities Act 1993 (parochial charities)" substitute "sections 298 to 303 of the Charities Act 2011 (parochial charities)".

23 In section 27F(6), for "section 79 of the Charities Act 1993 (parochial charities)" substitute "sections 298 to 303 of the Charities Act 2011 (parochial charities)".

24 In section 27H(6), for "section 79 of the Charities Act 1993 (parochial charities)" substitute "sections 298 to 303 of the Charities Act 2011 (parochial charities)".

25 In section 29(6), for "section 79 of the Charities Act 1993 (parochial charities)" substitute "sections 298 to 303 of the Charities Act 2011 (parochial charities)".

26 In section 127(4) for "the Charities Act 1993" substitute "the Charities Act 2011".

27 In section 131(3)—

(a) for "section 36 of the Charities Act 1993 (restrictions on disposition of charity land)" substitute "sections 117 to 121 of the Charities Act 2011 (restrictions on dispositions of charity land)", and

(b) for "section 36(9)(a) of that Act (certain statutorily authorised transactions not to require the sanction of the Charity Commission)" substitute "section 117(3)(a) (certain statutorily authorised dispositions not to require the sanction of the Charity Commission)".

28 In Schedule 12A, for paragraphs 8(f) and 19(f) substitute—

"(f) the Charities Act 2011."

Consumer Credit Act 1974 (c. 39)

29 In section 189(1), in the definition of "charity", for "the Charities Act 1993" substitute "the Charities Act 2011".

Friendly Societies Act 1974 (c. 46)

30 In section 32A(6), for "as defined by section 1(1) of the Charities Act 2006," substitute "as defined by section 1(1) of the Charities Act 2011,".

House of Commons Disqualification Act 1975 (c. 24)

31 Part 2 of Schedule 1 continues to include, at the appropriate place—

"The Charity Commission."

Northern Ireland Assembly Disqualification Act 1975 (c. 25)

32 Part 2 of Schedule 1 continues to include, at the appropriate place—

"The Charity Commission."

Theatres Trust Act 1976 (c. 27)

33 In section 2(2)(d), for "sections 36 and 38 of the Charities Act 1993" substitute "sections 117 to 121 and 124 of the Charities Act 2011".

Endowments and Glebe Measure 1976 (No. 4)

34 In section 11(2), for "the Charity Commission or in accordance with such provisions of section 36(2) to (8) of the Charities Act 1993 as are applicable" substitute "the Charity Commission or in accordance with such provisions of sections 117(2) and 119 to 121 of the Charities Act 2011 as are applicable".

Interpretation Act 1978 (c. 30)

35 In Schedule 1, for the definition of "Charity Commission" substitute—

""“Charity Commission" means the Charity Commission for England and Wales (see section 13 of the Charities Act 2011)."

Ancient Monuments and Archaeological Areas Act 1979 (c. 46)

36 In section 49(3), for "the Charities Act 1993" substitute "the Charities Act 2011".

Disused Burial Grounds (Amendment) Act 1981 (c. 18)

37 For section 6 substitute—

"6 Saving for Charity Commission

"6 Saving for Charity Commission

Nothing in this Act affects the charitable jurisdiction of the High Court or the Charity Commission and in particular, in the absence of appropriate provisions in the governing instrument of the charity concerning—

(a) the future use of the said land, or

(b) the application of the proceeds of sale of the whole or any part of it,

it is under section 61 of the Charities Act 2011 the duty of the church or religious body owning the land or other trustees of the said land to make an application for the appropriate relief by way of a scheme."

Pastoral Measure 1983 (No. 1)

38 For section 55(1) substitute—

"(1) The power of the court (as defined by the Charities Act 2011) to make schemes under its jurisdiction with respect to charities, and the power of the Charity Commission to make schemes under that Act, extend to the making of schemes with respect to consecrated chapels belonging to charities which are no longer needed for the purposes of the charity, and section 10(2)(c) of that Act shall not be taken as preventing the making of any such scheme."

39 In section 63(3), for "the Charities Act 1993" substitute "the Charities Act 2011".

40 In section 87(1), in the definition of "charity", for "section 96 of the Charities Act 1993" substitute "section 10 of the Charities Act 2011".

41 (1) Amend Schedule 3 as follows.

(2) In paragraph 11(6)—

(a) for "section 16 of the Charities Act 1993" substitute "section 69 of the Charities Act 2011", and

(b) for "that section" substitute "sections 69 to 71 of that Act".

(3) In paragraph 16(1)(e) for "section 16 of the Charities Act 1993" substitute "section 69 of the Charities Act 2011".

Greater London Council (General Powers) Act 1984 (c. xxvii)

42 In section 10(2)(n), for "the Charities Act 1993" substitute "the Charities Act 2011".

Housing Act 1985 (c. 68)

43 In section 6A(5), for "in accordance with section 3A of the Charities Act 1993" substitute "in accordance with section 30 of the Charities Act 2011".

44 In section 525, in the definition of "charity trustees", for "the Charities Act 1993" substitute "the Charities Act 2011".

Housing Associations Act 1985 (c. 69)

45 In section 10(1), for "sections 36 and 38 of the Charities Act 1993" substitute "sections 117 to 121 and 124 of the Charities Act 2011".

46 In section 35(2)(c), for "section 36 of the Charities Act 1993 (restrictions on dispositions of charity land)" substitute "sections 117 to 121 of the Charities Act 2011 (restrictions on dispositions of charity land)".

Coal Industry Act 1987 (c. 3)

47 (1) In section 5(7), for "the Charities Act 1993" substitute "the Charities Act 2011".

(2) For section 5(8) to (8B) substitute—

"(8) Sections 70(1), 71, 73(1) to (6), 74, 88 and 89 of the Charities Act 2011 apply in relation to the powers of the Commission and the making of schemes under this section as they apply in relation to its powers and the making of schemes under that Act and sections 337 and 339 of that Act apply to orders and decisions under this section as they apply to orders and decisions under that Act.

(8A) The Commission must not proceed under section 73 of that Act (as applied by subsection (8)) without the same application and notice to the trustees of the trust in question, as would be required if the Commission was proceeding under subsection (1); but on any application made with a view to a scheme under subsection (1) the Commission may proceed under that subsection or under section 73 of that Act (as so applied) as appears to it appropriate.

(8B) Chapter 2 of Part 17 of, and Schedule 6 to, the Charities Act 2011 (appeals and applications to Tribunal) apply in relation to an order made under this section as they apply in relation to an order made under section 69(1) of that Act."

Reverter of Sites Act 1987 (c. 15)

48 For section 4(2) and (4) substitute—

"(2) Chapter 2 of Part 17 of, and Schedule 6 to, the Charities Act 2011 (appeals and applications to Tribunal) apply in relation to an order made under section 2 above as they apply in relation to an order made under section 69(1) of that Act, except that the persons who may bring an appeal against an order made under section 2 above are—

(a) the Attorney General;
(b) the trustees of the trust established under the order;
(c) a beneficiary of, or the trustees of, the trust in respect of which the application for the order had been made;
(d) any person interested in the purposes for which the last-mentioned trustees or any of their predecessors held the relevant land before the cesser of use in consequence of which the trust arose under section 1 above;

(e) any two or more inhabitants of the locality where that land is situated;

(f) any other person who is or may be affected by the order.

(4) Sections 337 and 339 of the Charities Act 2011 (supplemental provisions with respect to orders) apply in relation to orders under section 2 above as they apply in relation to orders under that Act."

Education Reform Act 1988 (c. 40)

49 In section 124(2)(fa), for "(within the meaning of section 69A of the Charities Act 1993)" substitute "(within the meaning of Part 11 of the Charities Act 2011)".

50 For section 125A substitute—

"125A Charitable status of a higher education corporation

"125A Charitable status of a higher education corporation

A higher education corporation shall be a charity and—

(a) an English higher education corporation is, in accordance with Schedule 3 to the Charities Act 2011, an exempt charity for the purposes of that Act, and

(b) a Welsh higher education corporation is, in accordance with regulations made in compliance with section 31(3) of that Act, excepted from registration under that Act."

51 In section 128(5), for ""charitable purposes" has the same meaning as in the Charities Act 1993" substitute ""charitable purposes" has the meaning given by section 11 of the Charities Act 2011".

Copyright, Designs and Patents Act 1988 (c. 48)

52 In Schedule 6, in paragraph 7(3), for "the Charities Act 1993" substitute "the Charities Act 2011".

Imperial College Act 1988 (c. xxiv)

53 In section 10, for ""the Commissioners" and "the court" have the same meanings as in the Charities Act 1993" substitute ""the Commission" and "the court" have the same meanings as in the Charities Act 2011".

54 (1) In section 17(1), for "section 22 of the Charities Act 1960" substitute "section 96 of the Charities Act 2011".

(2) In section 17(2)—

(a) for "the Commissioners" substitute "the Commission", and

(b) for "the said section 22" substitute "section 96 of the 2011 Act".

Courts and Legal Services Act 1990 (c. 41)

55 In Schedule 11, for the entry beginning "Member of the Charity Commission" substitute—

"Member of the Charity Commission appointed as provided in Schedule 1 to the Charities Act 2011."

London Local Authorities Act 1991 (c. xiii)

56 In section 4, in paragraph (d) of the definition of "establishment for special treatment" for "in accordance with section 3A of the Charities Act 1993 or is not required to be registered (by virtue of subsection (2) of that section)" substitute "in accordance with section 30 of the Charities Act 2011 or is not required to be registered (by virtue of subsection (2) of that section)".

Further and Higher Education Act 1992 (c. 13)

57 In section 19(4)(bc), for "(within the meaning of section 69A of the Charities Act 1993)" substitute "(within the meaning of Part 11 of the Charities Act 2011)".

58 For section 22A substitute—

"22A Charitable status of a further education corporation

"22A Charitable status of a further education corporation

A further education corporation shall be a charity (and, in accordance with Schedule 3 to the Charities Act 2011, is an exempt charity for the purposes of that Act)."

59 In section 27(5), for ""charitable purposes" has the same meaning as in the Charities Act 1993" substitute ""charitable purposes" has the meaning given by section 11 of the Charities Act 2011".

60 In section 33F(6)(d), for "(within the meaning of section 69A of the Charities Act 1993)" substitute "(within the meaning of Part 11 of the Charities Act 2011)".

61 In section 33M, for "(and, as a result of its inclusion in Schedule 2 to the Charities Act 1993, is an exempt charity for the purposes of that Act)" substitute "(and, as a result of its inclusion in Schedule 3 to the Charities Act 2011, is an exempt charity for the purposes of that Act)".

62 In section 33N(10), for ""charitable purposes" has the same meaning as in the Charities Act 1993" substitute ""charitable purposes" has the meaning given by section 11 of the Charities Act 2011".

63 In section 69—

(a) in subsection (1A), for "section 13 of the Charities Act 2006)" substitute "section 25 of the Charities Act 2011)", and

(b) in subsection (1B), for "section 10A of the Charities Act 1993" substitute "section 56 or 57 of that Act".

64 In section 79A—

(a) for "section 13 of the Charities Act 2006)" substitute "section 25 of the Charities Act 2011)", and

(b) for "subsection (2) of that section" substitute "section 26(2) of that Act".

Charities Act 1992 (c. 41)

65 (1) In section 58(1), in the definition of "company" for "section 97 of the Charities Act 1993" substitute "section 353 of the Charities Act 2011".

(2) In section 58(4), for "as defined by section 2(1) of the Charities Act 2006" substitute "as defined by section 2(1) of the Charities Act 2011".

66 In section 63(2), for "section 3 of the Charities Act 1993" substitute "section 29 of the Charities Act 2011".

Leasehold Reform, Housing and Urban Development Act 1993 (c. 28)

67 In section 93(6)(a), for "section 36 of the Charities Act 1993" substitute "sections 117 to 121 of the Charities Act 2011".

Environment Act 1995 (c. 25)

68 In Schedule 9, in paragraph 15, for "Sections 76 to 78 of the Charities Act 1993" substitute "Sections 294 to 297 of the Charities Act 2011".

Reserve Forces Act 1996 (c. 14)

69 (1) In Schedule 5, in paragraph 2, in the definition of "charity", for "as it has under section 1(1) of the Charities Act 2006" substitute "as it has under section 1(1) of the Charities Act 2011".

(2) In paragraph 5 of that Schedule, for sub-paragraphs (2) and (3) substitute—

"(2) An application under this paragraph—

(a) may be made at any time within the period of 6 months beginning with the day on which the warrant comes into force; and

(b) is subject to subsections (2) to (5) of section 115 of the Charities Act 2011 (proceedings not to be begun without the consent of the Charity Commission or leave of a judge of the High Court),

and for the purposes of subsection (5) of that section an application for an order of the Commission authorising proceedings under this paragraph is deemed to be refused if it is not granted during the period of one month beginning with the day on which the application is received by the Commission.

(3) In this paragraph "the court" has the same meaning as in the Charities Act 2011."

(3) For paragraph 6 substitute—

"6 In any case where—

(a) the Secretary of State requests the Charity Commission to make provision with respect to any charitable property which is held for the purposes of a unit of a reserve force that has been or is to be disbanded, or

(b) an order is made under paragraph 4 or 5 excluding any charitable property so held from the operation of paragraph 3(1),

the Commission may, regardless of anything in section 70(2) of the Charities Act 2011 (limit on jurisdiction to make schemes etc. for the protection of charities), exercise its jurisdiction under section 69 with respect to the property to which the request or order relates."

Trusts of Land and Appointment of Trustees Act 1996 (c. 47)

70 In Schedule 1, in paragraph 4(2)—

(a) in paragraph (a), for "section 37(1) nor section 39(1) of the Charities Act 1993" substitute "section 122(2) nor section 125(1) of the Charities Act 2011", and

(b) in paragraph (b), for "section 37(2) nor section 39(2)" substitute "section 122(3) nor section 125(2)".

Housing Act 1996 (c. 52)

71 In section 58, for subsection (1) substitute—

"(1) In this Part—

(a) "trusts", in relation to a charity, has the same meaning as in the Charities Act 2011 and "trustee" means a charitable trustee within the meaning of that Act, and

(b) "registered charity" means a charity which is registered in accordance with section 30 of that Act."

72 (1) Amend Schedule 1 as follows.

(2) In paragraph 4(2)(d), for "section 72 of the Charities Act 1993" substitute "section 178 of the Charities Act 2011".

(3) For paragraph 18(4) substitute—

"(4) The charity must appoint a qualified auditor ("the auditor") to audit the accounts prepared in accordance with sub-paragraph (3) in respect of each period of account in which—

(a) the charity's gross income arising in connection with its housing activities exceeds the sum for the time being specified in section 144(1)(a) of the Charities Act 2011, or

(b) the charity's gross income arising in that connection exceeds the accounts threshold and at the end of that period the aggregate value of its assets (before deduction of liabilities) in respect of its housing activities exceeds the sum for the time being specified in section 144(1)(b) of that Act;

and in this sub-paragraph "gross income" and "accounts threshold" have the same meanings as in section 144 of that Act."

(4) In paragraph 18A(2)(b), for "the Charities Act 1993" substitute "the Charities Act 2011".

Housing Grants, Construction and Regeneration Act 1996 (c. 53)

73 In section 95(6), for "but otherwise has the same meaning as in the Charities Act 1993" substitute "but otherwise has the same meaning as it has under section 10 of the Charities Act 2011".

Education Act 1996 (c. 56)

74 In section 537C—

(a) in subsection (1)(a), for "section 13 of the Charities Act 2006)" substitute "section 25 of the Charities Act 2011)", and

(b) in subsection (2), for "section 10A of the Charities Act 1993" substitute "section 56 or 57 of the Charities Act 2011".

School Standards and Framework Act 1998 (c. 31)

75 (1) In section 23, for subsection (1A) substitute—

"(1A) Any body to which subsection (1)(a) or (b) applies is, as a result of its inclusion in Schedule 3 to the Charities Act 2011, an exempt charity for the purposes of that Act."

(2) In subsection (3), for ", and is an institution to which section 3A(4)(b) of the Charities Act 1993 applies" substitute "and is an institution which is to be treated for the purposes of section 31(3) of the Charities Act 2011 as if that provision applied to it."

(3) For subsection (4)(a) substitute—

"(a) institution" has the same meaning as in the Charities Act 2011;".

76 In section 23A(10), in the definitions of "charity trustee" and "institution", for "the Charities Act 1993" substitute "the Charities Act 2011".

77 In section 23B(2), for "section 18 of the Charities Act 1993" substitute "section 76 or sections 79 to 81 of the Charities Act 2011".

78 In Schedule 1, for paragraph 10 substitute—

"10 An Education Action Forum shall be a charity and is an institution which is to be treated for the purposes of section 31(3) of the Charities Act 2011 (institutions required to be excepted from registration under that Act) as if that provision applied to it."

79 In Schedule 22, in paragraph 8A(2)(c), for "removed under subsection (4) of section 3 of the Charities Act 1993 from the register of charities kept under that section," substitute "removed under section 34 of the Charities Act 2011 from the register of charities kept under section 29 of that Act,".

National Institutions Measure 1998 (No. 1)

80 (1) In section 3(1), for "Part VI of the Charities Act 1993" substitute "Part 8 of the Charities Act 2011".

(2) In section 3(2), for "under subsection (2) of section 43 of that Act to carry out an audit under that subsection" substitute "under subsection (2) of section 144 of that Act to carry out an audit under that subsection".

(3) In section 3(3), for "Part VI, to have been appointed in pursuance of the said section 43" substitute "Part 8, to have been appointed in pursuance of the said section 144".

Finance Act 1999 (c. 16)

81 In Schedule 19, in paragraph 15—

(a) in sub-paragraph (a), for "or section 24 of the Charities Act 1993," substitute ", section 24 of the Charities Act 1993 or section 96 of the Charities Act 2011," and
(b) in sub-paragraph (b), for "or section 25 of the Charities Act 1993" substitute ", section 25 of the Charities Act 1993 or section 100 of the Charities Act 2011".

Cathedrals Measure 1999 (No. 1)

82 In section 4(4), for "section 72(1) of the Charities Act 1993" substitute "section 178 of the Charities Act 2011".

83 In section 15(1), in paragraph (iii) of the proviso, for "section 36 of the Charities Act 1993," substitute "sections 117 to 121 of the Charities Act 2011,".

84 In section 27(1), for "section 43 of the Charities Act 1993" substitute "section 144 of the Charities Act 2011".

85 In section 34, for "same meaning as in the Charities Act 1993" substitute "meaning given by section 10 of the Charities Act 2011".

Financial Services and Markets Act 2000 (c. 8)

86 In Schedule 11A, in paragraph 7(2)(a), for the words from "within the meaning of —" to "(ii)" substitute "—

(i) as defined by section 1(1) of the Charities Act 2011, or
(ii) within the meaning of".

87 In Schedule 11B, in paragraph 12(4)(b), for "or section 24 or 25 of the Charities Act 1993 (c. 10)" substitute "section 24 or 25 of the Charities Act 1993 or section 96 or 100 of the Charities Act 2011".

Learning and Skills Act 2000 (c. 21)

88 In section 143(6)(d), for "the Charities Act 1993)" substitute "the Charities Act 2011)".

Trustee Act 2000 (c. 29)

89 In section 38—

(a) in paragraph (a), for "section 24 of the Charities Act 1993" substitute "section 96 of the Charities Act 2011", and
(b) in paragraph (b), for "section 25" substitute "section 100".

90 In section 39(1)—

(a) in the definition of "charitable purposes", for "has the same meaning as in the Charities Act 1993" substitute "has the meaning given by section 11 of the Charities Act 2011", and
(b) in the definition of "exempt charity" for "the Charities Act 1993" substitute "the Charities Act 2011".

Criminal Justice and Court Services Act 2000 (c. 43)

91 In section 42(1), for "“charity trustee” has the same meaning as in the Charities Act 1993" substitute "“charity trustee” has the same meaning as in the Charities Act 2011".

Criminal Justice and Police Act 2001 (c. 16)

92 In Part 1 of Schedule 1, for paragraph 56A and its heading substitute—

"*56A Charities Act 2011*

56A The power of seizure conferred by section 48(3) of the Charities Act 2011 (seizure of material for the purposes of an inquiry under section 46 of that Act)."

Churchwardens Measure 2001 (No. 1)

93 In section 2(1), for "under section 72(1) of the Charities Act 1993 (c 10) and the disqualification is not for the time being subject to a general waiver by the Charity Commission under subsection (4) of that section or to a waiver by it under that subsection" substitute "under section 178 of the Charities Act 2011 and the disqualification is not for the time being subject to a general waiver by the Charity Commission under section 181 of that Act or to a waiver by it under that section".

Land Registration Act 2002 (c. 9)

94 In section 4(1)(aa), for "section 83 of the Charities Act 1993" substitute "section 334 of the Charities Act 2011".

Licensing Act 2003 (c. 17)

95 In section 16(3), omit the definition of "charity".

96 In Schedule 2, for paragraph 5(4) substitute—

"(4) In sub-paragraph (1)(d) "registered charity" means--

(a) a charity which is registered in accordance with section 30 of the Charities Act 2011, or

(b) a charity which by virtue of subsection (2) of that section is not required to be so registered."

Higher Education Act 2004 (c. 8)

97 In section 40—

(a) in subsection (1A), for "section 13 of the Charities Act 2006)" substitute "section 25 of the Charities Act 2011)",

(b) in subsection (1B), for "section 10A of the Charities Act 1993" substitute "section 56 or 57 of the Charities Act 2011", and

(c) in subsection (3) for "section 13 of the Charities Act 2006)" substitute "section 25 of the Charities Act 2011)".

Companies (Audit, Investigations and Community Enterprise) Act 2004 (c. 27)

98 In section 54C(3), for "''exempt charity" has the same meaning as in the Charities Act 1993 (see section 96 of that Act)" substitute "''exempt charity" has the same meaning as in the Charities Act 2011 (see section 22 of that Act)."

99 In section 63(1), in the definition of "English charity" for "as defined by section 1(1) of the Charities Act 2006" substitute "''as defined by section 1(1) of the Charities Act 2011".

100 In Schedule 3, for paragraph 4 substitute—

"4 The person appointed to chair the Charity Commission may make available to the Regulator, to assist in the exercise of the Regulator's functions—

(a) any other member of the Commission appointed under paragraph 1(1) of Schedule 1 to the Charities Act 2011, or

(b) any member of staff of the Commission appointed under paragraph 5(1) of that Schedule."

Pensions Act 2004 (c. 35)

101 In Schedule 3, for the entry relating to the Charity Commission substitute—

"The Charity Commission	Functions under the Charities Act 2006 or the Charities Act 2011."

102 In Schedule 8, for the entry relating to the Charity Commission substitute—

"The Charity Commission	Functions under the Charities Act 2006 or the Charities Act 2011."

Serious Organised Crime and Police Act 2005 (c. 15)

103 In section 146(3)(b), for "charity trustee (within the meaning of the Charities Act 1993 (c. 10))" substitute "charity trustee (within the meaning of the Charities Act 2011)".

Education Act 2005 (c. 18)

104 In section 92(5), for "section 13 of the Charities Act 2006)" substitute "section 25 of the Charities Act 2011)".

Gambling Act 2005 (c. 19)

105 In section 19(2)(a), for "purposes which are exclusively charitable according to the law of England and Wales" substitute "purposes which are exclusively charitable purposes (as defined by section 2 of the Charities Act 2011)".

Charities and Trustee Investment (Scotland) Act 2005 (asp 10)

106 In section 36(1), for paragraphs (a) and (b) substitute—

"(a) which is registered as a charity in England and Wales in accordance with section 30 of the Charities Act 2011, or

(b) which, by virtue of subsection (2) of that section, is not required to register as a charity under that section."

107 In section 69(2)(d)(i), after "Wales under" insert "section 79(2)(a) of the Charities Act 2011 or" and for "18(2)(i) of that Act" substitute "18(2)(i) of the 1993 Act".

108 In section 96(3), for "sections 24 and 25 of the Charities Act 1993 (c. 10)" substitute "sections 96 and 100 of the Charities Act 2011".

Natural Environment and Rural Communities Act 2006 (c. 16)

109 In section 81(2)(h), for "section 13 of the Charities Act 2006)" substitute "section 25 of the Charities Act 2011)".

Education and Inspections Act 2006 (c. 40)

110 In Schedule 2, in paragraph 10(2)(b), for "charity trustee (within the meaning of the Charities Act 1993 (c. 10))" substitute "charity trustee (within the meaning of the Charities Act 2011)".

National Health Service Act 2006 (c. 41)

111 In section 217(5), for "the court (as defined in the Charities Act 1993 (c. 10))" substitute "the court (as defined in the Charities Act 2011)".

National Health Service (Wales) Act 2006 (c. 42)

112 In section 165(5), for "the court (as defined in the Charities Act 1993 (c. 10))" substitute "the court (as defined in the Charities Act 2011)".

Companies Act 2006 (c. 46)

113 In section 21(2)(a), for "section 64 of the Charities Act 1993 (c. 10)" substitute "sections 197 and 198 of the Charities Act 2011".

114 In section 31(4)(a), for "section 64 of the Charities Act 1993 (c. 10)" substitute "sections 197 and 198 of the Charities Act 2011".

115 In—

(a) section 1140(2)(c)(ii), and

(b) section 1154(1)(b) and (2)(b),

for "section 18 of the Charities Act 1993 (c. 10)" substitute "section 76 of the Charities Act 2011".

116 In Schedule 1, in paragraph 6(4)(b) for "or section 24 or 25 of the Charities Act 1993 (c. 10)," substitute ", section 24 or 25 of the Charities Act 1993 or section 96 or 100 of the Charities Act 2011,".

Safeguarding Vulnerable Groups Act 2006 (c. 47)

117 In Schedule 4, in—

(a) paragraph 4(7) and

(b) paragraph 8(6),

for "“charity trustee” has the same meaning as in the Charities Act 1993 (c. 10)" substitute "“charity trustee” has the same meaning as in the Charities Act 2011".

Charities Act 2006 (c. 50)

118 In section 54(2), for “section 9 of the 1993 Act” substitute “section 52 of the Charities Act 2011”.

119 In section 72(3), for “section 10(2) to (4) of the 1993 Act” substitute “section 55 of the Charities Act 2011”.

120 (1) In section 73(5)(b), for “the appointed day (within the meaning of section 10 of this Act)” substitute “31 January 2009”.

(2) After section 73(5) insert—

“(6) This section has effect, in relation to any time occurring on or after the commencement of the Charities Act 2011 as if—

(a) the reference in subsection (1) to the operation of this Act included (in relation to provisions of this Act repealed and re-enacted by the 2011 Act) a reference to the operation of the 2011 Act,

(b) the reference in subsection (2)(a) to the effect of the Act included (in relation to provisions of this Act repealed and re-enacted by the 2011 Act) a reference to the effect of the 2011 Act, and

(c) the reference in subsection (5)(a) to paragraph (b) or (c) of section 3A(2) of the 1993 Act (as amended by section 9 of this Act) were a reference to paragraph (b) or (c) of section 30(2) of the 2011 Act.”

121 (1) In section 74(4), omit—

(a) paragraphs (a) and (b), and

(b) in paragraph (e), “76 or”.

(2) In section 74(5), omit “(a), (b),”.

(3) Omit section 74(6).

122 Omit section 76.

123 (1) In section 78(2)—

(a) omit paragraph (a);

(b) in paragraph (b), for “(in accordance with section 2(6)) the meaning given by section 2(1)” substitute “(in accordance with section 2(2) of the Charities Act 2011) the meaning given by section 2(1) of that Act”;

(c) in paragraph (c), for “the 1993 Act” substitute “that Act”;

(d) omit the words following paragraph (c).

(2) Omit section 78(3).

(3) In section 78(4)(c), omit “6(5) or”.

124 In section 79(1), omit—

(a) paragraph (a), and

(b) in paragraph (g), the words from “paragraph 104” to “paragraph 174(d)”.

125 In section 80—

(a) omit subsections (3)(a), (b) and (d) (but not the "and" following it), (4), (5)(a) to (c) and (e) (but not the "and" following it), (6) and (8),
(b) in subsections (3)(e) and (5)(f), for "76" substitute "77", and
(c) in subsection (9)—
(i) omit "also" and paragraph (a) (together with the "or" following it), and
(ii) in paragraph (b), for "those" substitute "the amendments".

Income Tax Act 2007 (c. 3)

126 (1) Amend section 558 as follows.

(2) Under the heading "Type 2", for "or" preceding paragraph (c) substitute—
"(bb) section 96 of the Charities Act 2011, or".

(3) Under the heading "Type 3", omit "or" preceding paragraph (b) and at the end of paragraph (b) insert "or
(c) section 100 of the Charities Act 2011."

Legal Services Act 2007 (c. 29)

127 In section 194(9)(a), for "in accordance with section 3A of the Charities Act 1993 (c. 10)," substitute "in accordance with section 30 of the Charities Act 2011,".

Dioceses, Pastoral and Mission Measure 2007 (No. 1)

128 In section 62(1), in the definition of "charity", for "section 78(2) of the Charities Act 2006 (c. 50)" substitute "section 10 of the Charities Act 2011".

129 In Schedule 2, in paragraph 13(2), for "charity trustee within the meaning of the Charities Act 1993 (1993 c. 10)" substitute "charity trustee within the meaning of the Charities Act 2011".

Regulatory Enforcement and Sanctions Act 2008 (c. 13)

130 In Schedule 3, omit "Charities Act 1993 (c. 10), sections 76 to 78" and after the entry relating to the Charities Act 2006 insert "Charities Act 2011, sections 294 to 297".

Housing and Regeneration Act 2008 (c. 17)

131 In section 135(6), for "sections 41 to 45 of the Charities Act 1993 (c. 10) (charity accounts)" substitute "Part 8 of the Charities Act 2011".

132 In section 136—
(a) in subsection (4), for "section 43(1)(a) of the Charities Act 1993" substitute "section 144(1)(a) of the Charities Act 2011",
(b) in subsection (5)(a), for "section 43(1) of the Charities Act 1993," substitute "section 144(1) of the Charities Act 2011,",
(c) in subsection (5)(b), for "section 43(1)(b)", substitute "section 144(1)(b)", and
(d) in subsection (6), for "section 43 of the Charities Act 1993 (c. 10)" substitute "section 144 of the Charities Act 2011".

133 In section 138(3)(a), for "the Charities Act 1993" substitute "the Charities Act 2011".

134 In section 266(6), for "section 72 of the Charities Act 1993 (c. 10)" substitute "section 178 of the Charities Act 2011".

135 In section 275—

(a) in the definition of "non-registrable charity", for "section 3A of the Charities Act 1993 (c. 10),", substitute "section 30 of the Charities Act 2011,", and

(b) in the definition of"registered charity", for "the Charities Act 1993 (c. 10)," substitute "the Charities Act 2011,".

Planning Act 2008 (c. 29)

136 (1) Amend section 210 as follows.

(2) In subsection (1)(b), for "section 2 of the Charities Act 2006 (c. 50)" substitute "section 2 of the Charities Act 2011".

(3) In subsection (4)—

(a) in paragraph (a), for "section 3 of the Charities Act 1993 (c. 10)," substitute "section 29 of the Charities Act 2011,", and

(b) in paragraph (b), for "section 1(1) of the Charities Act 2006 but is not required to be registered in the register kept under section 3 of the Charities Act 1993" substitute "section 1(1) of the Charities Act 2011 but is not required to be registered in the register kept under section 29 of that Act".

(4) In subsection (5), for "section 2(2) of the Charities Act 2006;" substitute "section 3(1) of the Charities Act 2011;".

Charities Act (Northern Ireland) 2008 (c. 12 (N.I.))

137 In section 56(1)(a), for "under section 3 of the Charities Act 1993 (c. 10), or which, by virtue of section 3A(2) of that Act, is not required to register as a charity under that section" substitute "in the register kept under section 29 of the Charities Act 2011, or which, by virtue of section 30(2) of that Act, is not required to be registered in that register".

138 In section 86(1)(e)—

(a) in sub-paragraph (i), after "under" insert "section 79(2)(a) of the Charities Act 2011 or", and

(b) in sub-paragraph (ii), for "that provision" substitute "section 18(2)(i) of the 1993 Act".

Apprenticeships, Skills, Children and Learning Act 2009 (c. 22)

139 In section 71A(1), for "section 13 of the Charities Act 2006)" substitute "section 25 of the Charities Act 2011)".

140 In Schedule 3, in paragraph 19(4)(c), for "(within the meaning of section 69A of the Charities Act 1993 (c. 10))" substitute "(within the meaning of Part 11 of the Charities Act 2011)".

141 In Schedule 4, in paragraph 9(4)(c), for "(within the meaning of section 69A of the Charities Act 1993 (c. 10))" substitute "(within the meaning of Part 11 of the Charities Act 2011)".

Corporation Tax Act 2010 (c. 4)

142 (1) Amend section 511 as follows.

(2) Under the heading "Type 2", for "or" preceding paragraph (c) substitute—

"(bb) section 96 of the Charities Act 2011, or".

(3) Under the heading "Type 3", omit "or" preceding paragraph (b) and at the end of paragraph (b) insert "or

(c) section 100 of the Charities Act 2011."

Finance Act 2010 (c. 13)

143 (1) Amend Schedule 6 as follows.

(2) In paragraph 1(4)—

(a) for "see section 2 of the Charities Act 2006" substitute "see section 2 of the Charities Act 2011", and

(b) in paragraph (b), for "(see section 80(3) to (6) of that Act)" substitute "(see sections 7 and 8 of that Act)".

(3) In paragraph 3(1)(a), for "within the meaning of the Charities Act 1993" substitute "within the meaning of section 10 of the Charities Act 2011".

(4) In paragraph 3(2), for "section 3 of the Charities Act 1993" substitute "section 29 of the Charities Act 2011".

Equality Act 2010 (c. 15)

144 In section 194(3)(a), for "section 1(1) of the Charities Act 2006" substitute "section 1(1) of the Charities Act 2011".

Church of England (Miscellaneous Provisions) Measure 2010 (No. 1)

145 In section 10(1), for "section 96(2) of the Charities Act 1993 (c. 10)" substitute "section 10 of the Charities Act 2011".

Mission and Pastoral Measure 2011 (No. 3)

146 For section 67(1) substitute—

"(1) The power of the court (as defined by the Charities Act 2011) to make schemes under its jurisdiction with respect to charities, and the power of the Charity Commission to make schemes under that Act, shall extend to the making of schemes with respect to consecrated chapels belonging to charities which are no longer needed for the purposes of the charity, and section 10(2)(c) of that Act shall not be taken as preventing the making of any such scheme."

147 In section 77(3), for "the Charities Act 1993" substitute "the Charities Act 2011".

148 In section 106(1), in the definition of "charity", for "section 78(2) of the Charities Act 2006 (c. 50)" substitute "section 10 of the Charities Act 2011".

149 (1) Amend Schedule 3 as follows.

(2) In paragraph 9(6)—

(a) for "section 16 of the Charities Act 1993" substitute "section 69 of the Charities Act 2011", and

(b) for "that section" substitute "sections 69 to 71 of that Act".

(3) In paragraph 14(1)(e) for "section 16 of the Charities Act 1993" substitute "section 69 of the Charities Act 2011".

SCHEDULE 8

Section 354

TRANSITIONALS AND SAVINGS

PART 1

GENERAL

Continuity of the law

1 The repeal and re-enactment of provisions by this Act does not affect the continuity of the law.

2 A reference, express or implied, in this Act, another enactment or an instrument or document, to a provision of this Act is, subject to its context, to be read as being or including a reference to the corresponding provision repealed by this Act, in relation to times, circumstances or purposes in relation to which the repealed provision had effect.

3 (1) A reference, express or implied, in any enactment, instrument or document to a provision repealed by this Act is, subject to its context, to be read as being or including a reference to the corresponding provision of this Act, in relation to times, circumstances or purposes in relation to which that provision has effect.

(2) Where a power conferred by an Act is expressed to be exercisable in relation to enactments contained in Acts passed before or in the same Session as the Act conferring the power, the power is also exercisable in relation to provisions of this Act that reproduce such enactments.

(3) The powers in—

(a) section 75(4) and (5) of the Charities Act 2006 (to make supplementary and consequential provision etc.), and

(b) section 77 of that Act (to make amendments in consequence of, or in connection with, changes to the provisions of company law relating to the accounts of charitable companies etc.),

are, so far as they were exercisable in relation to any provision repealed and re-enacted by this Act, exercisable in relation to the corresponding provision of this Act.

(4) Sub-paragraphs (2) and (3) do not affect the generality of sub-paragraph (1).

4 Anything done, or having effect as if done, under (or for the purposes of or in reliance on) a provision repealed by this Act, and in force or effective immediately before the commencement of this Act, has effect after that commencement as if done under (or for the purposes of or in reliance on) the corresponding provision of this Act.

5 Paragraphs 1 to 4 have effect in place of section 17(2) of the Interpretation Act 1978; but nothing in this Schedule affects any other provision of that Act.

Effect of old transitionals and savings

6 The repeals made by this Act do not affect the operation of any transitional provision or saving relating to the coming into force of a provision reproduced in this Act in so far as the transitional provision or saving is not specifically reproduced in this Act but remains capable of having effect in relation to the corresponding provision of this Act or otherwise.

7 (1) The repeal by this Act of an enactment previously repealed subject to savings does not affect the continued operation of those savings.

(2) The repeal by this Act of a saving on the previous repeal of an enactment does not affect the operation of the saving in so far as it is not specifically reproduced in this Act but remains capable of having effect.

Use of existing forms etc.

8 Any reference to an enactment repealed by this Act which is contained in a document made, served or issued after the commencement of the repeal is, subject to its context, to be read as being or including a reference to the corresponding provision of this Act.

PART 2

RECREATIONAL ETC. PURPOSES

General

9 In this Part of this Schedule "the 1958 Act" means the Recreational Charities Act 1958.

10 (1) Where section 2 of the 1958 Act applied to any trusts immediately before the day on which section 5(3) of the Charities Act 2006 came into force, the repeal by this Act of paragraph 2 of Schedule 10 to the 2006 Act does not prevent the trusts from continuing to be charitable if they constitute a charity in accordance with section 1(1) of this Act.

(2) Sub-paragraph (1)—

(a) affects the law of Scotland only so far as it affects the construction of references to charities or charitable purposes in enactments which relate to matters falling within Section A1 of Part 2 of Schedule 5 to the Scotland Act 1998 (reserved matters: fiscal policy etc.);

(b) affects the law of Northern Ireland only so far as it affects the construction of references to charities or charitable purposes in enactments which relate to matters falling within paragraph 9 of Schedule 2 to the Northern Ireland Act 1998 (excepted matters: taxes and duties).

11 The repeal by this Act of subsections (2) and (3) of section 3 of the 1958 Act does not affect any saving in either of those subsections which is capable of having continuing effect.

Scotland

12 Sections 1 and 2 of the 1958 Act as in force before the commencement of section 5 of the Charities Act 2006 continue to have effect in relation to the law of Scotland so far as they affect the construction of any references to charities or charitable purposes which—

(a) are to be construed in accordance with the law of England and Wales, but

(b) are not contained in enactments relating to matters falling within Section A1 of Part 2 of Schedule 5 to the Scotland Act 1998 (reserved matters: fiscal policy etc.).

Northern Ireland

13 Sections 1 and 2 of the 1958 Act as in force before the commencement of section 5 of the Charities Act 2006 continue to have effect in relation to the law of Northern Ireland so far as they affect the construction of any references to charities or charitable purposes which—

(a) are to be construed in accordance with the law of England and Wales, but

(b) are not contained in enactments relating to matters falling within paragraph 9 of Schedule 2 to the Northern Ireland Act 1998 (excepted matters: taxes and duties).

PART 3

MISCELLANEOUS

Regulations relating to fees

14 Despite the revocation by this Act of the Charities (Pre-consolidation Amendments) Order 2011 (S.I. 2011/1396), regulations having effect as if made under section 19 continue to have effect as if any reference to the furnishing of a document were a reference to the provision of the document.

Exempt charities

15 (1) Despite the repeal by this Act of section 11(13) of the Charities Act 2006 (power to make amendments or modifications of enactments in connection with changes in exempt charities), the Minister may by order make such amendments or other modifications of any enactment as the Minister considers appropriate in connection with—

(a) charities of a particular description becoming, or ceasing to be, exempt charities, or

(b) a particular charity becoming, or ceasing to be, an exempt charity,

as a result of provision made by or under section 11 of the 2006 Act.

(2) In sub-paragraph (1) "enactment" includes—

(a) any provision of subordinate legislation (within the meaning of the Interpretation Act 1978), and

(b) a provision of a Measure of the Church Assembly or of the General Synod of the Church of England;

and references to enactments include enactments whenever passed or made.

16 The repeal and re-enactment by this Act of—

(a) section 11(13) of the Charities Act 2006 (power to make amendments or modifications of enactments in connection with changes in exempt charities), and

(b) section 13(5) of that Act (power to make amendments or modifications of enactments in connection with principal regulator regulations),

is not to be treated as preventing any amendment or modification being made of an enactment contained in this Act which re-enacts an enactment of which an amendment or modification could have been made under section 11(13) or 13(5).

Application cy-près: donors unknown or disclaiming or treated as disclaiming

17 Sections 63, 64 and 67 apply to property given for charitable purposes whether before or on or after the commencement of this Act.

Official custodian as successor to official trustee of charity lands and official trustees of charity funds

18 (1) Despite the repeal by this Act of paragraph 26 of Schedule 10 to the Charities Act 2006, the official custodian for charities is to continue to be treated as the successor for all purposes both of the official trustee of charity lands and of the official trustees of charitable funds as if—

(a) the functions of the official trustee or trustees had been functions of the official custodian, and

(b) the official trustee or trustees had been, and had discharged the functions of the official trustee or trustees as, holder of the office of the official custodian.

(2) Despite the repeal of paragraph 26 of that Schedule (and without affecting the generality of sub-paragraph (1))—

(a) any property which immediately before the commencement of that repeal was, by virtue of paragraph 26(2) of that Schedule, held by the official custodian continues to be so held, as if vested in the official custodian under section 90, and

(b) any enactment or document referring to the official trustee or trustees mentioned above continues to have effect, so far as the context permits, as if the official custodian had been mentioned instead.

Savings for consequential amendments

19 (1) The repeal by this Act of paragraph 23(a) of Schedule 10 to the Charities Act 2006 (saving for consequential amendment made by the Charities Act 1960) does not affect the amendment made by Schedule 6 to the Charities Act 1960 in section 9 of the Places of Worship Registration Act 1855.

(2) The repeal by this Act of paragraph 23(d) of Schedule 10 to the Charities Act 2006 (saving for consequential amendment made by the Charities Act 1960) does not affect

the amendment made by Schedule 6 to the Charities Act 1960 in section 31 of the New Parishes Measure 1943.

(3) The repeal by this Act of paragraph 30 of Schedule 6 to the Charities Act 1993 does not affect the amendments made by that paragraph in—

(a) section 90(4) of the Local Government Act 1985, or

(b) section 192(11) of the Education Reform Act 1988.

Universities of Durham and Newcastle-upon-Tyne Act 1963

20 Despite the revocation by this Act of the Charities (Pre-consolidation Amendments) Order 2011 (S.I. 2011/1396), the Universities of Durham and Newcastle-upon-Tyne Act 1963 continues to have effect as if Schedule 7 to the Charities Act 1993 (repeals) had never referred to section 10 of the 1963 Act.

SCHEDULE 9

Section 354

TRANSITORY MODIFICATIONS

Commission's general functions—public charitable collections

1 (1) Sub-paragraph (2) applies if Chapter 1 of Part 3 of the 2006 Act (public charitable collections) has not been brought into force before the commencement of this Act.

(2) Section 15 (the Commission's general functions) has effect until the appointed day as if—

(a) paragraph 4 of section 15(1), and

(b) section 15(6),

were omitted.

(3) "The appointed day" means the day on which Chapter 1 of Part 3 of the 2006 Act is brought into force by virtue of an order made under section 79 of that Act.

"Exempt charity" and common investment and deposit funds

2 (1) Sub-paragraph (2) applies if—

(a) section 11(10) of the 2006 Act (amendment of section 24(8) of the 1993 Act), and

(b) paragraph 173(3)(a) of Schedule 8 to the 2006 Act (amendment of definition of "exempt charity" in section 96(1) of the 1993 Act),

have not been brought into force before the commencement of this Act.

(2) Subsection (3) of—

(a) section 99 (further provisions relating to common investment schemes and funds), and

(b) section 103 (further provisions relating to common deposit schemes and funds),

has effect until the relevant commencement date as if at the end of the subsection there were inserted "; and if the scheme admits only exempt charities, the fund is an exempt charity for the purposes of this Act".

"Exempt charity" and church funds

3 (1) Sub-paragraph (2) applies if section 11(9) of the 2006 Act (removing certain exempt charities from Schedule 2 to the 1993 Act), so far as relating to—

(a) an Investment Fund or Deposit Fund within the meaning of the Church Funds Investment Measure 1958, or

(b) an investment fund or deposit fund within the meaning of the Methodist Church Funds Act 1960,

has not been brought into force before the commencement of this Act.

(2) Schedule 3 (exempt charities) has effect until the relevant commencement date as if paragraphs (a) and (b) of paragraph 1(2) were omitted.

"Exempt charity" and registered societies etc.

4 (1) Sub-paragraph (2) applies if section 11(8) of the 2006 Act (changing the exemption under paragraph (y) of Schedule 2 to the 1993 Act) has not been brought into force before the commencement of this Act.

(2) Schedule 3 (exempt charities) has effect until the relevant commencement date as if, in paragraph 27, for "if the society is also registered in the register of social landlords under Part 1 of the Housing Act 1996" there were substituted "and any registered society or branch within the meaning of the Friendly Societies Act 1974".

5 (1) Sub-paragraph (2) applies if section 2 of the Co-operative and Community Benefit Societies and Credit Unions Act 2010 (re-naming the Industrial and Provident Societies Acts) has not been brought into force before the commencement of this Act.

(2) In the application of paragraph 26 or 27 of Schedule 3 (exempt charities) before the commencement of section 2 of the 2010 Act the reference to the Co-operative and Community Benefit Societies and Credit Unions Act 1965 (c. 12) is to be read as a reference to the Industrial and Provident Societies Act 1965 (c. 12).

Power to amend enactments in connection with changes in exempt charities

6 (1) Sub-paragraph (2) applies if paragraph 2, 3 or 4 applies in relation to charities of a particular description or to a particular charity.

(2) In relation to those charities or that charity, section 23 has effect as if for subsection (3) there were substituted—

"(3) The Minister may by order make such amendments or other modifications of any enactment as the Minister considers appropriate in connection with—

(a) charities of a particular description ceasing to be exempt charities on the relevant commencement date, or

(b) a particular charity ceasing to be an exempt charity on the relevant commencement date."

Exempt charities and the principal regulator

7 (1) Sub-paragraph (2) applies if, in relation to charities of a particular description or a particular charity—

(a) section 13(1) to (3) of the 2006 Act (general duty of principal regulator), and

(b) section 86A of the 1993 Act (duty of Commission to consult principal regulator),

have not been brought into before the commencement of this Act.

(2) In relation to those charities or that charity, Part 3 has effect until the relevant commencement date as if—

(a) section 26 (general duty of principal regulator), and

(b) section 28 (duty of Commission to consult principal regulator),

were omitted.

Voluntary registration

8 (1) Sub-paragraph (2) applies if section 3A(6) of the 1993 Act (voluntary registration) has not been brought into force before the commencement of this Act.

(2) Part 4 (registration and names of charities) has effect until the relevant commencement date with the omission of section 30(3) (but subject to the modifications specified in the Charities Act 2006 (Commencement No. 5, Transitional and Transitory Provisions and Savings) Order 2008 (S.I. 2008/3267) as it has effect in accordance with Part 1 of Schedule 8).

Regulations to secure that any institution ceasing to be an exempt charity on the relevant commencement date is excepted

9 (1) Sub-paragraph (2) applies if paragraph 2, 3 or 4 applies and, on the date which is the relevant commencement date in relation to that paragraph, an institution ceases to be an exempt charity.

(2) In relation to that institution, section 31 has effect as if for subsection (3) there were substituted—

"(3) Such regulations must be made under section 30(2)(c) as are necessary to secure that the institution is excepted under section 30(2)(c) (subject to compliance with any conditions of the exception and the financial limit mentioned in section 30(2)(c))."

Change of name and exempt charities

10 (1) Sub-paragraph (2) applies if, in relation to charities of a particular description or a particular charity, paragraph 1 of Schedule 5 to the 2006 Act (removal of exception for exempt charities from power to require charity's name to be changed) has not been brought into before the commencement of this Act.

(2) In relation to those charities or that charity, section 42 (power to require name to be changed) has effect until the relevant commencement date as if at the end there were inserted—

"(6) Nothing in this section applies to an exempt charity."

Power to institute inquiries and exempt charities

11 (1) Sub-paragraph (2) applies if, in relation to charities of a particular description or a particular charity, paragraph 2 of Schedule 5 to the 2006 Act (restriction of exclusion

of exempt charities from power to institute inquiries) has not been brought into force before the commencement of this Act.

(2) In relation to those charities or that charity, section 46 (general power to institute inquiries) has effect until the relevant commencement date as if, in subsection (2), "except where this has been requested by its principal regulator" were omitted.

Maximum term of imprisonment for offence under section 49(8)

12 In relation to an offence committed before the commencement of section 281(5) of the Criminal Justice Act 2003 (alteration of penalties for summary offences), the reference to 51 weeks in section 49(9) is to be read as a reference to 3 months.

Power to call for documents etc. and exempt charities

13 (1) Sub-paragraph (2) applies if, in relation to charities of a particular description or a particular charity, paragraph 3 of Schedule 5 to the 2006 Act (removal of exclusion of exempt charities from power to call for documents etc.) has not been brought into force before the commencement of this Act.

(2) In relation to those charities or that charity, section 52 (power to call for documents) has effect until the relevant commencement date with the insertion after subsection (1) of—

"(1A) No person properly having the custody of documents relating only to an exempt charity is required under subsection (1) to transmit to the Commission any of those documents, or to provide any copy of or extract from any of them."

Maximum term of imprisonment for offence under section 57(3)

14 In relation to an offence committed before the commencement of section 154(1) of the Criminal Justice Act 2003 (general limit on the magistrates' court's power to impose imprisonment) the reference to 12 months in section 57(4) is to be read as a reference to 6 months.

Exempt charities and disclosure to and by principal regulator

15 (1) Sub-paragraph (2) applies if, in relation to charities of a particular description or a particular charity, the main provisions of section 10B of the 1993 Act (disclosure to and by principal regulators of exempt charities) have not been brought into force before the commencement of this Act.

(2) In relation to those charities or that charity, this Act has effect until the relevant commencement date as if section 58 (disclosure to and by principal regulators of exempt charities), except in so far as it confers power to make regulations, were omitted.

(3) In sub-paragraph (1), "the main provisions of section 10B of the 1993 Act" means section 10B except in so far as it confers power to make regulations.

Exempt charities and Commission's concurrent jurisdiction with High Court

16 (1) Sub-paragraph (2) applies if, in relation to charities of a particular description or a particular charity, paragraph 4 of Schedule 5 to the 2006 Act (removal of exclusion of exempt charities from Commission's concurrent jurisdiction) has not been brought into force before the commencement of this Act.

(2) In relation to those charities or that charity, section 70 (restrictions on Commission's concurrent jurisdiction) has effect until the relevant commencement date as if—

(a) at the beginning of subsection (2)(c) there were inserted "in the case of a charity other than an exempt charity", and

(b) in subsection (3), after "In the case of a charity" there were inserted "which is not an exempt charity and".

Exempt charities and restriction on expenditure on promoting Bills

17 (1) Sub-paragraph (2) applies if, in relation to charities of a particular description or a particular charity, paragraph 5 of Schedule 5 to the 2006 Act (restriction on expenditure on promoting Bills to apply to exempt charities) has not been brought into force before the commencement of this Act.

(2) In relation to those charities or that charity, section 74 (restriction on expenditure on promoting Bills) has effect until the relevant commencement date as if, at the end of subsection (2), there were inserted "but does not apply in the case of an exempt charity".

Exempt charities and power to act for protection of charities

18 (1) Sub-paragraph (2) applies if, in relation to charities of a particular description or a particular charity, paragraph 6 of Schedule 5 to the 2006 Act (restriction of exception for exempt charities from Commission's powers to act for protection of charities) has not been brought into force before the commencement of this Act.

(2) In relation to those charities or that charity, Part 6 (cy-près powers etc.) has effect as if sections 80(4) and 81(3) were omitted and after section 82 there were inserted—

Exempt charities

"82A **Exempt charities**

Sections 76 to 82 (powers to act for protection of charities) do not apply to an exempt charity."

Reference to Mission and Pastoral Measure 2011

19 (1) Sub-paragraph (2) applies if the Mission and Pastoral Measure 2011 has not been brought into force before the commencement of this Act.

(2) In the application of section 105(10) before the commencement of the 2011 Measure the reference to the Mission and Pastoral Measure 2011 is to be read as a reference to the Pastoral Measure 1983.

Exempt charities and power to give directions about dormant bank accounts

20 (1) Sub-paragraph (2) applies if, in relation to charities of a particular description or a particular charity, paragraph 7 of Schedule 5 to the 2006 Act (removal of exclusion of exempt charities from power to give directions about dormant accounts) has not been brought into force before the commencement of this Act.

(2) In relation to those charities or that charity, section 107 (power to direct transfer of credits in dormant bank accounts) has effect until the relevant commencement date as if after subsection (5) there were inserted—

"(6) Subsection (1) does not apply to any account held in the name of or on behalf of an exempt charity."

Exempt charities and Commission's consent to proceedings etc.

21 (1) Sub-paragraph (2) applies if, in relation to charities of a particular description or a particular charity, paragraph 8 of Schedule 5 to the 2006 Act (proceedings relating to exempt charity must be authorised by Commission etc.) has not been brought into force before the commencement of this Act.

(2) In relation to those charities or that charity, section 115 (proceedings by persons other than the Commission) has effect until the relevant commencement date as if—

(a) in subsection (2), after "relating to a charity", and

(b) in subsection (7)(a), after "with reference to any charity",

there were inserted "(other than an exempt charity)".

Exempt charities and duty of auditors etc. to report matters to Commission

22 (1) Sub-paragraph (2) applies if, in relation to charities of a particular description or a particular charity, section 29(2) of the 2006 Act (amendments of section 46 of the 1993 Act about application to exempt charities of duty of auditors etc. to report matters to Commission) has not been brought into force before the commencement of this Act.

(2) In relation to those charities or that charity, section 160 (audit or examination of accounts: exempt charities) has effect until the relevant commencement date as if—

(a) in subsection (1) (provision corresponding to section 46(1)), for "sections 144 to 155 (audit or examination of accounts)" there were substituted "sections 144 to 157 (audit or examination of accounts and duty of auditors etc. to report matters to Commission)", and

(b) subsection (2) (provision corresponding to section 46(2A) and (2B)) were omitted.

(3) Sub-paragraph (4) applies if, in relation to charities of a particular description or a particular charity, section 46(3A) of the 1993 Act (application to certain excepted charities which are also exempt charities of duty of auditors etc. to report matters to Commission) has not been brought into force before the commencement of this Act.

(4) In relation to those charities or that charity, section 161 (audit or examination of accounts: excepted charities) has effect until the relevant commencement date as if subsection (4) (provision corresponding to section 46(3A)) were omitted.

(5) Sub-paragraph (6) applies if—

(a) sub-paragraph (2) applies and, on the date which is the relevant commencement date in relation to that sub-paragraph, section 160 applies without the modifications in that sub-paragraph, or

(b) sub-paragraph (4) applies and, on the date which is the relevant commencement date in relation to that sub-paragraph, section 161 applies without the modifications in that sub-paragraph.

(6) Section 160(2) or (as the case may be) 161(4) applies in relation to matters ("pre-commencement matters") of which a person became aware at any time falling—

(a) before the relevant commencement date, and

(b) during a financial year ending on or after that date,

as well as in relation to matters of which the person becomes aware on or after that date.

(7) Any duty imposed by virtue of sub-paragraph (6) must be complied with in relation to any such pre-commencement matters as soon as practicable after the relevant commencement date.

Disqualification and references to section 429(2) of Insolvency Act 1986

23 (1) This paragraph applies if paragraph 7 of Schedule 16 to the Tribunals, Courts and Enforcement Act 2007 (administration orders: consequential amendments) has not been brought into force before the commencement of this Act.

(2) Section 178(1) has effect until the relevant commencement date as if in Case F for "section 429(2) of the Insolvency Act 1986 (disabilities on revocation of county court administration order)" there were substituted "section 429(2)(b) of the Insolvency Act 1986 (failure to pay under county court administration order)".

(3) Section 180(2) has effect until the relevant commencement date as if for "section 429(2) of the Insolvency Act 1986" there were substituted "section 429(2)(b) of the Insolvency Act 1986".

Maximum term of imprisonment for offence under section 183(1)

24 In relation to an offence committed before the commencement of section 154(1) of the Criminal Justice Act 2003 (general limit on the magistrates' court's power to impose imprisonment) the reference to 12 months in section 183(3)(a) is to be read as a reference to 6 months.

Exempt charities and power to order disqualified trustee to repay sums

25 (1) Sub-paragraph (2) applies if, in relation to charities of a particular description or a particular charity, paragraph 9 of Schedule 5 to the 2006 Act (Commission to have power to order disqualified charity trustee or trustee to repay sums to exempt charity) has not been brought into force before the commencement of this Act.

(2) In relation to those charities or that charity, section 184 (civil consequences of acting while disqualified) has effect until the relevant commencement date as if in subsection (2)(a), after "for a charity", there were inserted "(other than an exempt charity)".

CIOs

26 (1) Sub-paragraph (2) applies if any provision of the 1993 Act relating to CIOs—

(a) has not been brought into force before the commencement of this Act, or

(b) has not been brought into force for all purposes or for all areas before the commencement of this Act;

and in sub-paragraph (2) "excluded purpose or area" means any purpose or area in relation to which that provision of the 1993 Act has not been brought into force.

(2) This Act has effect until the relevant commencement date as if the provision of this Act corresponding to that provision of the 1993 Act—

(a) were omitted, or

(b) were omitted in relation to the excluded purpose or area.

(3) For the purposes of this paragraph, the provisions of the 1993 Act relating to CIOs, and the corresponding provisions of this Act, are—

provision of the 1993 Act	*corresponding provision of this Act*
section 45(3B)	section 163(3)
in section 48(1A), "(but this subsection does not apply if the charity is constituted as a CIO)"	in section 169(2), "(but this subsection does not apply if the charity is constituted as a CIO)"
any provision of Part 8A, including Schedule 5B but excluding section 69O	the corresponding provision of Part 11
section 69O	section 267(2)
section 73E(2)(b)	section 192(2)(b)
section 75C(11)	section 314
in section 97(1), the definition of "CIO"	section 204
paragraph 1 of Schedule 1C in relation to a decision of the Commission under a provision of Part 8A or Schedule 5B mentioned in column 1 of the Table in Schedule 1C	section 319 in relation to a decision of the Commission under a provision of Part 11 mentioned in column 1 of Schedule 6.

27 (1) Sub-paragraph (2) applies if section 2 of the Co-operative and Community Benefit Societies and Credit Unions Act 2010 (re-naming the Industrial and Provident Societies Acts) has not been brought into force before the commencement of this Act.

(2) In the application of subsection (1) or (5) of section 229 (application for conversion by registered society) before the commencement of section 2 of the 2010 Act the reference to the Co-operative and Community Benefit Societies and Credit Unions Act 1965 (c. 12) is to be read as a reference to the Industrial and Provident Societies Act 1965 (c. 12).

References to re-named Acts in Schedule 7

28 (1) Sub-paragraph (2) applies if section 2 of the Co-operative and Community Benefit Societies and Credit Unions Act 2010 (re-naming the Industrial and Provident Societies Acts) has not been brought into force before the commencement of this Act.

(2) In the application of Schedule 7 before the commencement of section 2 of the 2010 Act—

(a) the reference to the Co-operative and Community Benefit Societies and Credit Unions Act 1965 is to be read as a reference to the Industrial and Provident Societies Act 1965 (c. 12), and

(b) the reference to the Co-operative and Community Benefit Societies and Credit Unions Act 1968 (c. 55) is to be read as a reference to the Friendly and Industrial and Provident Societies Act 1968 (c. 55).

Meaning of "the relevant commencement date"

29 (1) Subject to sub-paragraph (2), in this Schedule "the relevant commencement date" means such day as the appropriate authority may by order appoint.

(2) If, in the case of a provision referred to in any paragraph above which has not been brought into force before the commencement of this Act, an order has been made before the commencement of this Act appointing a day for the coming into force of that provision, "the relevant commencement date" in relation to that provision means that appointed day.

(3) "The appropriate authority" means—

(a) in relation to paragraph 23 (disqualification and references to section 429(2) of Insolvency Act 1986), the Lord Chancellor;

(b) otherwise, the Minister.

(4) An order made in relation to paragraph 23 may make different provision for different purposes.

(5) An order made in relation to any other paragraph of this Schedule may—

(a) appoint different days for different purposes or different areas;

(b) make such provision as the Minister considers necessary or expedient for transitory, transitional or saving purposes in connection with the coming into force of the order.

(6) Any power to make an order under this paragraph is exercisable by statutory instrument.

References to Acts

30 In this Schedule—

"the 1993 Act" means the Charities Act 1993;

"the 2006 Act" means the Charities Act 2006.

SCHEDULE 10

Section 354

REPEALS AND REVOCATIONS

Short title or title	*Extent of repeal or revocation*
Recreational Charities Act 1958 (c. 17)	The whole Act.
Charities Act 1992 (c. 41)	In Schedule 6, paragraphs 1, 3 to 8, 13(1) and (3) and 14 to 16.
Charities Act 1993 (c. 10)	The whole Act.
Welsh Language Act 1993 (c. 38)	Sections 32 and 33.
Local Government (Wales) Act 1994 (c. 19)	In Schedule 16, paragraph 101.
Deregulation and Contracting Out Act 1994 (c. 40)	Section 29(1) to (6).
	Section 30.
	In Schedule 11, paragraph 12.
Charities (Amendment) Act 1995 (c. 48)	The whole Act.
Trusts of Land and Appointment of Trustees Act 1996 (c. 47)	In Schedule 3, paragraph 26.
Education Act 1996 (c. 56)	In Schedule 37, paragraphs 119 and 121.
Education Act 1997 (c. 44)	In Schedule 7, paragraph 7.
Bank of England Act 1998 (c. 11)	In Schedule 5, paragraph 42.
School Standards and Framework Act 1998 (c. 31)	In Schedule 30, paragraph 49.
Insolvency Act 2000 (c. 39)	In Schedule 4, paragraph 18.
Land Registration Act 2002 (c. 9)	In Schedule 11, paragraph 29.
Licensing Act 2003 (c. 17)	In section 16(3), the definition of "charity".
Civil Partnership Act 2004 (c. 33)	In Schedule 21, paragraph 38.
	In Schedule 27, paragraph 147.
National Health Service (Consequential Provisions) Act 2006 (c. 43)	In Schedule 1, paragraphs 160 to 162.
Companies Act 2006 (c. 46)	Section 181(4).
	Section 226.
Charities Act 2006 (c. 50)	Sections 1 to 9 and 11 to 44.
	In section 74, in subsection (4), paragraphs (a) and (b) and in paragraph (e) "76 or", in subsection (5) "(a), (b)," and subsection (6).
	Section 76.

Short title or title	*Extent of repeal or revocation*
	In section 78, in subsection (2), paragraph (a) and the words following paragraph (c), subsection (3) and, in subsection (4)(c), "6(5) or".
	In section 79(1), paragraph (a) and in paragraph (g) the words from "paragraph 104" to "paragraph 174(d)".
	In section 80 subsections (3)(a), (b) and (d) (but not the "and" following it), (4), (5)(a) to (c) and (e) (but not the "and" following it), (6) and (8) and in subsection (9) "also" and paragraph (a) (together with the "or" following it).
	Schedules 1, 2 and 4 to 7.
	In Schedule 8, paragraphs 1, 2, 6, 8, 13(4), 30, 33(3), 37(3), 39, 50 to 52, 54, 55, 57, 59, 61, 65, 69, 73, 77(3), 80(5)(d) (together with the "and" preceding it), (6) to (8), 83(3) and (4), 85 to 88, 90(4), 96 to 178, 180, 181(4) and (5), 191, 192(4), 193 to 195, 198, 199, 204 to 207, 210(b) (together with the "and" following it) and (c) and 212.
	In Schedule 10, paragraphs 1 to 14, 17 to 20, 23(a), (b) and (d) (together with the "or" preceding it), 24 and 26.
Income Tax Act 2007 (c. 3)	In section 558, under the heading "Type 3", the word "or" preceding paragraph (b).
	In Schedule 1, paragraph 353.
Tribunals, Courts and Enforcement Act 2007 (c. 15)	In Schedule 16, paragraph 7.
Further Education and Training Act 2007 (c. 25)	In Schedule 1, paragraph 8.
Local Government and Public Involvement in Health Act 2007 (c. 28)	In Schedule 9, paragraph 1(2)(i).
Regulatory Enforcement and Sanctions Act 2008 (c. 13)	In Schedule 3, "Charities Act 1993 (c. 10), sections 76 to 78".
Apprenticeships, Skills, Children and Learning Act 2009 (c. 22)	In Schedule 12, paragraph 8.
Corporation Tax Act 2010 (c. 4)	In section 511, under the heading "Type 3", the word "or" preceding paragraph (b).
	In Schedule 1, paragraphs 273 to 275 and 491 to 493.
Academies Act 2010 (c. 32)	Section 12(4).
Church of England (Miscellaneous Provisions) Measure 2000 (No. 1)	Section 11.

Short title or title	Extent of repeal or revocation
Companies Act 1985 (Audit Exemption) Regulations 1994 (S.I. 1994/1935)	In Schedule 1, paragraphs 6 and 7.
Charities Act 1993 (Substitution of Sums) Order 1995 (S.I. 1995/2696)	The whole Order.
Financial Services and Markets Act 2000 (Consequential Amendments and Repeals) Order 2001 (S.I. 2001/3649)	Article 339.
Insolvency Act 2000 (Company Directors Disqualification Undertakings) Order 2004 (S.I. 2004/1941)	In the Schedule, paragraph 5.
Regulatory Reform (National Health Service Charitable and Non-Charitable Trust Accounts and Audit) Order 2005 (S.I. 2005/1074)	Article 3.
Qualifications, Curriculum and Assessment Authority for Wales (Transfer of Functions to the National Assembly for Wales and Abolition) Order 2005 (S.I. 2005/3239 (W.244))	In Schedule 1, paragraph 4.
Charities and Trustee Investment (Scotland) Act 2005 (Consequential Provisions and Modifications) Order 2006 (S.I. 2006/242 (S.2))	In the Schedule, paragraph 6.
Enterprise Act 2002 (Disqualification from Office: General) Order 2006 (S.I. 2006/1722)	In Schedule 2, paragraph 4.
Transfer of Functions (Third Sector, Communities and Equality) Order 2006 (S.I. 2006/2951)	In the Schedule, paragraph 4.
Companies Act 2006 (Commencement No. 3, Consequential Amendments, Transitional Provisions and Savings) Order 2007 (S.I. 2007/2194)	In Schedule 4, paragraphs 78 to 82.
Charities Act 2006 (Charitable Companies Audit and Group Accounts Provisions) Order 2008 (S.I. 2008/527)	The whole Order.
Companies Act 2006 (Consequential Amendments etc.) Order 2008 (S.I. 2008/948)	In Schedule 1, paragraphs 1(rr), 17 and 192. In Schedule 3, paragraphs 7 to 12.

Short title or title	*Extent of repeal or revocation*
Charities Acts 1992 and 1993 (Substitution of Sums) Order 2009 (S.I. 2009/508)	Articles 7 to 11.
Transfer of Functions of the Charity Tribunal Order 2009 (S.I. 2009/1834)	In Schedule 1, paragraphs 6 to 15.
Companies Act 2006 (Consequential Amendments, Transitional Provisions and Savings) Order 2009 (S.I. 2009/1941)	In Schedule 1, paragraph 139.
Legal Services Act 2007 (Consequential Amendments) Order 2009 (S.I. 2009/3348)	Article 4.
Charities Act 2006 (Changes in Exempt Charities) Order 2010 (S.I. 2010/500)	Article 2. In Schedule 1, paragraphs 3 and 4.
Income Tax Act 2007 (Amendment) Order 2010 (S.I. 2010/588)	Article 4.
Housing and Regeneration Act 2008 (Consequential Provisions) Order 2010 (S.I. 2010/866)	In Schedule 2, paragraph 78.
Charities (Pre-consolidation Amendments) Order 2011 (S.I. 2011/1396)	The whole Order.
Charities Act 2006 (Changes in Exempt Charities) Order 2011 (S.I. 2011/1725)	Article 2. In the Schedule, paragraphs 1 to 4.

SCHEDULE 11

Section 357

INDEX OF DEFINED EXPRESSIONS

aggregate gross income (in Part 8)	section 175
the appropriate registrar (in sections 230 to 233)	section 230(2)
application for amalgamation (in sections 237 to 239)	section 237(7)
application for conversion (in sections 230 to 233)	section 230(3)
available endowment fund (in Parts 13 and 14)	section 281(7) (and see also sections 282(5) and 288(7))
benefit (in sections 185 and 186, 198 and various provisions in Part 11)	sections 187, 199 and 248
charitable company	section 193

charitable purpose or purposes	sections 2(1) and 11
charitable purposes, failure of (in sections 63 and 65)	section 66(1)
charity	sections 1 and 10 (and see also section 12)
charity law (in Chapter 3 of Part 17)	section 331(1)
charity trustees	section 177
child (in sections 118(2)(c), 188(1)(a), 200(1)(a) and 249(2)(a))	section 350(1)
CIO	section 204
CIO regulations (in Part 11)	section 247
civil partner (in sections 118(2)(e), 188(1)(b), 200(1)(b) and 249(2)(b))	section 350(2)
the Commission	section 13(1)
common deposit scheme (in sections 100 to 103)	section 100(2)
common investment scheme (in sections 96 to 99)	section 96(2)
company	section 353(1)
connected institution or body (in section 156(2))	section 157
connected person, in relation to a charity (in section 117(2))	section 118
connected person—person connected with: a charity trustee or trustee (in sections 185 and 186); a director or member of a charitable company (in section 198(2)(c)); or a charity trustee or member of a CIO (in various provisions in Part 11)	sections: 188; 200; and 249
constitutional capacity, lack of (in sections 218 and 219)	section 218(7)(a)
constitutional limitations (in sections 218 and 219)	section 218(7)(b)
constitutional powers (in sections 218 and 219)	section 218(7)(b)
control of institution (in sections 118(2)(g), 157(1)(a), 188(1)(d), 200(1)(d) and 249(2)(d))	section 351
the court	section 353(1)
document	section 353(2)
donor (in sections 63 to 66)	section 66(2)
dormant account (in sections 107 to 109)	section 109(2)
ecclesiastical charity	section 353(1)
enactment (extended meanings)	sections 9(1), 23(4) and 27(2), 58(7), 245(4), 246(5) and 331(1); Schedule 7, paragraph 2(2) and Schedule 8, paragraph 15(2)
exempt charity	section 22 and Schedule 3
financial year	section 353(1)

gross income (generally and in section 30)	sections 353(1) and 30(4)
the group (in Part 8)	section 141(5)
group accounts (in Part 8)	section 142
incorporated body (in Part 12)	section 265
independent examiner	section 353(1)
institution	section 9(3)
land (in sections 117 to 126)	section 129(1)
maximum amount, in relation to remuneration (in sections 185 and 186)	section 187
members, in relation to a charity with a body of members distinct from the charity trustees	section 353(1)
members, in relation to a group (in Part 8)	section 141(5)
the Minister	section 353(1)
mortgage (in sections 124 to 126)	section 129(2)
Northern Ireland charity (in sections 97 and 101)	section 104(2)
the official custodian	section 21(1)
parent charity (in Part 8)	section 141(2)
parochial charity (in sections 299 and 300)	section 303(1)
permanent endowment	section 353(3)
the principal regulator	section 25
prescribed (in sections 63 and 65)	section 66(4)
the public benefit requirement	section 4(1)
the register	section 29(3)
registered	section 29(3)
the relevant charity, in relation to an incorporated body (in Part 12)	section 265
the relevant charity, in relation to power to spend capital subject to special trust (in Part 14)	section 288(1)
relevant charity merger (in Part 16)	section 306(1)
the relevant commencement date (in Schedule 9)	Schedule 9, paragraph 29
relevant institution (in sections 107 to 109)	section 109(3)
remit (in column 3 of Schedule 6)	section 323
remuneration (in sections 185 and 186)	section 187
reviewable matter (in Chapter 2 of Part 17)	section 322
Scottish recognised body (in sections 97 and 101)	section 104(1)
services (in sections 185 and 186)	section 187

special trust	section 28[illegible]
spouse (in sections 118(2)(e), 188(1)(b), 200(1)(b) and 249(2)(d))	section 350(2)
subsidiary undertaking, in relation to a parent charity (in Part 8)	section 141(2) and (4)
substantial interest in a body corporate (in sections 118(2)(f), 158(1)(b), 188(1)(e), 200(1)(e) and 249(2)(e))	section 352
transfer of property (in sections 268 to 274)	section 275(4)
transfer of property (in sections 306 to 308)	section 306(4)(a)
transferee and transferor (in Part 16)	sections 306(1) and 312
transferor's property etc. (in Part 16)	sections 306(1)(a) and 312(1)(c)
the Tribunal	section 315(1)
trusts, in relation to a charity and to an institution	section 353(1)
unincorporated charity (in certain specified parts)	sections 267(1) and 281(1)
vesting declaration (in sections 306 to 308)	section 306(1)(b)
the 1993 Act (in Part 2 of Schedule 8)	Schedule 8, paragraph 8
the 1987 Act (and references to sections of the 1987 Act, including in sections 32 to 35)	section 92[illegible]
the [illegible] Act (in Schedule 9)	Schedule 9, paragraph [illegible]
the 2006 Act (in Schedule 9)	Schedule 9, paragraph [illegible]

Adapted and published by GRANGIS under the OGL Licence 3.0.

www.nationalarchives.gov.uk/doc/open-government-licence/version/3/

GRANGIS - UK PUBLISHING 2022.

Thank you for taking the time to leave us a review regarding this version

★★★★★

For further inquiries, contact us at:
www.grangis.com / contact@grangis.com

www.ingramcontent.com/pod-product-compliance
Lightning Source LLC
LaVergne TN
LVHW060211210926
848481LV00008B/2695
9798885590099